HUMAN CAPITAL
OR CULTURAL CAPITAL?

SOCIAL INSTITUTIONS AND SOCIAL CHANGE

An Aldine de Gruyter Series of Texts and Monographs

EDITED BY

James D. Wright

Larry Barnett, **Legal Construct, Social Concept: A Macrosociological Perspective on Law**

Vern L. Bengtson and W. Andrew Achenbaum, **The Changing Contract Across Generations**

Thomas G. Blomberg and Stanley Cohen (eds.), **Punishment and Social Control: Essays in Honor of Sheldon L. Messinger**

Remi Clignet, **Death, Deeds, and Descendants: Inheritance in Modern America**

Mary Ellen Colten and Susan Gore (eds.), **Adolescent Stress: Causes and Consequences**

Rand D. Conger and Glen H. Elder, Jr., **Families in Troubled Times: Adapting to Change in Rural America**

Joel A. Devine and James D. Wright, **The Greatest of Evils: Urban Poverty and the American Underclass**

G. William Domhoff, **The Power Elite and the State: How Policy is Made in America**

G. William Domhoff, **State Autonomy or Class Dominance? Case Studies on Policy Making in America**

Paula S. England, **Comparable Worth: Theories and Evidence**

Paula S. England, **Theory on Gender/Feminism on Theory**

George Farkas, **Human Capital or Cultural Capital? Ethnicity and Poverty Groups in an Urban School District**

Ronald F. Inglehart, Neil Nevitte, Miguel Basañez, **North American Trajectory: Growing Cultural, Economics, and Political Ties between the United States, Canada, and Mexico**

Gary Kleck, **Point Blank: Guns and Violence in America**

Dean Knudsen and JoAnn L. Miller (eds.), **Abused and Battered: Social and Legal Responses to Family Violence**

James R. Kluegel, David S. Mason, and Bernd Wegener (eds.), **Social Justice and Political Change: Public Opinion in Capitalist and Post-Communist States**

Theodore R. Marmor, **The Politics of Medicare** (*Second Edition*)

Thomas S. Moore, **The Disposable Work Force: Worker Displacement and Employment Instability in America**

Clark McPhail, **The Myth of the Madding Crowd**

Steven L. Nock, **The Costs of Privacy: Surveillance and Reputation in America**

Talcott Parsons on National Socialism (*Edited and with an Introduction by Uta Gerhardt*)

James T. Richardson, Joel Best, and David G. Bromley (eds.), **The Satanism Scare**

Alice S. Rossi and Peter H. Rossi, **Of Human Bonding: Parent-Child Relations Across the Life Course**

Joseph F. Sheley and James D. Wright: **In the Line of Fire: Youth, Guns, and Violence in Urban America**

David G. Smith, **Paying for Medicare: The Politics of Reform**

James D. Wright, **Address Unknown: The Homeless in America**

James D. Wright and Peter H. Rossi, **Armed and Considered Dangerous: A Survey of Felons and Their Firearms, (Expanded Edition)**

James D. Wright, Peter H. Rossi, and Kathleen Daly, **Under the Gun: Weapons, Crime, and Violence in America**

Mary Zey, **Banking on Fraud: Drexel, Junk Bonds, and Buyouts**

HUMAN CAPITAL
OR CULTURAL CAPITAL?

Ethnicity and Poverty Groups in an Urban School District

GEORGE FARKAS

About the Author

George Farkas is Professor of Sociology and Political Economy and Founding Director of the Center for Education and Social Policy at the University of Texas-Dallas, in Richardson, Texas. He is the author (with Paula England) of *Households, Employment, and Gender* (Aldine, 1986) and he edited (with Paula England) *Industries, Firms, and Jobs* (expanded edition, Aldine, 1994) and (with Ernst Stromsdorfer) *Evaluation Studies Review Annual: Volume 5*. His articles have appeared in numerous journals.

Copyright © 1996 Walter de Gruyter, Inc., New York

ALDINE DE GRUYTER
A division of Walter de Gruyter, Inc.
200 Saw Mill River Road
Hawthorne, New York 10532

This publication is printed on acid free paper ∞

Library of Congress Cataloging-in-Publication Data
Farkas, George, 1946–
    Human capital or cultural capital? : ethnicity and poverty groups in an urban school district / George Farkas.
      p. cm. — (Social institutions and social change)
    Includes bibliographical references (p.   ) and index.
    ISBN 0-202-30523-6 (alk. paper) — ISBN 0-202-30524-4 (pbk. : alk. paper)
    1. Minorities—Education—Social aspects—United States. 2. Poor—Education—Social aspects—United States. 3. Academic achievement—United States. 4. Human capital—United States. 5. Educational anthropology—United States. 6. Minorities—Education—Texas—Dallas—Reading—Case Studies. 7. Reading comprehension—Texas—Dallas—Case studies. 8. Reading—Remedial teaching—Texas—Dallas—Case studies. 9. Remedial teaching—Texas—Dallas—Case studies. I. Title. II. Series.
LC3731.E37 1996
370.19'34'0973—dc20   96-6394
                                          CIP

Manufactured in the United States of America

10 9 8 7 6 5 4 3 2 1

For Linda and David, who make it all worthwhile

But pray remember, children are not to be taught by rules. . . . What you think necessary for them to do, settle in them by an indispensable practice. . . . This will beget habits in them which being once established, operate of themselves easily and naturally . . .

This method of teaching children by a repeated practice and the same action done over and over again, under the eye and direction of the tutor, till they have got the habit of doing it well . . . has so many advantages . . . that I cannot but wonder (if ill customs could be wondered at in any thing) how it could possibly be so much neglected.

John Locke (1692)

Contents

Acknowledgments

This study began as a joint project with Daniel Sheehan and Robert Grobe, who served, at the time, as principal evaluator and executive evaluator, respectively, in the Department of Planning, Evaluation, and Testing of the Dallas Independent School District. Even though their professional responsibilities kept them too busy to join me in authoring this work, it is clearly the case that the data would not have been collected, and the study would not have occurred, without their collaboration. I am enormously grateful for all the work they did, and for their continued friendship. I am also grateful to William Webster, the Director of the Division of Program Evaluation Services, for creating and maintaining a professional environment with high intellectual standards, where work of this sort is encouraged.

Yuan Shuan, at the time a doctoral student in political economy at the University of Texas at Dallas, ran many of the regressions reported here. He did this with enormous skill and care, for which I am grateful. Kurt Beron coauthored Chapter 3 with me. Paula England, Barbara Kilbourne, and Keven Vicknair coauthored Chapter 4. Keven Vicknair coauthored Chapter 11. Johnnye Heaton input the final tables with skill and dispatch.

If Richard Koffler hadn't kept after me, I might never have completed this volume. John Kain provided moral support and valuable advice on this project over a period of many years. He also read the manuscript and offered important suggestions on how to restructure it. In addition, good advice was provided by Ross Koppel, the (previously) anonymous Aldine reviewer. The manuscript was also read by Paula England, Paul Jargowsky, and Ernie Stromsdorfer, who provided useful comments and advice.

From the very beginning, Reading One-One has been a joint effort of a great many dedicated people. Mary Warren was there at the beginning and continues as director to this day. So very much of the program—both curricular and emotional/supportive—is her work. She is the program's heart and soul. June Vernier was also there at the beginning, taking care of many things that just needed to be done. In addition, Richard Marquez, Jim Fischer, Ralph Doshier, Kerney Laday, Royce Hanson, Hobson Wildenthal, Janeen Hock, Sabrina Perdue, Chichita Rice, Dana Patrick, Audrey Scano, Elizabeth Wiggins, Sharon Rowe, Kurt Beron, Diane Walters, Sue Sewell, Laurie Bolton, Cristela Garza, Gilbert Barrera, Ray Hernandez, Jane Lampton, Bud Gifford, James Nodeland, Aileen Johnson, Chrys Daugherty, and Liz Hartmann deserve special mention for believing in the program and working hard for it.

For the past twenty years, Linda Perry has taught me about culture and so much more. Everyday life with Linda and David has provided much of the motivation for the work reported here.

PART I

Culture, Cognitive Skill, and Earnings

Chapter 1

Introduction

If culture is the savior against the hereditarians and those persuaded by *The Bell Curve*, culture must contain the answer as we search for an explanation of the pathological sink into which some 10 million Americans have fallen.

—Orlando Patterson, "For Whom the Bell Curves"

[I]f admitted on merit alone, ethnic Asians would make up a clear *majority* at UC Berkeley, arguably the most esteemed public university in the nation. . . . If the vast majority of American homes were still employing the kinds of values that most Asian immigrants have brought with them and kept through one or more generations, we might not be having a quota debate in the U.S. Yes, poverty and isolation would be problems indicating a basis for special help just as they are today, but we wouldn't be looking at the prospect of 1% African-Americans and 3% Hispanics in an objectively selected freshman class at Berkeley.

—*Wall Street Journal*, May 30, 1995

THE *BELL CURVE* CONTROVERSY, CULTURAL EFFECTS, AND INTERVENTION

The Bell Curve by Herrnstein and Murray (1994) set off nationwide discussion of the lower standardized test scores typically achieved by low-income and African-American or Hispanic as opposed to middle-class and Anglo children and adults. Particularly inflammatory were these authors' claims that such class and ethnic differentials are hereditary, and not amenable to improvement via compensatory education programs.

The response by social scientists and public intellectuals was immediate and strong. With few exceptions, the resulting review essays were hostile, strongly attacking the book's conclusions. (For collections of these pieces, see Jacoby and Glauberman 1995; Fraser 1995.) Typical of the reviews, Nisbett summarized Herrnstein and Murray's handling of evidence as follows:

3

For the question of genetic contribution to the IQ gap, almost all of the direct evidence has been left out, and the single study that is treated at any length is the only one consistent with a genetic component of the gap. . . . For the question of intervention, most of the relevant evidence has not been presented, and that which has is presented in a one-sidedly negative light. (1995:53–54)

The controversy also stimulated additional empirical examination of the issues. Among empirical pieces, Crane (1995) used the same National Longitudinal Survey of Youth (NLSY) database as Herrnstein and Murray to show that the black/white cognitive-skills gap can be completely accounted for by cultural/environmental variables, particularly measures of the cognitive and emotional support that children are provided in the home. This provides a capstone to much related empirical work in this area (Brooks-Gunn, Duncan, Klebanov, and Sealand 1993a; Brooks-Gunn, Klebanov, Liaw, and Spiker, 1993b; Brooks-Gunn, Klebanov, and Duncan, 1995; Duncan, Brooks-Gunn, and Klebanov, 1994; Parcel and Menaghan 1994).

The results of this flurry of activity have been twofold. First, the scholarly and lay communities have been alerted to the significance of the black/white cognitive-skills gap for unequal societal success, and this topic has been moved out of its "politically incorrect" status to a central place in public policy discussion. Second, the issue of the cultural/environmental determination of these outcomes, and the search for successful interventions to compensate for the less advantageous home environments experienced by at-risk children, has become *the* issue for people concerned to ameliorate the poverty problem. Five years previously, a similar evolution of attention constituted a key step within an ongoing personal odyssey.

A PERSONAL ODYSSEY

From 1978 to 1984 I was involved in evaluating the Youth Incentive Entitlement Pilot Projects, a pilot program for what was to have been a nationwide initiative tying school and work together for at-risk teenagers. Unfortunately, the results of these studies showed that this intervention was too little, too late (Farkas, Smith, and Stromsdorfer 1983; Farkas, Olsen, Stromdorfer, Sharpe, Skidmore, Smith, and Merrill 1984). Impressed that viable answers to the problems of at-risk youth must focus on instruction in basic cognitive skills and occur earlier in the youths' schooling careers, I set out in 1985 to conduct research within the public schools in my locality—Dallas. This was the second phase of my Odyssey. In the period from 1988 to 1992 I completed a briefer version of the empirical research presented in Part II (Chapters 5 to 9) (originally published as Farkas, Grobe, Sheehan, and Shuan 1990a; Farkas, Grobe, Sheehan, and Shuan 1990b; Farkas 1993). More recently, I and others completed analyses showing that (a) family linguistic culture is a central determinant of the child's cognitive-skill development, and (b) controlling for the African-American/white cognitive-skill gap completely explains the wage rate gap between the groups. (These studies constitute Chapters 3 and 4 of this volume.) This research confirmed my view that culture, expressed as skills, habits, and styles, is the key to properly understanding ethnic and class differentials in cognitive achievement, and that these differences are the key to understanding earnings inequality in American society. The theoretical perspective underlying this view is treated at length in Chapter 2. The purpose of the present volume is to present this material in an extended and fleshed-out form. The resulting synthesis of arguments typically attributed to "human capital economists" and "cultural-capital sociologists" provides the appropriate foundation for further empirical studies of social inequality.

However, my research did not stop here, and neither does the present volume. Instead, the third phase of my odyssey occurred in 1989, when I gave a public talk on this research, and in 1990, when I was invited to join the Dallas Citizens' Council, a business group involved with school reform. I was soon challenged to indicate which interventions were most likely to increase student achievement and decrease dropping out of school. Following the logic of the findings reported here, accompanied by personal experience,[1] I told the group that reading skills are key and that the most cost-effective program would result from early intervention when these skills are first learned—in elementary school.

I soon identified two program models that are consistent with this view. Both use teachers to work one-on-one with elementary school students who are behind in reading. One of these—Reading Recovery—is centered at the Ohio State University School of Education. Its practitioners exist in hundreds of school districts, typically funded by the Title I program (federal aid to local schools). The second of these is Success for All, centered at a federal research center at Johns Hopkins University, and also disseminated widely throughout the country.

Working with the business group within a Dallas elementary school, I realized that the only way to try such interventions was to run one myself. I began to do this in January 1991. Thus began Reading One-One, an intervention aimed at increasing the reading skills, habits, and styles of low-performing elementary-school students. The implementation and evaluation of this program have been ongoing since 1991. My experience with this and related interventions, their success and reception by school district bureaucracies, and the implications of these outcomes, are the subject of Part III of this volume (Chapters 10–12).

THE PLACE OF THIS STUDY WITHIN A SERIES OF STUDIES

The nation's discussion of how to understand and remedy the underclass's plight continues. My own odyssey continues, as I seek to improve, study, and disseminate the Reading One-One program. It is my hope, therefore, that this volume will be the first of a series. Its principal contribution is to provide an intellectual framework for further studies of the role played by culture—skills, habits, and styles—in achievement. It also provides an initial evaluation of Reading One-One, a program intervention erected on this intellectual foundation. My intention is to pursue these topics in the years ahead. Other researchers, some of whose work is cited in the chapters below, will no doubt pursue related agendas. My hope for the present study is that its ideas will be fruitful in two typically disparate lines of inquiry: first, in purely intellectual attempts to understand the role of culture in the differential cognitive and earnings success of groups defined by ethnicity and poverty status; and second, in attempts to formulate, implement, and evaluate program interventions designed to improve the outcomes experienced by the most disadvantaged. I argue in this volume that within each of these lines of inquiry a focus on skills, habits, and styles, their determinants and consequences is crucial for success.

NOTE

1.   Our son, David, who was born in 1986, is African-American. (We adopted him at three months of age.) Accordingly, we arranged for an African-American babysitter, the son of an acquaintance of ours. In 1989, this babysitter was in eighth grade and having difficulty with his schoolwork, so I offered to tutor him. It was then that I discovered that although he was in eighth grade, he was reading at only the fourth-grade level. He had come to believe that he was stupid, even though there was nothing wrong with his mind. As a result he had developed a "bad attitude" about schooling and many psychological defenses. My (ultimately failed) attempts to work closely with him showed me the centrality of reading skill in learning, as well as the human reality of the statistical results presented later in this volume.

Chapter 2

Skills, Habits, Styles, and School Success

Culture . . . is more like a style or a set of skills and habits than a set of preferences or wants. If one asked a slum youth why he did not take steps to pursue a middle-class path to success . . . the answer might well be not "I don't want that life," but instead, "Who, me?" One can hardly pursue success in a world where the accepted skills, styles, and informal know-how are unfamiliar. One does better to look for a line of action for which one already has the cultural equipment.
        —Anne Swidler, "Culture in Action: Symbols and Strategies"

[O]ur sunk costs are us . . . we are largely stuck with the knowledge we have gained in the past and used enough to keep actively in mind.
        —Russell Hardin, *One for All. The Logic of Group Conflict*

THE PROBLEM

The most interesting science often emerges from the attempt to solve a practical problem and/or to understand an anomaly. Where sociology and economics meet over public policy toward human resources—the education and training of populations—one of the greatest social problems and anomalies concerns the systematically different schooling performance of entire nations as well as of subgroups of different national origin within individual nations. In particular, there has been great public attention to the better performance of Japanese and other national groups than of American public school students, as well as to the relatively poor schooling performance of low-income Mexican-American and African-American students in the large central school districts of American cities. Related to this, seemingly endless discussion of "school reform" has occupied newspapers and magazines, as well as the time and energy of public officials at the local, state, and national levels. Yet little progress seems to occur.

I address these issues by focusing on the experience of the Dallas Independent School District (DISD). The DISD, centrally located within one of our largest cities, exemplifies conditions typical of all of them. Standardized test scores are low, and the need to improve student performance is a constant topic of local discussion. So, too, is school finance. Intertwined with these issues is the politics of race. Busing and court-ordered desegregation and oversight are continuing aspects of a long history. White flight has produced a district within which, by 1995, approximately 143,000 students are less than 15 percent Anglo. African-Americans constitute approximately 45 percent of the school population; Mexican-Americans approximately 40 percent. There is a small, but significant Asian-American population.

The first African-American school superintendent in Dallas was appointed in 1988, brought in from a small midwestern school district. He left the district, under fire for stagnating test scores, in 1993. He was succeeded by a white administrator who had spent his career within the district. Racial politics are a continuing aspect of school board elections and deliberations. So too are the currently fashionable topics for debate and experiment: decentralization, site-based management, accountability, and parental choice and empowerment.

I have employed two strategies to wrest some understanding from this situation. First, statistical data on student performance are used to understand patterns of basic skill acquisition, mastery of assigned coursework, and course grades. Second, statistical as well as qualitative data gained from my involvement in creating Reading One-One, an intervention employing large numbers of hourly paid, trained college students and community residents to increase the reading proficiency of elementary-school students, are used in an effort to understand the day-to-day operation of schools and the possibilities for improved student performance.

Student basic skills and teacher/student interaction occupy the center of the analysis. Specifically, I focus on the reward structure used by teachers in allocating course grades and on the skills, habits, styles, and coursework mastery manifested by male and female, poor and nonpoor, and Mexican-American, African-American, Asian-American, and Anglo students. Basic skills and coursework mastery are measured by test scores; habits and styles are reported from a specially conducted teacher questionnaire, with statistical controls for the teacher's race. Issues include: To what extent, and why, do Asian-American students perform so successfully at school? To what extent, and why, do Mexican-American and African-American students perform relatively unsuccessfully at school? Do schools systematically discriminate against minority youths and those from low-income households? What can be done to improve student performance?

These questions are addressed within a conception of behavior in which student and teacher background characteristics combine in classroom interaction along with home and peer influences to determine student skills, habits, and styles. These skills, habits, and styles in turn determine coursework mastery, and this variable, together with its antecedents in skills, habits, and styles, determines the teacher-assigned course grade. In the following sections I present an intellectual framework that can durably support continued inquiry in these areas. In this effort I juxtapose and build upon the two competing paradigms that have dominated previous discussions in this area: human capital theory and cultural-capital theory.

HUMAN CAPITAL OR CULTURAL CAPITAL?

The Nobel Prizes awarded in 1979 to T. W. Schultz and in 1992 to Gary Becker recognized the enormous influence and essentially complete triumph of what at first had been a controversial idea: that topics as diverse and "sociological" as schooling attainment; childbearing and child care; housework; worker training, productivity, and earnings; geographic mobility; and health can by unified as *human capital investment* and assigned to economists for study. In this view, present consumption and competing investments are forgone in order to reap a later reward, much as with investment in capital equipment. However, in human capital investment, the resulting increased productive capacity resides in the person rather than in a piece of machinery or a building (Becker 1964; Mincer 1958, 1974; Schultz 1960, 1981).

The emphasis in this paradigm upon optimizing actors engaged in trading off different activities based upon rate-of-return calculations is typical of the economist's perspective. Atomistic individuals engage in rational (economizing) action, based upon their exogenously given tastes and endowments of biologically determined skills and abilities. Consequently, group differentials in schooling and training attainment, and in consequent outcomes such as earnings, must be attributable to essentially "accidental" group differences in such tastes and natural abilities. Thus, the human capital perspective—the predominant view of these matters within economics—has emphasized atomistic individual behavior, with little attention to the group structure of society.

Matters are somewhat different within sociology. On the one hand, there is the *status attainment* school, whose approach to schooling and occupational and earnings attainment is quite similar to that of human capital economists. That is, its proponents focus on essentially atomistic individuals and their families, with relatively little attention to group and contextual social structure. (For a review of exceptions within status attainment research, focusing on studies of network affiliations, see Granovetter 1994.)

On the other hand, there are those sociologists who emphasize group membership and the shared understandings that constitute group culture.

The *conflict synthesis* paradigm is one version of this perspective. A key feature of the conflict synthesis is the theory of *cultural capital*, which builds upon Max Weber's notion of society as composed of status groups, each with its own status culture controlling access to the rewards and privileges of group membership. Collins (1975, 1979, 1985, 1986, 1988) has shown that the Weberian perspective, with its emphasis upon culture as a key determinant of stratification outcomes, can be integrated with the theories of Emil Durkheim and Erving Goffman, among others, to yield a unified theory of society. This viewpoint has now gained wide acceptance within sociology, and other scholars have joined Collins in seeking to expand the scope of the paradigm. Of particular note is the work of DiMaggio (1982; DiMaggio and Mohr 1985), who began the task of providing empirical support for the paradigm's claims (see also Lamont and Lareau 1988; Farkas et al. 1990a).

As presented by Collins (1971, 1979), the conflict/cultural-capital paradigm directly contradicts the functionalism/human capital paradigm. This is because the former sees educational and earnings stratification as resulting from credentialing systems wherein the cultural hegemony of middle- and upper-class status groups operates through school and workplace reward systems that are only loosely, if at all, tied to actual productivity. By contrast, the latter sees an open competition in which individuals invest in their own skill and productivity, so that those achieving greater educational performance simply receive their just deserts. When scholars from the conflict view look at the differential school success of groups defined by ethnicity and poverty status, they see ascriptive criteria in the service of Anglo, middle-class cultural hegemony. The schools become a cultural battleground within which minority and poverty group children are fundamentally disadvantaged. By contrast, when human capital scholars look at schools, they see a meritocratic competition based upon skill and performance. Here, atomistic individuals assess their own tastes and naturally endowed skills, and invest in themselves accordingly.

INTEGRATING THE TWO VIEWS

The goal of this book is to integrate the two views within an empirical study of group differentials in schooling outcomes. Such an integration is called for as a consequence of the partial inadequacy exhibited by each view when considered alone. Thus, on the one hand, human capital economists offer no realistic understanding of what appears to be extremely different educational "investment" by poor and minority groups. That is, the economists' emphasis on individual choice is blind to patterns of cultural resources and influence as well as choices that are made for the individual by others. On the other hand, conflict sociologists appear to maintain that performance plays little role in stratification outcomes, so that social achievement is a shell game, and real skills embodied in individuals and developed through arduous educational efforts are considered to be largely irrelevant to productivity.

The key for a synthesis is found in a paper by Swidler (1986). While citing Bourdieu, one of the founders of the cultural-capital school, she maintains that beginning with Max Weber, sociologists of culture have been too intent on seeing culture determining action through its effect on *values*, the end toward which action is directed. Instead, she argues for viewing culture as a tool kit of *skills*, the means by which strategies of action are constructed. This notion of culture as a resource, providing real skills for real production, but differentially available to members of different groups via parents' skills and their socialization of their children, as well as by peer group pressures, is used to bridge the gap between the human capital and cultural-capital perspectives. As we shall see, the resulting viewpoint is compatible with Ogbu's (1974, 1978, 1986) emphasis upon the negative schooling effects of castelike minority status, as well as with recent attempts to extend the human capital viewpoint so as to specify the mechanisms by which cultural resources become a form of social capital (Lamont and Lareau 1988; Lareau 1987, 1989). It also responds to Aaron's (1994) plea for an economics that is more relevant to observed behavior.

This volume's central question is, Human capital or cultural capital? My response to the apparent hostility between these two research paradigms is to create a new paradigm from pieces of each old one. This new paradigm has two key features: First, it defines culture as skills, habits, and styles, and identifies these skills with those which are central to the human capital paradigm. It thereby moves beyond typical practice for students of cultural capital, by asserting that real skills for real production constitute a central determinant of stratification outcomes. Second, it rejects the naive "long-run optimization" calculus commonly employed within the human capital paradigm to account for the differential acquisition of such skills. In its place I posit a more complex view in which parental skills, habits, and styles determine the very early cognitive skills of their children, and these influence the child's habits and styles via his/her estimation of the success they can expect from hard effort at tasks that both require and increase cognitive skill. The resulting differential time-on-task and concentration-on-task feed back to affect the level of cognitive skill itself, creating a powerful mechanism by which large cognitive-skill gaps between groups of children from different backgrounds come into being by relatively young ages. In sum, skills, habits, and styles are central to stratification outcomes, but these are formed at young ages and essentially without conscious intent on the children's part. Instead, they result from outcomes that are taught, modeled, and reinforced by events occurring in households and schools. These events may pass relatively unnoticed at the time, but they constitute the central mechanisms by which stratification outcomes are determined.

SKILLS, HABITS, AND STYLES AS MECHANISMS
OF CULTURAL INFLUENCE

Swidler notes that despite considerable argument in the "culture-of-poverty" literature, empirical studies clearly show that lower-class youth and their parents share middle-class values regarding the attainment of higher education, secure friendships, stable marriages, steady jobs, and high incomes. Thus:

> The culture-of-poverty example suggests a misdirection of our explanatory efforts. Students of culture keep looking for cultural values that will explain what is distinctive about the behavior of groups or societies, and neglect other distinctively *cultural* phenomena which offer greater promise of explaining patterns of action. These factors are better described as culturally-shaped skills, habits, and styles than as values or preferences. (1986:275)

This view is consistent with Ogbu's (1986) discussion of castelike minority status as an explanation of the relatively poor school performance of African-Americans. Noting that, throughout the world, membership in a castelike minority leads to lower test scores and school performance (the Burakumin of Japan are a particularly striking example), Ogbu seeks to describe the mechanisms of this effect for African-Americans. Primary causal emphasis is placed upon the job ceiling, and its feedback effect upon the development of cognitive competency:

> The restricted opportunity structure that confined blacks to menial jobs and comparable sociopolitical positions obviously ensured that generations of blacks developed certain instrumental competencies, including the cognitive skills required for such menial positions. At the same time their exclusion from high-status, more desirable, white middle-class jobs and positions meant that they did not participate in activities that require and stimulate the cognitive competencies associated with such activities. (p. 37)

According to the author, restricted opportunity has led to black disillusionment with schooling, and an absence of "effort optimism" and focused concern toward test scores and schoolwork:

It is in this context that one begins to understand why the children studied in Stockton were not particularly worried by their poor performance. Many of them appeared to have learned to blame the system for their low test scores and school failures, just as local adult blacks blamed the system for their social and economic problems. However, we emphasize that the children did not learn this discouraging message from explicit or deliberate teachings of their parents. Rather, it is the actual texture of parents' lives that comes through strongly, producing a message powerful enough to undercut parents' own exhortations that their children should work hard to succeed in school. (p. 47)

The congruency between this and Swidler's view of the processes by which "viable lines of action" are constructed is revealed by Ogbu's discussion of three alternative "survival strategies" under the job ceiling:

Among these are *collective struggle* or "civil rights" struggle, *clientship* or "Uncle Tomming," and *hustling*. The attitudes, knowledge, skills, and rules of behavior for achievement fostered by these survival strategies often are not compatible with those required to do well in school or to do well on IQ tests. . . . Children who enter school with some degree of competence in the survival strategies are likely to perform poorly in school and on IQ tests; and as the children get older and become more competent in the survival strategies, their academic and other difficulties increase. (p. 48)

Finally, two other responses to the job ceiling tend to reinforce these effects: One of these is hostility and distrust toward the public schools, which makes it "difficult for black children to accept and internalize the school's goals, standards and teaching and learning approaches" (Ogbu 1986:49). The other is *cultural inversion*, the tendency to define certain activities and styles as *not* black because they are characteristic of whites or vice versa. A consequence is that blacks who enroll in college preparatory courses, try hard at schoolwork, and/or engage in activities such as student government may be accused of trying to "act white" and ostracized as Uncle Toms. Fordham and Ogbu (1986) and Fordham (1988) expand upon this point and buttress it with new ethnographic data. They report immense peer pressure directed against youths manifesting high levels of school effort and performance. Of course, adolescent society has always rewarded the budding athlete over the budding scholar (Coleman 1961). And black and white styles of talking and acting differ in ways that are particularly generative of conflict within school and classroom settings (Kochman 1981). But Fordham and Ogbu go beyond these observations to report the particular strength of African-American student peer pressure against school effort and achievement. When these observations are phrased in Swidler's language, we see that African-American students who wish to succeed at school must adopt elaborate strategies—habits and styles—if they are to avoid peer sanctions. Many instead opt for low effort and performance, and this is particularly the case when they are socially isolated in the inner city (Wilson 1987).

The argument that intergroup differentials in schooling success are at least partially due to culturally driven habits, skills, and styles can be extended to account for the relative success of other ethnicity/race groups—Mexican- and Asian-Americans—as well as groups defined by the youth's family social-class background.

For youths of Mexican ancestry, there is a growing literature that largely parallels that for African-Americans. Thus, Ogbu (1986) and Fordham and Ogbu (1986) include Mexican-Americans alongside blacks as castelike minorities whose relative disconnection to school is at least partially traceable to habits, skills, and styles that have developed in response to the job ceiling. For a discussion of "second-generation discrimination" and its consequences for Mexican-American as well as for African-American students, see Meier, Stewart, and England (1989) and Meier and Stewart (1991). Other researchers have focused on language difficulties and their pervasive effects upon socioeconomic attainment (Carliner 1981; McManus, Gould, and Welch 1983; Grenier 1984; Kossoudji 1988; Tainer 1988; Stolzenberg 1990; Chiswick 1991).

Where Asians are concerned, researchers' emphasis upon habits and styles of "good school citizenship" date back more than fifty years:

> How shall we explain the fact that the Japanese pupils in Los Angeles have about the same IQ as the average pupil and score about the same on educational tests but obtain strikingly better grades? It may be that they possess to a greater degree than whites those qualities which endear pupils to a teacher; that is, they are more docile, occasion less disciplinary trouble, and give the appearance of being busy and striving to do their best. (Strong 1934:2)

This statement suggests that Asian students may receive better course grades for their demeanor than is strictly justified by their coursework mastery. Whether or not this is the case and how, if at all, it relates to the basic skills of these students will be investigated in the present study.

Of course, the most influential research on group differentials in schooling attainment and their relationship to cultural interaction and school organization has focused on social class (Bernstein 1977; Bourdieu 1977; Bowles and Gintis 1976; MacLeod 1987). A related literature has focused on self-fulfilling prophecies and patterns of teacher discriminatory behavior toward females and lower-class African-American students (Rosenthal and Jacobson 1968; Rist 1973). I will test for these effects by measuring the role of skills, habits, and styles as mediating variables between gender, ethnicity, and poverty group membership on the one hand, and schooling outcomes (coursework mastery and course grades) on the other.

CULTURE AND STRUCTURE: AN INTERACTIONIST SYNTHESIS

More than twenty-five years ago, Herbert Gans (1968) struggled to find an appropriate perspective from which to view the problems summarized by the culture-of-poverty literature, and to thereby provide a realistic foundation for antipoverty policy. His conclusion was that social structure and culture are closely interrelated. The attempt to treat either in isolation from the other is doomed to failure.

How striking then that when, in 1991, Jencks and Peterson edited a volume that is in many ways a successor to the classic Moynihan (1968) volume containing the Gans piece, that book contained a paper seemingly rediscovering the point made by Gans. Thus, as noted by the author of that paper:

> Debates . . . typically regard underclass behavior as either a response to an economic predicament or the result of cultural commitments to dysfunctional values. . . . Each side offers a carefully explicated and argued position. Yet neither is able to fully resolve the issues. Much of the difficulty follows from the complexity of the pivotal terms "culture" and "rationality." Among the many aspects of "culture" are a community's fundamental beliefs, ethical and esthetic values, revered rituals, and material preferences. But culture also includes the tools—material and linguistic, practical and theoretical—that people employ in their purposive and reflective activities. Again, the instrumental side of "rationality" specifies those actions, techniques, and skills necessary to achieve specific goals, but rationality also includes the capacity to make human experience bearable by rendering it intelligible. Once these more complex meanings are recognized, a sharp distinction between culture and rationality becomes untenable. (Greenstone 1991:399)

This is fully consistent with Swidler's (1986) definition of culture as embodying skills, habits, and styles. As Camic reminds us, this forgotten focus on habit was a central concern of the sociological masters:

> In his last new lecture course, Durkheim brought into the open a fundamental claim that had long been in the recesses of his work. . . . This was the idea that, by its very nature, human action, whether individual or collective, oscillates between two poles, that of consciousness or reflection on the one side, and that of habit on the other side, with the latter pole being the stronger. . . . [I]t is not enough to direct our attention to the superficial por-

tion of our consciousness; for the sentiments, the ideas which come to the surface are not, by far, those which have the most influence on our conduct. What must be reached are the habits—these are the real forces which govern us. (1986:1052)

A similar perspective was held by Weber:

> If Durkheim's reformist zeal propelled him to examine the micro-level development of specific moral habits, Weber's comparative-historical orientation led him away from this issue and into a more thoroughgoing investigation of the larger social and cultural conditions under which general societal patterns of habitual action wax and wane. It was Weber's belief that habitual action does not occur at random. While individuals everywhere may act out of habit on occasion, they are not all equally inclined in this direction in all domains of their activity, for there is a strong affinity between the way of life within different social groups and the propensity of group members toward various sorts of habitual or reflective conduct. (p. 1062)

The habits and styles we are concerned with result from a mixture of reflective (e.g., purposive, rational) and unreflective actions, which affect school-related skills and success (coursework mastery and course grades), which in turn feed back upon habits and styles. The resulting self-definition, self-presentation, efforts, and goals are summarized by Swidler and Ogbu as the individual's "strategy."

Yet such strategies are neither shaped nor played out within a vacuum. Rather, at the macrolevel, gatekeeper (in this case, schoolteacher) as well as peer group and parental preferences and practices define reward structures. These reward structures are themselves shaped by bureaucratic, historical, cultural, and personal factors extending across space and time. And at the microlevel, individuals respond to these reward structures with strategies of action determined by their access to differentially valued cultural resources. Gatekeeper and other authority figures recognize and reward a broad list of characteristics, including habits, skills, and styles as well as attitudes, preferences, knowledge, goods, and credentials (Lamont and Lareau 1988).

This provides a basis for the interactive synthesis we seek. I follow DiMaggio's (1982) example by focusing on the reward structure used by secondary-school teachers in allocating course grades. However, where DiMaggio operationalizes cultural resources as highbrow music and arts activities, I seek to discover the informal academic standards by which teachers reward more general skills, habits, and styles. The results will be seen to provide empirical content for Lamont and Lareau's (1988) argument that the cultural resources rewarded by school (and other) stratification systems go far beyond those defined by the elite consumption activities of high culture.

Cultural resources may be classified according to whether they represent cognitive or noncognitive performance. By estimating the net contribution of each of these to course grades, I join the cultural-resources literature to an older research tradition within the sociology of education. This tradition has long argued that school reward outcomes are based upon teacher judgments of students' noncognitive traits as well as of their cognitive performance.[1] Relevant noncognitive traits include behaviors that are clearly related to cognitive performance, such as homework; behaviors that may be marginally related to cognitive performance, such as disruptiveness; and purely ascriptive characteristics, such as gender, ethnicity, and social-class background.

Previous studies differ on whether teacher bias is a factor in assignment of course grades. The studies finding teacher bias typically picture a "middle-class hegemony" within the schools such that teachers discriminate against students from low-income and/or minority households (e.g., Sexton 1961; Rosenthal and Jacobson 1968; Rist 1973; Bowles and Gintis 1976). Two causal mechanisms behind teacher bias can be distinguished. The first is a theory of "perceptual bias." Some teachers sometimes *perceive* lower levels of performance when evaluating poor, African-American, or female students, and give lower grades even when the students' *actual* performance is no different from that of children with more favored characteristics. The second mechanism is a "self-fulfilling prophecy," which involves a feedback loop that affects real student behavior. Here, the teacher's reduced expectations lower students' self-image and effort and lead the teacher to present less-demanding material, resulting in reduced cognitive achievement.

Other studies find no evidence of teacher bias based on class or race. These studies report little success in detecting either teacher expectation effects on student cognitive performance (Dusek 1975; Williams 1976; Entwisle and Hayduk 1982, 1983) or socioeconomic bias in teacher evaluations net of such performance (Rehberg and Rosenthal 1978; Alexander and Eckland 1980; Sewell and Hauser 1980; Natriello and Dornbusch 1983, 1984; Leiter and Brown 1985). The evidence is more fragmentary regarding bias against minority students since studies based on large data sets (Williams 1976; Rehberg and Rosenthal 1978; Alexander and Eckland 1980; Sewell and Hauser 1980) contain too few such students to test for these effects. Small-scale studies that are able to perform appropriate tests (Entwisle and Hayduk 1982; Natriello and Dornbusch 1984; Leiter and Brown 1985) have failed to find evidence of racial bias among teachers. Regarding gender, results are mixed. Some researchers report that, net of aptitude test score, girls receive somewhat higher course grades than boys (Brophy and

Good 1974; Rehberg and Rosenthal 1978; Alexander and Eckland 1980) while others do not (Entwisle and Hayduk 1982; Natriello and Dornbusch 1984; Leiter and Brown 1985).

Both groups of studies relate closely to the cultural-resources research agenda. The "unbiased teacher" literature implies that group differences in grades should be attributed to family and cultural background characteristics, peer group culture, and/or societywide (structural) arrangements (such as job ceilings for some groups). The "teacher bias" literature directly implicates teachers in the differential school success of particular social groups: it posits grading on ascribed characteristics. Such a direct form of discrimination should be detectable with a simple statistical test examining course grades by gender, ethnicity, and social-class background, net of performance. The failure of some studies to detect teacher bias may be due to the fact that a more subtle form of bias is occurring: the self-fulfilling prophecy with its emphasis on feedback effects. When Lamont and Lareau (1988) count "good citizenship" and "the ability to signal competence" as examples of cultural resources, they recognize the necessity for gatekeepers to be able to *perceive* such signals and to *feed back* appropriate rewards. That is, both cultural-resource and self-fulfilling prophecy views acknowledge the centrality of skills, habits, and styles, but see them as evolving within a dynamic process in which student conduct is shaped by student/teacher interaction.

Two studies illustrate the different emphases that can be placed upon such interaction. Natriello and Dornbusch (1983, 1984), analyzing objective data on student behavior, report that teachers have unbiased perceptions of this behavior and grade their students accordingly. They conclude that previous reports of teacher bias may be invalid because researchers failed to measure and control behavior variables. Alexander, Entwisle, and Thompson (1987) focus on the teacher, arguing that attempts to find a pervasive middle-class hegemony have misspecified the effect. Instead, patterns of teacher bias are produced by the interaction between the personal backgrounds of teachers and students. These researchers report that teachers with high-status backgrounds relate poorly to low-status and African-American students, and this acts to depress the aptitude test scores and grades of these students. Of course, both of these attempts to "bring behavior back in" and to "bring the teacher back in" to school achievement studies are potentially consistent with the cultural-resources view. They simply provide alternative specifications of the important causal mechanisms.

In sum, cultural-resource theory posits a general set of student skills, habits, and styles, which figure in student/teacher interaction and are differentially rewarded by teachers; prior studies simply assert the importance of some of these variables, or of ascriptive characteristics. Yet these prior studies suffer from several limitations. First, most employ basic cognitive-skill ("aptitude") test scores to measure cognitive performance, whereas mastery of assigned coursework is the appropriate criterion underlying course grades. Second, the majority of these studies lack measures of student noncognitive attitudes and behavior, and when such measures are available, they are rarely combined with appropriate cognitive performance measures. Finally, these studies have typically searched for a pervasive pattern of middle-class hegemony and teacher bias. Few have tested for interactions between student and teacher characteristics in the incidence of bias.

PLAN OF THE STUDY

The remainder of the volume is organized as follows. Chapter 3 demonstrates the important role played by family linguistic culture in determining the child's cognitive-skill development. Chapter 4 then shows that these cognitive skills strongly determine later earnings. Part II of the volume (Chapters 5 to 9) uses Dallas data to analyze the process by which student skills, habits, and styles determine coursework mastery and course grades. Chapter 5 describes the research setting, data, and methods. Chapter 6 reports the determinants of student basic skills, measured by Iowa Test of Basic Skills (ITBS) scores. Chapter 7 reports the determinants of teacher judgments of student habits and styles. Chapter 8 focuses on coursework mastery, as measured by curriculum-referenced tests that were uniformly administered within the district at the end of each school term. Both background variables and students skills, habits, and styles are used as predictors of these outcomes. Chapter 9 then repeats this analysis for teacher-assigned course grades, using all causally prior variables as predictors.

Part III focuses on intervention. Chapter 10 provides further information about the magnitudes of the skills deficits experienced by low-income and minority group children in the early grades, and the most promising programs to reduce these deficits. Chapter 11 reports on Reading One-One, a one-on-one tutoring intervention I implemented within the Dallas schools. We see that such tutoring intervention, applied during the early elementary grades, offers the best hope for creating meaningful improvement in the skills, habits, and styles of at-risk students. Yet, despite the apparent success of this intervention, it ran afoul of bureaucratic politics within the school district, and after five years of dramatic growth was significantly scaled back. How this occurred is examined in Chapter 12, which also reflects upon the educational governance issues that must be addressed if the urban poverty problem is to be ameliorated.

NOTE

1.   Both "functionalists" and "conflict theorists" agree on the importance of citizenship and work habits for course grade assignment, net of cognitive performance. For example, see Parsons (1959) and Bowles and Gintis (1976).

Chapter 3

Family Linguistic Culture and the Child's Cognitive-Skill Development[1]

with Kurt Beron

[S]ince the mid-sixties a great deal has been made of how language codes may affect early schooling (Bernstein 1960, 1962). These sociolinguistic issues involving racial and sociocultural backgrounds seem especially relevant for children learning to read.

—Doris K. Entwisle and Karl Alexander, "Winter Setback:
The Racial Composition of Schools and Learning to Read."

I didn't even know there was something called Black English when I began to realize that many of the difficulties my students were having were rooted in language. It was the incongruence of the obvious intelligence and determination of these students with the unusual kinds of misunderstanding that persisted in their work that drove me to find answers. What I arrived at is an acute awareness of the function in English of prepositions, conjunctions, and relative pronouns in the identification of quantitative ideas. . . . For students whose first language is black English vernacular, language can be a barrier to success in mathematics and science.

—Eleanor Orr, *Twice as Less: Black English and the Performance of Black Students in Mathematics and Science*

In the previous chapter I argued that culture, represented as skills, habits, and styles, is the crucial link between family background, on the one hand, and educational, occupational and earnings attainment, on the other. But what are the detailed family actions and behaviors that help determine the skills, habits, and styles of their children? In particular, over and above the family's influence on the child's work habits and communicative styles, what is the *mechanism* by which the family influences the child's development of cognitive skill, particularly reading skill?

In this chapter I use a national data set to empirically address this question. Building on a long research tradition (see Woodcock 1990; McGrew,

Werder, and Woodcock 1991; and the literature cited there) regarding the basic cognitive abilities that underlie the development of reading skill, I test three possibilities: (1) minority group children and the children of poorly educated mothers, because of differences between their family linguistic culture and standard English, have unusual difficulty with *auditory processing*, the ability to fluently comprehend patterns among auditory stimuli; (2) minority group children and the children of poorly educated mothers have special difficulty with *long-term retrieval*, the memory-related skills involving the storing of information and the fluency of retrieving it later through association; and (3) minority group children and the children of poorly educated mothers have special difficulty with *processing speed*, the ability to work quickly, particularly when measured under pressure to maintain focused attention. We will see that the lower reading skills of African-American children are essentially completely explained by their deficits in auditory processing. Similar, although somewhat less dramatic findings are observed for Hispanic children and the children of poorly educated mothers. These findings suggest that family linguistic culture plays an important role in determining the lower reading skills of these students. Further, as discussed by Orr (1987) and others, such lower linguistic and reading skills are, in turn, determinants of the lower mathematics and science skills of these students.

BASIC COGNITIVE ABILITIES WITHIN A MODEL
OF READING SKILL DEVELOPMENT

I begin by specifying a set of basic cognitive abilities, which are hypothesized to mediate the relationship between family ethnic and social-class background on the one hand, and reading achievement on the other. Central to this approach is reliance on the work of Richard Woodcock, a psychometrician who has gone further than other researchers in developing and administering a set of distinct test measures of both basic cognitive abilities and scholastic achievement. Using data from the nationally representative norming sample of the Woodcock-Johnson Psycho-Educational Battery–Revised (WJ-R), I am able to estimate the causal model of Figure 3.1.

In this figure, family ethnicity and mother's education (social-class background) determine three basic cognitive abilities—auditory processing, long-term retrieval, and processing speed—which in turn determine reading achievement. As we shall see, these intermediate variables almost completely explain the relationship between social-class/racial background and reading achievement. This explanatory power is largely attributable

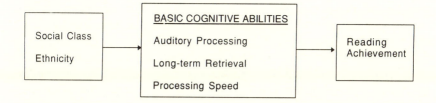

Figure 3.1. Causal model of the reading achievement process.

to auditory processing, which supports the linguistic cultural explanation posited by Entwisle and Alexander (1994). On the other hand, processing speed is of much less importance, arguing against a common version of the inheritance interpretation (Gottfredson 1996:20,21). Since the analyzed data have no direct measures of student work habits and communicative styles, we cannot simultaneously assess the roles played by these variables in the reading achievement process. However, as suggested in the previous chapter, student work habits and communicative styles are likely part of a feedback process connecting time-on-task for cognitive skills and achievement with the development of such skills and achievement. Later analyses (Chapters 5 to 9) focus on the detailed roles played by skills, habits, and styles in school achievement. In this chapter I simply strive to better understand why children from certain family backgrounds tend to achieve differential basic reading skills.

MEASUREMENT AND DATA

I have followed Woodcock's advice (personal communication) in selecting the most appropriate measures of basic cognitive skills to serve as determinants of reading achievement. They are as follows (these descriptions are taken from McGrew et al. 1991):

1. *Auditory processing* is defined as the ability to fluently comprehend patterns among auditory stimuli. It includes temporal tracking, the perception of speech under distorting or distracting conditions, the detection or transformation of tonal patterns, and the anticipation of an auditory form that can be synthesized from a stream of sounds. It is measured by two tests, *Sound Blending* and *Incomplete Words*. The first of these tests the ability to integrate and then say whole words after hearing parts (syllables and/or phonemes) of the words. An audiotape is used to present word parts in their proper order for each item. The second of these is a tape-

recorded test that measures auditory closure. After hearing a recorded word that has one or more phonemes missing, the subject names the complete word.

2.   *Long-term retrieval* involves the storing of information and the fluency of retrieving it later through association. The length of intervening time is not the essence, but rather that intervening tasks have engaged working memory during the interim and the information must be retrieved. It is measured by *Memory for Names* and *Visual-Auditory Learning*. The first of these measures the ability to learn associations between unfamiliar auditory and visual stimuli. At each step in the test, the subject is shown a picture of a space creature and told the creature's name. The subject is then shown a page of nine space creatures and is asked to point to the creature just introduced and to previously introduced space creatures as named by the examiner. The second test measures the ability to associate new visual symbols (rebuses, that is, drawings) with familiar words in oral language and to translate a series of symbols into verbal sentences.

3.   *Processing speed* is the ability to work quickly, particularly when measured under pressure to maintain focused attention. Examples include speed of scanning, comparison, printing, or writing. Whatever the task, it must be so easy that most people would get all items correct if the test were not highly speeded up. In a broader sense, it is the ability to maintain focused and steady concentration during thinking. Speediness in intellectual tasks relates to carefulness, processing strategies, mood, and persistence, as well as to features of physiological structures (neural, hormonal). It is measured by *Visual Matching* and *Cross Out*. The first of these measures the ability to locate and circle the two identical numbers in a row of six numbers. The task proceeds in difficulty from single-digit numbers to triple-digit numbers and has a three-minute time limit. The second test measures the ability to quickly scan and compare visual information. The subject must mark the five drawings in a row of twenty drawings that are identical to the first drawing in the row. The subject is given a three-minute time limit to complete as many rows of items as possible.

Distinct from these measures of basic cognitive skill, we have four measures of reading achievement. These are (a) *Letter-Word Identification*, which measures the subject's reading identification skills, (b) *Passage Comprehension*, which measures the subject's skill in reading a short passage and identifying a missing key word, (c) *Word Attack*, which measures the subject's skill in applying phonic and structural analysis skills to the pronunciation of unfamiliar printed words, and (d) *Reading Vocabulary*, which measures the subject's skill in reading words and supplying appropriate meanings.

Exogenous variables are as follows: Social-class background is measured by the mother's years of schooling, race/ethnicity is measured by dummy variables for whether the child is black, American-Indian, or Asian, with a Spanish language background being measured by a dummy variable for whether or not Spanish is spoken in the home. We also control the child's age in years.

The data are the national norming sample for the WJ-R, collected continuously, 1986–1988, and kindly supplied by Richard Woodcock. These data were collected from students in over one hundred geographically diverse U.S. communities. For a detailed description of sampling procedures and other aspects of data collection, see Chapter 4 of McGrew et al. (1991).

Particularly important is that these tests are the result of more than twenty years of development by a group of psychologists seeking to operationalize the work of Cattell and Horn on the Gf-Gc theory of intellectual capabilities. (See, for example, Cattell 1941; Horn and Cattell 1966; Horn 1976, 1978, 1985, 1988, 1991.) This theory of multiple intelligences represents an important generalization of earlier models such as Spearman (1904), Terman's (1916) Stanford-Binet, and the Wechsler scales (Wechsler 1981). For a review see Horn (1991).

Today, the Woodcock-Johnson battery is one of the most widely utilized cognitive and program evaluation research tools. (For examples of its use see Madden, Slavin, Karweit, Dolan, and Wasik 1993; Slavin, Madden, Dolan, Wasik, Ross, Smith, and Dianda 1995; Pinnell, Lyons, DeFord, Bryk, and Seltzer 1994.) It is also very widely used by practicing psychologists and by school psychologists. The latter use it for testing for special education placements. The fact that the test is administered one-on-one makes it superior to tests such as the Iowa Test of Basic Skills (ITBS), which are typically administered to entire classes at one time. This can be particularly important for achieving high validity and reliability when testing low-performing children and/or those for whom English is a second language. Such children often fail to understand the test instructions when the test is administered to an entire class at one time. The WJ-R has high validity and reliability, and compares favorably to its competitors. [For extensive discussion see Woodcock (1990) and McGrew et al. 1991:Chapters 4–6).] The large, nationally representative norming sample of these one-on-one administered tests has never before been used to determine differential outcomes for social class/ethnicity groups (Richard Woodcock, personal communication).

RESULTS

Table 3.1 shows the means and standard deviations of the variables. The average level of mother's education is 12.9 years. The sample is about

Table 3.1. Means and Standard Deviation of Variables

Variables	Mean	Std. dev.	Cases (N)
Moth Ed	12.86	2.47	1640
Black	0.17	0.37	1640
Female	0.51	0.50	1640
Amerind	0.01	0.09	1640
Asian	0.02	0.15	1640
Hispanic	0.10	0.31	1640
Memory for Names	4994.20	124.67	1637
Visual Matching	4974.80	285.14	1635
Incomplete Words	4977.70	118.80	1637
Visual-Auditory Learning	4975.50	122.31	1640
Cross Out	4990.00	181.75	1634
Sound Blending	4974.60	191.35	1639
Letter-Word Identification	4888.70	466.26	1637
Passage Comprehension	4870.80	392.99	1632
Word Attack	4901.80	271.18	1332
Reading Vocabulary	4925.80	317.53	1327

evenly divided between males and females. It is 17 percent black, 10 percent Hispanic, and much smaller percentages Asian and American Indian. The average scores for the cognitive and reading variables are around 4900, with standard deviations in the 100–400 range.

Table 3.2 shows the regression results for predicting each of the six tests measuring the three basic cognitive skills: auditory processing, long-term retrieval, and processing speed. The first two columns of this table show results for predicting skill at Sound Blending and Incomplete Words, the measures of auditory processing. We see that mother's education (MOTHED) is positively and significantly associated with both skills, whereas being black is negatively associated with these skills. The largest effects are for blacks, who score, on average, 113 points lower on Sound Blending and 59 points lower on Incomplete Words than do whites. The first of these effects is 59 percent of the variable's standard deviation; the second is 50 percent of the standard deviation. Both effects are therefore quite substantial in magnitude. Negative effects are also found for Hispanics, but these are much smaller in magnitude.

We also find a positive and significant effect of social class, as measured by mother's education, on these auditory processing variables. A one-standard-deviation increase in mother's education increases Word Blending by 22 points and Incomplete Words by 9.5 points. However, this effect is much smaller than that of being black.

Table 3.2. Regression of Basic Skills Variables[a]

Explanatory variables	Sound Blending	Incomplete Words	Memory for Names	Visual-Auditory Learning	Visual Matching	Cross Out
Constant	4533.60	4746.50	4731.80	4698.70	4157.70	4480.40
	(190.04)	(303.14)	(270.41)	(297.82)	(174.21)	(284.07)
Moth Ed	8.84	3.85	7.70	6.03	6.30	4.13
	(5.75)	(3.81)	(6.83)	(5.92)	(4.09)	(4.07)
Age	2.50	1.46	1.33	1.57	5.28	3.33
	(31.46)	(27.88)	(22.95)	(29.84)	(66.25)	(63.27)
Female	17.83	−1.98	−18.07	−4.65	44.72	24.12
	(2.45)	(0.41)	(3.41)	(0.97)	(6.13)	(5.02)
Black	−113.38	−59.28	−33.69	−40.20	1.18	−35.54
	(11.32)	(9.02)	(4.62)	(6.07)	(0.12)	(5.38)
Amerind	30.90	−29.03	−19.08	−4.02	−27.57	12.72
	(0.75)	(1.08)	(0.64)	(0.15)	(0.67)	(0.47)
Asian	−31.90	−28.13	−0.38	−2.54	38.23	30.50
	(1.28)	(1.72)	(0.02)	(0.15)	(1.51)	(1.85)
Hispanic	−3.93	−30.44	−15.49	−33.56	−5.46	−7.56
	(0.31)	(3.71)	(1.70)	(4.06)	(0.44)	(0.92)
N	1639	1637	1637	1640	1635	1634
Adj. R^2	0.41	0.34	0.26	0.37	0.73	0.72

[a] The absolute value of the *t*-statistic is in parentheses.

Effects on the long-term retrieval variables—Memory for Names and Visual-Auditory Learning—are similar. That is, blacks score 34 and 40 points, respectively, lower on these variables. While significantly negative, these effects are much closer to those for Hispanics than was the case for auditory processing. The mother's education (social-class) effect on these variables is once again positive, and of the same order of magnitude as was the case for auditory processing. In sum, the race/ethnicity and social-class differentials are larger for auditory processing than for the memory abilities measured as long-term processing.

The final two columns of this table show the determinants of the processing speed variables: Visual Matching and Cross Out. Here we find even weaker relationships with race/ethnicity and a somewhat weaker effect of mother's education. For blacks there is no significant effect on Visual Matching, although there is one on Cross Out. For Hispanics there is no significant effect on either variable. The black and Hispanic effects on processing speed are low to nonexistent. This contradicts those who argue that the relatively low reading performance of low-income and ethnic minority children is associated with their being "less intelligent" or "slow" (Herrnstein and Murray 1994). On the other hand, the relatively large positive effects of mother's education and the relatively large negative effects of being black on auditory processing support those who attribute these differentials to linguistic culture (Entwisle and Alexander 1994).

Table 3.3 shows the regressions to predict the four reading measures. The first four columns regress each of these on the class and race variables only. Columns 5–8 then repeat these calculations with the six basic cognitive-skill variables added to the equation. Thus, the first four columns show the total effect of class and race, whereas columns 5–8 show the direct effect of class and race after the basic cognitive skills are held constant. These calculations, combined with those of Table 3.2, also permit us to calculate the indirect effects of class and race on reading, as these operate through the mediating basic skills variables.

Columns 1–4 show a significant positive effect of social class (mother's education) on each of the four measures of reading achievement. One additional year of schooling increases each of these scores by somewhere between 9 and 19.5 points. Being black exerts a significant and negative effect on reading. This effect is relatively uniform across the four reading indicators, with a magnitude between 50 and 63 points. American Indians and Hispanics also show negative effects, but these are more variable.

Columns 5–8 of this table repeat these calculations with measures of the three basic cognitive abilities added to the equation. The results are dramatic: very substantial portions of the effects of the mother's education are explained, and the effects of being black are completely explained. In particular, for mother's education, the effects in columns 5–8 are, respectively, 28, 21, 0, and 41 percent of those in columns 1–4. That is, controls for basic cognitive abilities explain between 59 and 100 percent of the social-class effect. For blacks, the explanatory power is even more complete. After controlling basic cognitive abilities, the black effect on Letter-Word Identification and Passage Comprehension actually switches from negative and significant to positive and significant! The swing is on the order of 100 points. (Compare the column 1 effect of -57.6 with the column 5 effect of 54.6.) The black effect on Word Attack and Reading Vocabulary switches from a statistically significant -63 and -50 to a not significant -4. Clearly, the basic cognitive ability measures largely explain the social-class effect and completely explain the black effect. That is to say, rather than being direct effects, net of basic cognitive skills, these effects are indirect, operating *through* the effects of social class and being black on basic cognitive skills.

Which of the children's basic cognitive skills play the major role in this transmission of the effect of family background variables to the child's reading ability? By the criterion of large t-statistics, the three most powerful variables in Table 3.3 are, in order, Sound Blending (a measure of auditory processing), Visual Matching (a measure of processing speed), and Incomplete Words (a measure of auditory processing). Of course, these in-

Table 3.3. Regression of Reading Variables[a]

Explanatory Variables	Letter-Word Identification	Passage Comprehension	Word Attack	Reading Vocabulary	Letter-Word Identification	Passage Comprehension	Word Attack	Reading Vocabulary
Constant	3528.70	3781.90	4251.40	3967.50	−6236.10	−4800.10	−2329.60	−2551.70
	(80.25)	(95.53)	(114.82)	(117.16)	(19.03)	(15.66)	(8.57)	(10.17)
Moth Ed	19.52	14.76	9.01	15.75	5.38	3.13	−1.37	6.41
	(6.87)	(5.79)	(3.75)	(7.17)	(2.61)	(1.63)	(0.79)	(3.96)
Age	8.24	6.73	4.00	5.67	2.14	1.43	−0.10	1.75
	(56.27)	(50.92)	(33.57)	(52.24)	(10.24)	(7.30)	(0.58)	(10.98)
Female	22.97	10.58	7.22	1.46	−9.21	−18.02	−10.12	−13.84
	(1.71)	(0.88)	(0.66)	(0.15)	(0.95)	(1.99)	(1.27)	(1.88)
Black	−57.56	−56.31	−62.69	−50.36	54.64	31.34	−3.91	−4.18
	(3.13)	(3.63)	(3.23)	(2.83)	(3.95)	(2.42)	(0.27)	(0.31)
Amerind	−124.76	−53.80	7.91	−89.97	−110.66	−41.65	13.52	−81.08
	(1.65)	(0.79)	(0.14)	(1.78)	(2.08)	(0.84)	(0.34)	(2.23)
Asian	45.42	9.96	49.55	32.50	49.51	11.89	64.85	36.00
	(0.99)	(0.24)	(1.20)	(0.87)	(1.51)	(0.39)	(2.16)	(1.30)
Hispanic	−56.03	−62.77	−2.69	−20.64	−24.62	−30.83	−13.90	−24.44
	(2.44)	(3.04)	(0.12)	(1.01)	(1.50)	(2.01)	(0.87)	(1.65)
Sound Blending					0.55	0.42	0.51	0.34
					(14.37)	(11.76)	(15.79)	(11.31)
Incomplete Words					0.38	0.35	0.24	0.29
					(6.66)	(6.52)	(5.0)	(6.63)
Memory for Names					0.23	0.06	0.12	−0.31
					(4.40)	(1.3)	(2.64)	(1.70)
Visual-Auditory Learning					0.33	0.46	0.25	0.32
					(5.41)	(7.95)	(4.90)	(6.69)
Visual Matching					0.58	0.49	0.41	0.34
					(12.66)	(11.57)	(10.54)	(9.51)
Cross Out					0.08	0.10	−0.06	0.08
					(1.18)	(1.62)	(1.08)	(1.55)
N	1637	1632	1332	1327	1624	1621	1325	1320
Adj. R^2	0.66	0.62	0.46	0.68	0.83	0.8	0.73	0.83

[a] The absolute value of the *t*-statistic is in parentheses.

termediate variables are important transmitters of the effect of mother's education and race only if they meet *two* criteria: they must be strongly related both to mother's education and race *and* strong predictors of reading. The magnitude of the resulting mediating effects are presented in Table 3.4.

Panel A of this table shows that all three basic cognitive abilities—auditory processing, long-term retrieval, and processing speed—play a role in mediating the relationship between mother's education. Overall, the indirect effect via these intermediate variables is typically much larger than the

Table 3.4. Indirect Effects of Class and Race on Reading, Mediated by Basic Cognitive Ability

Mediated by	Letter-Word Identification	Passage Comprehension	Word Attack	Reading Vocabulary
A. Effects of mother's education on each of the reading variables				
Auditory processing				
Sound Blending	4.9	3.7	4.5	3.0
Incomplete Words	1.5	1.3	0.9	1.1
Sum	6.4	5.0	5.4	4.1
Long-term retrieval				
Memory for Names	1.8	0.5	0.9	−2.4
Visual-Auditory Learning	2.0	2.8	1.5	2.1
Sum	3.8	3.3	2.4	−0.3
Processing speed				
Visual Matching	3.6	3.1	2.6	2.1
Cross Out	0.3	0.4	−0.3	0.3
Sum	3.9	3.5	2.3	2.4
Total indirect effect	14.1	12.8	10.1	6.2
Direct effect	5.4	3.1	−1.4	6.4
B. Effects of being black on each of the reading variables				
Auditory processing				
Sound Blending	−62.8	−48.1	−57.7	−38.1
Incomplete Words	−22.7	−20.8	−14.1	−17.4
Sum	−85.5	−68.9	−71.8	−55.5
Long-term retrieval				
Memory for Names	−7.8	−2.2	−3.9	−10.5
Visual-Auditory Learning	−13.5	−18.5	−10.2	−12.8
Sum	−21.3	−20.7	−14.1	−23.3
Processing speed				
Visual Matching	0.7	0.6	0.5	0.4
Cross Out	−2.9	−3.7	2.2	−2.9
Sum	−2.2	−3.1	2.7	−2.5
Total indirect effect	−109.0	−92.7	−83.2	−81.3
Direct effect	54.6	31.3	−3.9	−4.2

direct effect of mother's education net of these variables, and of the intermediate variables, the largest effect is due to auditory processing. Following this, long-term retrieval and processing speed have approximately
equal effects.

Panel B shows a far more dramatic finding for the effects of being
African-American. Here the effects are overwhelmingly due to the basic
cognitive skills, and within these they are overwhelmingly due to auditory processing. By comparison, those of long-term retrieval are a distant
second, and those of processing speed are essentially nonexistent. This
finding of the powerful effects of auditory processing in determining the
lower reading skill of African-American youngsters is strong evidence in
support of the linguistic-culture interpretation of the etiology of black
reading deficits (Entwisle and Alexander 1994). Further, there is *no evidence
that black children "think slower,"* in contradiction to one commonsense
mechanism sometimes associated with arguments for their "genetic infe-
riority" (Gottfredson 1996:20,21).[2]

DISCUSSION

Basic cognitive abilities—auditory processing, long-term retrieval, and
processing speed—have been introduced as mediating variables for the relationship between class/race background and reading ability for children
in grades 1–12. Unique data containing one-on-one-administered measures of these variables have been used to estimate the magnitudes of effect in this model. The results show that basic cognitive abilities explain
most of the relationship between social-class background and children's
reading ability, and all of the relationship between being black and reading ability. The effects of social class are mediated by all three cognitive
abilities, but the strongest effect is due to auditory processing. The effects
of being black are mediated almost entirely by auditory processing. By contrast, processing speed plays no role in the relationship between being
black and reading achievement.

Important implications flow from these findings. At the theoretical level, we have direct empirical evidence for the importance of linguistic culture in the determination of lower-class and African-American reading
deficits. This suggests many lines of further research in the cultural-capital tradition (Chapter 2). At the level of policy prescription, these findings
lend support to programmatic efforts to offer one-on-one remediation
of auditory processing skills (Chapters 10–12). Since Chapter 4 will demonstrate that reading and mathematics ability are the primary determinants of lower African-American than white earnings, the implications for

reducing the inheritance of inequality within American society are profound.

Finally, the results in this chapter suggest that the child's copying and "learning by doing" of his or her family linguistic culture is a key causal mechanism by which students from different family backgrounds acquire differential basic reading skills during their schooling years. Chapters 5 through 9 will further detail the antecedents, correlates and consequences of this differential skill achievement for schooling success.

NOTE

1. This chapter is coauthored with Kurt Beron. We are grateful to Richard Woodcock for making the norming sample data for the Woodcock-Johnson test battery available to us.

2. The two auditory processing variables measure the ability to extract standard English words from audiotape sounds. They are likely to be strongly affected by the extent to which a child has been immersed in standard English. By contrast, the memory and speed variables are "nonsense tasks," which are more likely to be involved with the biological, inherited "wiring of the brain." Once one sees that a complex reading task like passage comprehension strongly covaries with these environmental immersion-in-standard-English variables, as opposed to, say, processing speed, one begins to believe that African-American students' relatively poor reading performance is due to their relatively meager exposure to standard English rather than because they are "not smart."

Chapter 4

Cognitive Skill and Earnings Determination

with Paula England, Keven Vicknair, and Barbara Kilbourne

A vice president of a television station complained of the inner-city work force: "They are frequently unable to write. They go through the Chicago public schools or they dropped out when they were in the eighth grade. They can't read. They can't write. They can hardly talk. . . . And I'm talking about the languages that are spoken in the ghetto. They are not English."
—Joleen Kirschenman and Kathryn M. Neckerman, "'We'd Love to Hire Them, But . . . ': The Meaning of Race for Employers."

The findings in the previous chapter suggest that family linguistic culture strongly determines the individual's reading and mathematics skills. But do these skills in turn affect labor market outcomes? This chapter addresses this question utilizing data on a nationally representative sample of full-time workers in 1991. As we shall see, the answer is unequivocal: a worker's cognitive skills in the English language and mathematics, as measured by standardized tests, are important determinants of the job an individual can attain and are the overwhelmingly most important determinant of the wage rate he or she is paid. Indeed, these cognitive-skill variables far outweigh such standard determinants of earnings as the years of schooling and work experience an individual has completed. Taken together, the findings in this and the preceding chapter suggest the great importance of family linguistic culture in the inheritance of inequality across generations.

MODELS OF EARNINGS DETERMINATION

Employment and earnings outcomes occur within markets for labor. On the demand side of these markets there is an occupational structure whose

33

role as a determinant of earnings inequality is at least partially due to the hierarchy of skill demands it embodies. On the supply side, skills are acquired through arduous activities of schooling and training. Thus the skill-related dimension of an individual's employment career might be usefully summarized in terms of skills acquired during youth, the transformation of these skills into occupation-specific membership and skills acquired in adulthood, and the earnings rewards that employers confer upon the holders of these skills within the jobs they occupy.

We might expect that empirical study of occupational and earnings attainment would focus on these skills and the rewards accruing to them. In particular, we would expect to see a full delineation of the processes by which different individuals come to acquire different levels of skill, these skill levels combine with ascriptive processes to lead to membership within occupations with differential skill and training demands, and these factors combine with differential earnings rates of return to skills and occupational membership to generate earnings variations across individuals. Yet surprisingly little empirical work has directly addressed these questions. Thus, for example, although the influential studies by Sewell and Hauser (1975) and by Jencks and his coauthors (1979, 1983) do focus on individual cognitive skills and their role in earnings attainment, they do not explicitly relate such individual-level skills to access to occupations defined by occupational-level skill demands. Such differential access to skilled occupations across societal groups, combined with (a) the fact that occupations' demands for skill and training affect earnings, and (b) the earnings returns to individual's cognitive skills may differ for ethnic minorities, constitute potentially key mechanisms by which group differences in rewards occur.

The goal of this chapter is to measure the magnitude of the effects flowing from these mechanisms. In particular, we will focus on African-Americans and Mexican-Americans and compare their early careers with those of whites. A key feature of this effort is the analysis of a unique data set containing information on both the actual cognitive skills of workers and the cognitive-skill and training demands of the jobs they occupy. Since the data are for workers who experienced their career beginnings during the 1980s and focus on full-time jobs held in 1991, they provide an assessment of crucial early career experiences that is relatively up-to-date.

I will answer the following questions:

1.   To what extent are African-American and Mexican-American workers still confined to jobs whose skill and training demands are modest at best?

2.   To what extent can any such confinement be attributed to the cognitive skills these individuals bring to the labor market?

3. To what extent can the differential wage rates earned by these group members be attributed to their individual cognitive skills and to the cognitive-skill and training demands of the jobs they occupy?

4. Finally, what patterns of differential returns to cognitive skill are in evidence?

In larger context, these issues return to an old debate over how schooling-related skills affect employment success in capitalist economies. As reviewed by Hunter (1988), this debate pits the "technical-functional" view against the "credentialist" view. Hunter's empirical work, in which the skill demands of occupations to which different individuals achieve access are regressed against those individuals' years of schooling completed, supports the technical-functional viewpoint. In this chapter, I expand upon this work by using United States data (Hunter studied Canada), as well as detailed individual-level measures of cognitive skill and work experience to be included along with years of schooling completed as determinants of occupational access. Most important, I focus on differences across whites and two historically subordinated racial/ethnic groups. The result is to refocus the discussion on the role, if any, played by individual cognitive skills in determining success for disadvantaged groups, who must seek this success within an occupational system characterized, among other things, by a "skill dimension": a hierarchy of jobs that differ in skill demands, which limit access and affect compensation across jobs.

The empirical work centers on two questions: First, to what extent do employers base their employment and compensation offers to workers on the cognitive skills possessed by those workers? Second, to what extent does such employer decision-making based on worker cognitive skill account for the differential labor market outcomes experienced by historically subordinated societal groups? These questions are addressed from within an emerging perspective in labor market studies: the theory of information processing within segmented labor markets. While not providing a complete test of this perspective, I test questions that it raises about the role of cognitive skills in earnings determination. In particular, I test a model of job and earnings determination that synthesizes the views usually advocated by human capital economists and cultural-capital sociologists (see Chapter 2 for further discussion).

For purposes of this analysis, it is useful to view the employment relationship from an information-processing perspective. This approach dates back to two works that appeared simultaneously within sociology and economics: the books by Granovetter (1974) and Spence (1974). Not surprisingly, the characteristic concerns of each discipline were present at this beginning point. Granovetter focused on networks of social relations as information transmitters, and consequent unequal labor market opportunity for differently placed societal groups. Spence focused on the differential potential productivity of workers, and the incentive- and efficiency-related features of alternative mechanisms for revealing this productivity to employers.

These literatures maintained their characteristic focuses as they evolved in the intervening years, with only occasional crossings over to a richer theory embodying both viewpoints. Recently, however, the possibility of this richer theory has been given concrete form by Stinchcombe (1990). In his view, much of what workers do can be seen as information processing, and the allocative and compensation decisions of employers involve imperfect attempts to obtain and process information about employees. The skills possessed by workers are seen as real differences in worker information-processing capacity, differences that are a central concern of employers as they make hiring and compensation decisions. Unfortunately for employers, accurate information about workers' cognitive skills is very difficult to come by, so that "not knowing what one is buying, or even what one has bought, makes the labor contract a perennial information problem for management" (p. 243). Thus while agreeing with economists that differences in worker skill levels are both real and appropriately central to employers' concerns, Stinchcombe presents a view of skill certification in which the skills acquired by workers are often a function of the unequal opportunities flowing to these workers via their placement within a network of social relations. Such network positions may also explain credentials, certificates, and jobs even in the absence of the real skills they generally signal. In this view,

> multiple personnel information systems in organizations and in the labor market are directed at filling in the gaps in this picture of poor measurement and poor prediction of the productivity of labor. These systems of information include certificates from the educational system and sometimes from the professional system as well . . . ; union membership in the crafts; promotion decisions in internal labor markets; informal respect in the work group; whatever experience firms have about whether men or women work out better under the salary, promotion, and incentive systems they typically set up for clerical workers; job evaluation schemes; recommendations by workers in the plant about new hires (a remarkable proportion of workers are recruited this way); footnote citations that distribute honors in the scientific community. (pp. 243–44)

Note that this explanation grants the existence of real skill differences across individuals while still being fundamentally *sociological* in the sense that it focuses on the *social embeddedness* (Granovetter 1985) of individuals and the practices that affect them. Stinchcombe extends this argument to show that socially embedded solutions to the employer's information problem lead naturally to segmented labor markets:

> The information that leads employers to prefer one kind of workers to another . . . means that different *segments* of the labor force will have different opportunities: different incomes, different levels of employment security, different chances of promotion, and the like. Consequently, labor market segmentation is fundamentally a solution to a problem of the information structure about people and their performance that confronts organizations and employees. (p. 244)

As regards workers disadvantaged by such segmentation, Stinchcombe notes that they are "disproportionately ethnic minorities, women reentering the labor market in middle age, teenagers, and people recently unemployed" (p. 270). He goes on to tie their position directly to the employer's information problem:

> [W]hat is distinctive about such populations is that they have very little opportunity to provide certification that will satisfy an employer with a good job on offer that they can be predicted to do well in that job. The main kind of certification that satisfies employers is that one already occupies such a job—and that is the hardest kind of certification for members of disadvantaged segments of the labor market to give. Those sorts of formalized information that justify promotion in internal labor markets are even more inaccessible to such people, and the bodies of peers that govern self-recruited status groups have no reason to regard such people as potential peers, and much interest in keeping out low-wage labor. Such lack of certificates no doubt reflects in part a true lack of competence, but this does not answer the sociological question of how such lack of certified competence (and perhaps of true competence) is systematically distributed. After all, people who end up with the good jobs were also born incompetent. (ibid.)

In its broadest form, Stinchcombe's overview provides the framework necessary for understanding a variety of labor market patterns, both on the supply and the demand sides. For example, the historical tendency of Irish immigrants and their descendants to seek employment in police departments or of Korean immigrants to open small businesses (for example, in the grocery trade) clearly results from their use of social networks to solve their supply side information problem. Similarly, the demand side of segmented labor markets involves core sector employers selecting relatively few employees from among the vast numbers queuing for the jobs they have available (Lang and Dickens 1988). In such a buyer's market, employers can be expected to exercise the luxury of selecting only workers high on skills *and* social acceptability.

The Returns to Skill

But what does this socially embedded, information-processing view of labor market functioning imply about the rewards accruing to the differential skills actually possessed by workers? The answer is unclear, for as
the employer decision-making process is described by Stinchcombe, two
rather different extremes seem possible. At one extreme, skills may be so
difficult to measure, and particularistic social connections so compelling,
that labor market rewards (employment and earnings) are essentially un-
correlated with real skill levels. At the other extreme, employers may be so
focused on skills and so enterprising in their pursuit of indicators highly
correlated with such skills that they typically succeed in solving their
information problem. In this event, labor market returns to skill may be
quite high.

No doubt the true state of affairs lies somewhere between these extremes. Exactly where, and whether this is closer to the low or high end, is
unknown. That is, granted that labor markets are segmented, and that certain population subgroups are disadvantaged by their social embeddedness and its alignment with this segmentation, we do not know what role
the actual skills of these workers currently play in determining their labor
market outcomes.

Consider the following competing views. First, mainstream labor economists assert that skills are a prime determinant of both individual economic success and the differential success of ethnic minorities. These
researchers claim that (a) the narrowing of the black-white earnings gap
prior to 1980 was due to increases in the "quality" of black schooling
(Smith and Welch 1989), and that (b) the slowdown in this narrowing during the 1980s was due to the continued existence of a skills gap combined
with higher returns to skill since 1980 (Smith and Welch 1989; O'Neill 1990;
Juhn, Murphy, and Pierce 1993; Murnane, Willett, and Levy 1995). In related work, economists have attributed the relative economic success of
language minority immigrants to supply and demand side aspects of the
market for skills, particularly language skills (Carliner 1981; McManus,
Gould, and Welch 1983; Grenier 1984; Borjas 1985; Chiswick 1986, 1991;
Kossoudji 1988; Tainer 1988; Baker and Benjamin 1994).

Second, Stinchcombe, a sociologist borrowing from information economics but asserting the primacy of social embeddedness, nevertheless concludes his volume by asserting that "skill pervades our analysis"
(1990:357). Other sociologists have demonstrated that, net of schooling and
work experience, there are positive returns to cognitive skill measured by
test scores (Jencks et al. 1983). Sociologists have also pursued the language
skill issue, reporting a finding of "conditional economic assimilation" for
Spanish-speaking immigrants. That is, these individuals experience *higher*

returns to English-language skill than do native speakers, so that when their skills are poor their earnings are particularly low, but when their skills are strong their earnings are close to those of natives (Stolzenberg 1990).

Finally, a long tradition within sociology argues that education acts in the labor market more as a credential than an indicator of skill and serves more as a cover for discriminatory behavior than as a "signal" of potential productivity (Berg 1970; Collins 1979). This widespread minimizing of cognitive skill by sociologists is indicated by the fact that even a sociologist who is generally sympathetic to the methods and findings of mainstream economics, such as Smith (1990), asserts that cognitive skills play little role in earnings attainment: "Thus, the small effect of I.Q. on income, net of education, may reflect the fact that, for most of the labor force, education affects personal productivity through its impact on personality in general and work habits in particular rather than its effect on cognition" (p. 829).

Which is it? Does cognitive skill powerfully affect labor market outcomes for individuals and groups? Or, after controlling years of schooling, is cognitive skill relatively unimportant for labor market outcomes? The view proposed by Stinchcombe could be reconciled with either assertion. For although information regarding the skills of employees is more difficult to obtain than admitted by economists' human capital models, employers may find signals other than race and sex that serve as good proxies. In this case, we should find strong effects of individuals' cognitive skills. On the other hand, social networks and norms of acceptability may be so linked to ethnicity and sex that employers cannot find proxies for skills not so correlated with these factors that they provide little information to differentiate workers by skill within gender/ethnicity groups. If this is true, then the analyses of this chapter, undertaken separately within each of six ethnic/gender groups and controlling for socioeconomic background and educational credentials, should show no net effect of cognitive skills on labor market outcomes. The results reported below permit a choice between these alternatives.

DATA, VARIABLES, METHODS

We analyze data from the youth cohort of the National Longitudinal Survey (NLSY). These data are from a national probability sample of individuals aged fourteen–twenty-one in 1979, and interviewed each subsequent year. For the present analysis we have focused on full-time jobs held by sample members in 1991, when respondents were twenty-six–thirty-three years of age. The analyses in all our tables are unweighted.

A central aspect of this chapter is its focus on historically subordinated groups, and the different cognitive test scores, schooling, occupations, and wages they experience by comparison with the group that has cultural, numerical, and socioeconomic dominance—whites. To classify persons as African-Americans and whites, respectively, we started with those the NLSY staff categorized as black and non-Hispanic nonblack, based on a question used for screening individuals into or out of the survey. From each of these we deleted anyone whose self-identified first ethnicity (on another question) was any Asian category, American Indian, Cuban, Puerto Rican, or any other Hispanic category. We classified as Mexican-Americans those whose response to the question about first ethnicity fell into the categories of Mexican or Mexican-American. Thus, the group does not include Hispanics whose ancestry is Puerto Rican, Spanish, Cuban, or Central or South American. Also, from those identifying themselves as Mexican or Mexican-American, we eliminated immigrants—based on a question asking whether one was born outside the United States. We wanted to avoid confounding effects of ethnicity with immigrant status or being a nonnative speaker of English. (We did not delete immigrants from the white and African-American categories, but less than 2.5 percent of these groups were born outside the United States.) Other groups (including American Indians, Asians, and non-Mexican Hispanic groups, immigrant and nonimmigrant) were excluded from the analysis. After excluding any sample members with missing values on any of our variables, we were left with the sample of six subgroups on which all our tables are based.

Separate regression analyses are conducted for six groups: white, African-American, and Mexican-American men, and white, African-American, and Mexican-American women. We estimated separate models by ethnicity and gender for two reasons. First, Chow tests led us to reject the hypotheses that the models estimated for Tables 4.2 and 4.3 were invariant by ethnicity and gender. We also conducted specific tests to see if each coefficient differed across the six groups and found some differences (detailed in Tables 4.2 and 4.3).[1]

In regressions to estimate the effects of individuals' cognitive skill on the cognitive-skill demands of the job held in 1991 (Table 4.2), control variables include years of schooling completed by 1991, weeks of full- or part-time employment experience between 1978 (the year before the first wave of the survey) and 1991, the youth's age in 1991, urban vs. rural residence in 1991 (residence in any county with less than half of its population in places of over fifty thousand was defined as rural), and family socioeconomic status (SES) background, measured by the mother's years of schooling completed. We used mother's education rather than father's education or occupational prestige as a measure of SES background because, in these recent cohorts, many grew up in households without a father present for all or part of the time. Thus, using data on fathers would lead to many cases deleted because of missing values.

When estimating effects on wages [natural log of hourly wage, ln(wage)] of individuals' cognitive skills (Table 4.3), we present models including and excluding occupational characteristics: cognitive-skill demands of one's occupation, its physical- and social-skill demands, and the extent to which the occupation is hazardous, involves the exercise of authority over others, or involves exposure to cold or to hot and/or wet conditions. Measurement of these occupational variables is described below. These models also contain the variables discussed in the paragraph above. In addition, some models not shown but discussed add whether or not the wage was set by collective bargaining between a union and management, and the size (number of workers) of the establishment where the respondent worked.

In regressions predicting occupational demands for cognitive skill, as well as in those predicting wages, we expect positive effects of education, experience, and cognitive skill, and negative effects of rural residence. We predict positive effects of occupational demands for cognitive skill on wages. Given the presence of predictions, if coefficients are not significant at the .05 level on two-tailed tests but are significant at this level on one-tailed tests, we indicate this in the tables and discuss the effects as significant.

Our interest focuses primarily on one independent variable: individuals' cognitive skill, measured utilizing the four ASVAB (Armed Services Vocational Aptitude Battery) subtests that most directly reflect language and mathematics performance: tests of word knowledge, paragraph comprehension, arithmetic reasoning, and math knowledge. [These four subtests make up the Armed Forces Qualifying Test (AFQT).] These tests were administered to the entire sample in 1980. Each of these four tests was converted to a Z-score, and these were averaged. We have used a single scale to measure individuals' cognitive skill, rather than separate scales for language and mathematical skill, because the high (about .7) correlation between them would create collinearity in our analyses, making estimates of differences between effects of the two unreliable.

The skill demands and working conditions of one's occupation are measured by scales we created, merged onto each case according to the (three-digit) detailed 1970 occupational codes provided on the NLSY. The measurement of these variables builds on previous work (Kilbourne, England, Farkas, Beron, and Weir 1994), which developed scales guided by a factor analysis of variables from the *Dictionary of Occupational Titles* (DOT). Each scale is an unweighted average of one or more Z-scores.

The first scale measures the demands for general cognitive skill in the occupation. It is similar to what others have termed "substantive complexity" (Cain and Treiman 1981; Parcel and Mueller 1989). The four DOT items in the scale are requirements for general educational development in reasoning, intellectual ability, and specific vocational training, and the complexity of the task with data.

The second scale measures demands for physical skill. The DOT items are requirements for motor coordination, finger dexterity, complexity with things, and the need to see. The scale contains many of the same variables loading high on a factor identified by Cain and Treiman (1981) as "motor skills" in their analysis of DOT items.

The third scale measures nurturant social-skill demands. The DOT items used are adaptability to dealing with people and demands for talking and hearing. Added to this is a dummy variable measuring whether the occupation involves substantial nurturing. The dummy variable was coded 1 if both of these criteria were met: the occupation requires providing a service while engaged in face-to-face contact with clients or customers, and this service providing occurs during a substantial portion of work time. It was coded by the second author of this chapter (Paula England) based on the occupational title. Z-scores of these three items were averaged to create the scale.

The remaining scales tap three dimensions of working conditions: hazardous conditions, exposure to cold, and exposure to heat or wet conditions. They are simply controls for physically onerous working conditions that might affect wages. (For further discussion of the scales, see Kilbourne et al. 1994.)

We restrict attention to full-time jobs (greater than or equal to thirty-five hours/week) held by sample members in 1991. The ultimate dependent variable is the natural logarithm of the hourly wage. To avoid problems associated with miscodings and outliers, all cases with wage rates below $2.50/hour and above $30.00/hour have been deleted. (Only 1.2 percent of cases fell below $2.50/hour; 1.4 percent fell above $30.00/hour.)

RESULTS

Table 4.1 shows the means and standard deviations of the key variables separately for each of the six groups and which group differences in means are significant. Hourly wages are highest for white men ($12.22), followed by Mexican-American men ($10.83), white women ($10.35), African-American men ($9.37), Mexican-American women ($8.75), and African-American women ($8.70). (See note to Table 4.1 for which of these differences are significant. Note that these significance tests are only approximate, since they are calculated under the assumption of zero covariance between the paired means, which is not true. However, they provide suggestive evidence regarding those differences that are most significant.)

Whereas earnings favor men over women within each ethnic group, and whites over both minority groups within each sex, group means for cognitive-skill scores do not follow this pattern. Here the large differences are by ethnicity, favoring whites. Differences in cognitive skill by sex within ethnic groups are not significant except for African-Americans, where employed women significantly outscore men by a small but significant amount. White/African-American differences are approximately one standard deviation; white/Mexican-American differences are about two-thirds of a standard deviation. All ethnic differences are statistically significant.

Ethnic differences are much less pronounced on schooling than on cognitive skills. White men, white women, and African-American women have the highest schooling means in this full-time employed sample, each between 13 and 14 years, and none of these differences are significant. African-American men and Mexican-American women are next, each with about 12.7 years, and Mexican-American men have the least schooling. Within each sex, African-Americans have more schooling than Mexican-Americans.

Within each sex, the rank order on employment experience is whites, Mexican-Americans, then African-Americans. It is worth noting the greater employment experience of white women than African-American women; this is a reversal of the well-known historic pattern of higher rates of employment by African-American than white women. African-American women's overall employment rates just held constant since 1980, although in recent cohorts rates for groups with low education declined. By contrast, white women's rates continued to increase, so that in relatively young cohorts, white women now have more experience (Corcoran and Parrot 1992). The severe problem of unemployment and discouraged workers in African-American communities is highlighted by the fact that these NLSY white women, in the peak of child-rearing ages, have more employment experience than African-American men. Within each sex, African-Americans have more schooling but less employment experience than Mexican-Americans.

Whites hold occupations with higher cognitive-skill demands within each sex; all white-minority differences are significant. As with individuals' cognitive skills, within ethnic groups, no significant differences in the cognitive-skill demands of occupations favor men. For one group, African-Americans, women's occupations demand slightly (but significantly) more cognitive skill.

We discuss regression results as follows: First, we examine cognitive skill and other determinants of being in an occupation with higher require-

Table 4.1. Means and Standard Deviations of Key Variables

	Male			Female		
	Whites	African-American	Mexican-American	Whites	African-American	Mexican-American
Cognitive skill	.393	−.608	−.268	.354	−.455	−.260
	(.832)	(.811)	(.751)	(.715)	(.688)	(.670)
Education (years completed)	13.399	12.774	12.294	13.553	13.404	12.740
	(2.365)	(1.998)	(1.742)	(2.259)	(1.864)	(2.071)
Experience (weeks)	548.898	473.548	531.239	519.732	455.821	463.377
	(124.489)	(144.603)	(127.828)	(138.926)	(153.144)	(156.866)
Mother's education (years)	12.055	10.837	7.730	11.964	11.197	7.603
	(2.269)	(2.485)	(3.791)	(2.256)	(2.569)	(3.770)
Age in 1991	29.566	29.449	29.399	29.378	29.586	29.466
	(2.292)	(2.226)	(2.011)	(2.204)	(2.267)	(2.314)
Rural residence in 1991 (1 = rural)	.210	.089	.092	.175	.069	.096
	(.408)	(.285)	(.290)	(.380)	(.254)	(.295)

Occupational demand for cognitive skill	.184 (.885)	−.344 (.903)	−.170 (.870)	.139 (.832)	−.153 (.847)	−.086 (.831)
Hourly wage ($)	12.22 (5.23)	9.37 (4.41)	10.83 (4.99)	10.35 (4.78)	8.70 (3.80)	8.75 (3.95)
Ln Hourly Wage	7.02 (.44)	6.74 (.44)	6.89 (.46)	6.84 (.45)	6.68 (.41)	6.68 (.43)
N	1,170	606	163	805	493	146

Note: Standard deviations are in parentheses. The following group differences (where WM, . . . , MF are the six groups from left to right in the table) in means are significant ($p < .05$, two-tailed):

Cognitive skill: WM & AM, WM & MM, AM & MM, WF & AF, WF & MF, AF & MF, WM & MF, AM & WF, AM & MF, MM & AF, AM & AF, MM & MF, MM & WF

Education: WM & AM, WM & MM, AM & MM, WF & MF, AF & MF, WM & MF, AM & AF, MM & MF

Experience: WM & AM, AM & MM, WF & AF, WF & MF, WM & WF, AM & AF, AM & AW, MM & AF, MM & MF

Mother's education: WM & AM, WM & MM, AM & MM, WF & AF, WF & MF, AF & MF, WM & MF, AM & WF, AM & AF, AM & MF, MM & AF, MM & WF

Age: none

Rural: WM & AM, WM & MM, WF & AF, WF & MF, WM & AF, WM & WF, MM & WF

Occupational demand for cognitive skill: WM & AM, WM & MM, AM & MM, WF & AF, WF & MF, WM & AF, WM & MF, AM & WF, AM & AF, AM & MF, MF, MM & WF

Earnings: WM & AM, WM & MM, AM & MM, WF & AF, WF & MF, WM & WF, WM & AF, WM & MF, AM & WF, AM & AF, MM & AF

ments for cognitive skill (Table 4.2). Then we examine effects of individual and occupational variables on earnings (Table 4.3). Then we use regression decomposition to assess how much group mean differences on individual-level skill-related variables explain group differences in pay (Table 4.4).

Table 4.2 displays regression results for models predicting the cognitive-skill demands of the occupations in which sample members are employed. Coefficients are unstandardized, so they can be compared between groups. For each group, the cognitive-skill test score positively and significantly affects access to jobs with high cognitive-skill demands; t-tests for differences in coefficients between groups show no significant differences between the coefficients of any pair of groups. These returns are *net* of years of schooling, work experience, SES background (as measured by mother's education), age, and whether one resides in a rural area. Thus, it is clear that employers do somehow access information about individuals' cognitive skills, over and above what they can ascertain from their years of education and work experience, and that they prefer individuals with higher cognitive skills for occupations demanding more cognitive skill.

Schooling also has positive and significant effects on getting a job in an occupation requiring more cognitive skill, even net of measured cognitive skill, and these effects are significant for all six groups except Mexican-American women (although their coefficient is not significantly different from that for either Mexican-American men or African-American women). Since the sample of Mexican-American women is the smallest of the six groups, we should perhaps not infer too much from the difference between Mexican-American women and three of the other groups in the significance of the effect. How do we interpret these effects of schooling? They suggest that employers use educational credentials to decide which workers to place in jobs demanding more cognitive skill. They may do this because it is expensive to measure cognitive skill directly, so they use schooling as an imperfect proxy. Since education and cognitive skills are positively correlated, this will generally lead workers with higher cognitive skills to be in the more demanding jobs. However, it will also produce the effect seen here: among people with equal test-measured cognitive skills, those with more education are in more cognitively demanding jobs. It is also possible that schooling imparts (or staying in school selects on) cognitive skills or other qualities that employers want but that are not captured by our test-score-based measure. Examples of such qualities may be habits and styles associated with cultural capital (see Chapter 2), a tendency to obey orders, or "stick-to-it-iveness." We cannot choose between these interpretations from our analysis.

Past work experience positively affects access to occupations requiring more cognitive skill for five of the six groups (all but African-American

Table 4.2. Unstandardized Coefficients from Regression Analysis of Occupational Demand for Cognitive Skill

	Male			Female		
	White	African-American	Mexican-American	White	African-American	Mexican-American
Cognitive skill	.1978*	.2821*	.1874+	.1992*	.1990*	.2937*
	(5.49)	(5.64)	(1.78)	(4.37)	(3.14)	(2.42)
Education (years)	.1383*	.1470*	.1571*	.1311*	.1099*	.0473
	(10.93)	(7.31)	(3.60)	(8.98)	(4.74)	(1.30)
Experience (weeks)	.0006*	.0003	.0009+	.0005*	.0007*	.0009*
	(2.73)	(1.25)	(1.66)	(2.55)	(2.94)	(2.02)
Mother's education	.0137	.0080	.0102	.0076	.0013	.0206
(years)	(1.26)	(.602)	(.594)	(.593)	(.086)	(1.16)
Age (years)	−.0185*	−.0287*	−.0736*	−.0203*	−.0334*	−.0056
	(1.69)	(1.83)	(2.02)	(1.65)	(1.98)	(.197)
Rural residence	−.0960+	−.2146+	.0353	−.0844	−.1515	.0521
(1 = rural)	(1.74)	(1.95)	(.164)	(1.24)	(1.09)	(.242)
R^2 (adjusted)	.276*	.279*	.176*	.258*	.159*	.182*
N	1,170	606	163	805	493	146

Note: The absolute value of the t-statistic is in parentheses.
Significance of coefficients: *, $p < .05$ (two-tailed tests); +, $p < .05$ (one-tailed tests).
The following group differences in coefficients are significant ($p < .05$, two-tailed):
  Cognitive skill: none
  Education: WM & MF, AM & MF, WF & MF
  Experience: none
  Mother's education: none
  Age: none
  Rural: none

men). The coefficients are never significantly different between groups, so we should not make much of the nonsignificance for one group.

Net of these measures of individuals' characteristics, socioeconomic background, indexed by mother's education, does not have a significant effect on being in an occupation with higher cognitive demands for any of the six groups.

Do individuals' cognitive skills only affect access to jobs requiring more cognitive skill in professional or managerial job categories? Put differently, is cognitive skill irrelevant to explaining the nonprofessional, nonmanagerial jobs held by the majority of workers? In results not shown, we ascertain that this is not the case. We deleted individuals holding occupations the census categorizes as professional, technical, or managerial, and repeated the regressions of Table 4.2 for clerical, sales, blue-collar, service, and farm workers. We find significant positive effects of cognitive skill for all of the six groups except Mexican-American men, but effects for them have a positive sign and are not significantly different from those for most groups. Thus, cognitive skills are important for access to jobs requiring more cognitive skill even in those portions of the occupational-skill hierarchy below the professional and managerial level. Years of schooling show reduced effects when professional, technical, and managerial employees are omitted; the models show significant coefficients for education for only one group (African-American men). This suggests that the use of educational credentials as proxies for cognitive skills is greater in professional and managerial jobs than in others.

Table 4.3 shows the effects of individual and occupational characteristics on the natural logarithm of hourly wages. For each group, the first column (model 1) shows the reduced-form regression of wages on individual characteristics; returns to individual's characteristics in this column include those operating indirectly through their role in facilitating access to detailed census occupations requiring more cognitive skill. For each group, the second column (model 2) shows the result of adding occupational-skill demands and working conditions to the equation; coefficients for individuals' characteristics in this column are returns to cognitive skills that exist even among individuals in occupations that are equal in cognitive demands (at least as we are able to assess with our DOT-based scale).

Results for model 1 in Table 4.3 show that all groups receive significant positive returns to schooling and employment experience. These returns are never significantly different between groups. For all groups, returns to each additional year of schooling are in the range of 3–7 percent; returns for each year of experience are in the range of 3–5 percent (multiplying the coefficient times 52 converts from weeks to years).

Our interest focuses on individuals' cognitive skill, which (in both models 1 and 2) exerts positive and significant effects on wages for all six

Table 4.3. Unstandardized Coefficients from Regression Analysis of Ln (Hourly Wages)

| | Male | | | | | | Female | | | | | |
| | White | | African-American | | Mexican-American | | White | | African-American | | Mexican-American | |
	(1)	(2)	(1)	(2)	(1)	(2)	(1)	(2)	(1)	(2)	(1)	(2)
Cognitive skill	.1045*	.0881*	.1392*	.1052*	-.0017	-.0251	.1101*	.0885*	.1726*	.1566*	.1205*	.0971+
	(5.58)	(4.73)	(5.55)	(4.21)	(.03)	(.44)	(4.78)	(3.88)	(6.26)	(5.67)	(2.40)	(1.89)
Education (years)	.0407*	.0311*	.0421*	.0331*	.0423+	.0245	.0682*	.0519*	.0442*	.0378*	.0640*	.0609*
	(6.19)	(4.56)	(4.18)	(3.17)	(1.73)	(.99)	(9.25)	(6.79)	(4.37)	(3.68)	(4.27)	(3.94)
Experience (weeks)	.0007*	.0007*	.0009*	.0009*	.0007*	.0006+	.0007*	.0007*	.0007*	.0007*	.0006*	.0005*
	(7.05)	(6.80)	(7.46)	(7.68)	(2.17)	(1.84)	(7.34)	(6.80)	(6.36)	(5.78)	(3.09)	(2.60)
Mother's education (years)	.0024	.0022	.0085	.0079	.0123	.0127	.0131*	.0133*	.0074	.0075	.0323*	.0306*
	(.43)	(.40)	(1.28)	(1.22)	(1.27)	(1.39)	(2.02)	(2.09)	(1.16)	(1.18)	(4.38)	(4.04)
Age (years)	.0027	.0038	-.0074	-.0060	.0118	.0209	-.0060	-.0033	-.0020	.0004	-.0120	-.0106
	(.48)	(.69)	(.94)	(.78)	(.58)	(1.06)	(.97)	(.55)	(.28)	(.05)	(1.03)	(.89)
Rural residence (1 = rural)	-.1084*	-.1057*	-.0577	-.0566	-.1478	-.1685	-.0748*	-.0679*	-.0638	-.0444	-.0447	-.0533
	(3.78)	(3.74)	(1.04)	(1.05)	(1.22)	(1.48)	(2.18)	(2.00)	(1.05)	(.74)	(.50)	(.59)
Occupational demand for cognitive skill		.0998*		.0967*		.1925*		.1237*		.0576*		.0859*
		(5.35)		(3.96)		(3.26)		(6.04)		(2.35)		(1.99)
R^2 (adjusted)	.208	.240	.245	.295	.075	.239	.343	.374	.323	.341	.485	.484
N	1,170	1,170	606	606	163	163	805	805	493	493	146	146

Note: Other variables included in the equations for model 2 are Physical Skill Demands of Job, Social Skill Demands of Job, Hazardous Working Conditions, and Hot/Wet Working Conditions.

Absolute value of t-statistics in parentheses. Significance of coefficients: *, $p < .05$ (two-tailed tests); +, $p < .05$ (one-tailed tests).

The following group differences in coefficients are significant ($p < .05$, two-tailed):

	Model 1	Model 2
Cognitive skill:	WM & AF, AM & MM, MM & AF	WM & AF, AM & MM, MM & AF
Education:	none	none
Experience:	none	none
Mother's education:	WM & MF, AM & MF, AF & MF	WM & MF, AM & MF, AF & MF
Age:	none	none
Rural:	none	none
Occ. cognitive skill:		MM & AF

groups except Mexican-American men (for whom the coefficient is non-significant). Yet, since Mexican-American men's returns are not significantly different from four out of the five groups that have significant positive returns, we should not infer much from the nonsignificance for one group with a small sample size. Rates of return are not significantly different between any pairs of groups except for African-American women's higher rate of return than white or Mexican-American men and African-American men's higher rate of return than Mexican-American men. There is certainly no systematic pattern for women and minorities to have lower rates of return to cognitive skill.

The findings from Table 4.2, discussed above, implied that employers somehow find indicators of cognitive skill in hiring or promotion, such that these skills affect getting into a job requiring more cognitive skill. The findings in model 1 of Table 4.3, just reviewed, show that cognitive skills of individuals affect their pay. Since model 1 did not control for cognitive demands of occupations, these estimates include effects operating indirectly through placement in jobs that are more cognitively demanding, as well as effects of skills on pay differences within jobs and between jobs equal in their cognitive demands.

The second column (model 2) for each group in Table 4.3 shows the result of adding occupational cognitive-skill demands, as well as other occupational variables, as controls. Being in an occupation requiring more cognitive skill has positive and statistically significant effects on wages for all six groups. Mexican-American men's rate of return, the highest among the six groups, is significantly different from only one group: African-American women, the group with lowest returns. (Recall, however, that African-American women had the highest returns to individual cognitive skill and Mexican-American men the lowest.) There are no other significant group differences in returns to occupational demand for cognitive skill.

What happens to the effects of variables measuring individuals' characteristics in model 2 of Table 4.3 when occupational demands for skill and onerous working conditions are controlled? If the effects of individual characteristics seen in model 1 disappear in model 2, this would indicate that all of the returns to cognitive skill, schooling, and employment experience operate indirectly through their access to more demanding occupations. The findings for model 2 show that the effects of employment experience are not changed much from model 1. The effects of both schooling and cognitive skill are reduced, typically by no more than 30 percent of their former magnitude. The extent of reduction demonstrates that some of the effect of both education and cognitive skill operates through access to more skilled jobs, as we would expect. Yet approximately 70–80 percent of the effect of cognitive skills on earnings remains even after we adjust for differences in the cognitive-skill demands of the occupation held; a similar situation holds for education. This implies that the education and cognitive skills of individuals also affect wages through other mechanisms than access to occupations requiring more cognitive skill. One such mechanism could be paying workers with more skill or education more than other workers in the same occupation (through promotions or "merit pay"). Another possibility is that workers with greater cognitive skills use them to engage in "smarter" job searches or to figure out the contingencies of reward in their organizations. The effects could also result from the ability of employers with higher profits to use higher wages to recruit workers with more skill and education, which would force employers who cannot pay such high wages but who are hiring in jobs with equal cognitive demands to settle for the cheaper workers with less education or cognitive skill. It is also possible that some of the effect is indirect through skill demands of jobs that our DOT- and census-occupation-based measures are too crude to pick up.

An interesting note on direct effects of socioeconomic background is the fact that the education of the worker's mother affects earnings, net of all the controlled qualifications, for white and Mexican-American women, but not for African-American women or any group of men. Past research assures us that there are many indirect effects of socioeconomic background, but we have not specified reduced-form equations to show these since we are only interested in this variable as a control.

As we did for predicting access to a more cognitively demanding occupation, we repeated the models predicting earnings in Table 4.3 with professional, technical, and managerial workers deleted. (Results are not shown.) We were curious about whether the effects of individuals' cognitive skill and of occupations' demands for cognitive skill on earnings are present in the nonelite jobs where the vast majority work. As with our findings on occupational attainment, the main effect of limiting the analysis to lower-level workers is to reduce the estimated effects of education, although for both models 1 and 2 they remained significant and positive for four of the six groups. Effects of employment experience were virtually unchanged. The effect of individuals' cognitive skill was positive for all groups and significantly so for all groups except Mexican-Americans of either sex (whose N were only 124 and 104 here). Overall then, the results suggest that effects of cognitive skill operate in all ranges of the occupational hierarchy.

We undertook another supplementary analysis to ascertain the extent to which the effects of cognitive skill on earnings occur via the ability of higher-skill workers to attain union jobs and/or jobs in larger establishments, since these two organizational characteristics are often assumed to predict higher wages. We added these two variables to models 1 and 2 of the equa-

tions in Table 4.3. The number of people employed in one's establishment had significant positive effects for African-American and Mexican-
American men, but no other groups; having the wages in one's job set by
collective bargaining between the employer and a union increased wages
significantly and substantially for all groups. However, the effects of cognitive skill in model 1 remained positive and significant for all five groups
for whom it was significant before adding these variables (all except Mexican-American men), and remained significant for all five except Mexican-
American women after controlling occupational characteristics (model 2).
The effects did not decrease nontrivially for any group with the addition
of these two variables, yielding the surprising conclusion that returns to
individual cognitive skill do not result from workers with higher cognitive
skills having greater access to jobs in larger firms or unionized jobs. This
does not deny the possibility, suggested above, that returns to cognitive
skills may operate through access to higher-paying employers; however, it
suggests that the dimensions of jobs or organizations along which such se-
lectivity occurs are other than size or unionization.

To the extent that the mechanism through which cognitive skills affect
wages is through access to better-paying jobs (rather than higher pay within jobs), this raises the question of how employers assess cognitive skills.
In cases where this is not the person's first job in the firm, but a job attained
by promotion or within-firm transfer, the employer has some direct information on performance. But we have undertaken supplementary analyses
that find a positive effect of cognitive skills on wages even when we only
consider entry-level wages within firms. Since the NLSY includes data on
firm changes, we reorganized the data so that spells of individuals' time in
one firm were units, pooled across all spells from the beginning of the survey, and regressed the wage at the first survey date after the spell began
(our best estimate of starting wages) on the variables in Table 4.3. We found
cognitive skill to affect these first wages, implying that somehow employers assess cognitive skills before hiring workers. How do employers make
such assessments of cognitive skill before hire? One possibility is the use
of written tests to decide whether applicants qualify for any—or more-
skilled and better-paying—jobs. Performance on such tests undoubtedly
correlates with the tests given NLSY respondents; the latter are used by the
army to help determine job assignments. Another possibility is that interviewers make rough assessments of cognitive skills, using cues such as
grammar, vocabulary, comprehension of questions, and logical relevance
of answers. If their estimates are better than random choices, this would
contribute to the effects observed.

Table 4.4 presents a partial regression decomposition showing the consequences of the lower average cognitive-skill levels of African-American
and Mexican-American workers for their wage attainment relative to

whites. Using the group means on the three skill-related variables, cognitive skills, education, and experience, we assess how much group differences in means contribute to group differences in wages. We determine how much a difference in mean score on a variable contributes to mean ln(wage) difference by taking the mean difference between the two groups times the rate of return for that variable. This presents us with the problem of which group's slope to use. Two different thought experiments are answered, depending on the choice made. For example, when comparing African-Americans and whites, if we use blacks' slopes, we answer the question of how much of the gap in mean ln(wage) would be closed if blacks moved to the white mean on the independent variables, but re-

Table 4.4. Decomposition of Ethnic Pay Gaps: Percentage Explained by Mean Differences on Selected Variables

	$X_H - X_L$ (mean diff.)	$b_H(X_H - X_L)$	% Gap explained	$b_L(X_H - X_L)$	% Gap explained
African-American & white men					
Cognitive skill	1.001	.1046	38.46%*	.1393	51.23%*
Education	0.625	.0254	9.35%*	.0263	9.67%*
Experience	75.350	.0527	19.39%*	.0678	24.93%*
Total		.1827	67.20%	.2334	85.83%
African-American & white women					
Cognitive skill	.809	.0891	55.69%*	.1396	87.25%*
Education	.149	.0102	6.37%	.0066	4.12%
Experience	63.911	.0447	27.94%*	.0447	27.94%*
Total		.1440	90.00%	.1909	119.31%
Mexican-American & white men					
Cognitive skill	.661	.0691	54.39%*	−.0011	−.88%
Education	1.105	.0450	35.41%*	.0467	36.80%*
Experience	17.659	.0124	9.73%	.0124	9.73%
Total		.1265	99.53%	.058	45.65%
Mexican-American & white women					
Cognitive skill	.614	.0676	41.73%*	.0739	45.67%*
Education	.813	.0554	34.23%*	.0520	32.12%*
Experience	56.455	.0395	24.39%*	.0339	20.91%*
Total		.1625	100.35%	.1598	98.7%

Note: X = mean; *b* = slope; H and L pertain to higher- and lower-earning group, respectively. % Gap explained = the column to the left divided by the ln (pay) gap. Slopes taken from model 1 in Table 4.3; means from Table 4.1.

*This percentage of gap explained based on a significant mean difference and a significant slope ($p < .05$, two-tailed test).

tained the slopes and intercept they currently have. If we use whites' slopes, we learn how much of the black/white gap would be closed if whites moved to the black mean on the independent variables and retained the slopes and intercept they currently have. Since the choice between these two is somewhat arbitrary, we present two estimates of the contribution to the gap for each variable, one using each group's slope, thus providing a range. Each contribution is then translated into a percentage of the gap between the two group's means on ln(wage). We use the slopes from model 1 in Table 4.3. Our choice of the reduced-form model 1 for decomposition means that we will include effects of individuals' characteristics on earnings that operate through the intervening variables of occupational demands, as well as those that do not work through occupation.

A full decomposition would also determine how much of the ln(wage) gap can be attributed to different intercepts and slopes. We do not present these components, in part because slopes for the variables of interest are generally not significantly different between ethnic groups within a sex. (The only exception is the lower returns for Mexican-American men than African-American men on cognitive skill.) A second reason is that we are persuaded by Jones and Kelley's (1984) argument that how much of a gap is attributed to intercepts versus slopes is sensitive to the choice of metric for independent variables.

The first column of Table 4.4 shows the mean difference in cognitive skill, education, and experience between each minority group and whites of the same sex, taken from Table 4.1. The second column gives the product of each mean difference times the slope of whites, the higher-earning group. This product is an estimate of ln(wage) explained by the mean difference. The third column translates this into a percent of the group difference in mean ln(wage). The fourth and fifth columns are analogous to the second and third, except that they use the lower-earning (minority) group's slope.

The percentages of ln(wage) gap explained by group differences in cognitive skills are generally high. Differences in cognitive skills explain 38–51 percent of the African-American/white pay gap for men and 56–87 percent for women. Differences in education explain 9–10 percent of the African-American/white pay gap for men and 4–6 percent for women. Differences in weeks of work experience explain another 19–25 percent for men and 28 percent for women. If we add the contributions of group differences in these three variables, we have explained 67–86 percent of the African-American/white gap among men and 90–119 percent among women. When the explained portion is over 100 percent using black women's slopes, this means that, given their current intercept and rates of return, if their means moved to those of white women, they would earn more than white women by 19 percent.

Examining the Mexican-American/white pay gaps, we find that differences in cognitive skills explain 42–46 percent for women. For men the case is more ambiguous, since Mexican-American men had a negative but nonsignificant coefficient for cognitive skill, although their slope was not significantly different than that of white men, who showed a significant positive coefficient. Thus, if we use white men's coefficient, the estimate is that differences in cognitive skills explain 54 percent of the ln(wage) gap; however, using Mexican-American men's slope, the estimate is −1 percent. Differences in years of education explain 35–37 percent of the Mexican-American/white pay gap among men, and 32–34 percent among women. Ethnic differences in experience explain 10 percent of the Mexican-American/white pay gap for men and 21–24 percent for women. Adding the contributions of these three variables, we have explained 46–100 percent of the Mexican-American/white gap among men and 99–100 percent among women.

Overall, we see a powerful role for cognitive skills in explaining ethnic differences in earnings in these young cohorts, and smaller but nontrivial roles for education and experience as well. Among women, we have explained virtually all (or by some estimates even more than all) of the minority/white gaps with these three variables. Since any current discrimination by employers—in the sense of differential pay for those with equal cognitive skills, education, and experience—would have to be represented in the extent to which less than 100 percent is explained by these variables, the findings suggest little role for such ethnic discrimination in recent years in these cohorts of women.

Among men, the estimates depend more on which groups' slopes are used; the combined contributions of group differences in cognitive skills, education, and experience explain 67–86 percent of the African-American/white and 46–100 percent of Mexican-American/white gaps. This suggests the possibility that there may be more ethnic discrimination among men than women in recent cohorts of employed workers. However, even for men, the explanatory power of cognitive skills is powerful; this is most unambiguous for the white/African-American gap. Further, an additional share of the white/African-American earnings gap would be explained if we adjusted for interregional wage differences (which may reflect cost-of-living differences); African-Americans are more concentrated in the low-wage South. (For a calculation detailing this, see Farkas and Vicknair, forthcoming.)

We consider only those with full-time jobs here, so it is possible that there is more discrimination in getting a job or getting a full-time job than in wage allocation; our analyses do not capture the former.

While our focus has been on ethnic differences within sex groups, we note, by way of contrast, that the only one of the skill-related variables (cognitive skill, education, and experience) to explain a nontrivial part of the sex gap in pay is employment experience. Depending on whether men's or women's slopes are used, sex differences in experience explain 12% of the pay gap among whites, 20–26 percent among African-Americans, and 19–23 percent among Mexican-Americans. Since neither cognitive skills nor education show significant sex differences in means favoring men in any ethnic group, these factors play *no* role in intraethnic sex differences in pay in these recent cohorts of full-time workers.

DISCUSSION: BRINGING SKILLS BACK IN

I might have titled this chapter, "Bringing Skills (Back?) into the Study of Unequal Labor Market Outcomes." That is, while sociologists of work have long been interested in skills, their antecedents and consequences [for example, consider the large literature running through works such as Blauner (1964) and Spenner (1983)], and stratification sociologists have occasionally included standardized test scores in their regressions (e.g., Sewell and Hauser 1975; Jencks et al. 1979, 1983), there has been little empirical work by sociologists focusing on the joint effects of individual skills and occupational-skill demands on unequal labor market outcomes for historically subordinated groups.

Of course, economists have long argued that "human capital," by which they mean productivity-enhancing skills, are *the* central determinants of earnings. And yet their empirical work typically employs years of schooling and years of work experience as (distant and inadequate) proxies for individual skill, while direct measures of occupational-skill demands are completely absent.

In place of these distinct disciplinary interpretations we prefer Stinchcombe's (1990) view that the differential skills of workers are real, that they are of great concern to employers, but that their distribution across workers and their certification by employers are the result of socially embedded processes affected by ascription. His view leaves several empirical questions unanswered; we have tried to answer them here. First, are the economic returns to individual-level skill and occupational-skill demands important determinants of earnings? Or are any such effects greatly attenuated by the difficulty experienced by employers in correctly measuring worker skill? Second, are these returns smaller for members of historically subordinated ethnic groups than they are for majority group members?

Some sociologists argue that skills play little role in access to good jobs or earnings. Yet we have found the opposite. Individual-level cognitive skills, even measured years before the hiring date, are powerful determinants of access to cognitively demanding jobs and higher wages. Further, these returns (slopes) are larger for some minority-group members, African-Americans in particular, than for whites. And this is true despite controls for years of schooling, work experience, and social-class background. These effects, combined with the lower average cognitive-skills scores of these workers, account for large shares of the lower wages of African-American relative to white workers.

Our findings answer some questions and raise many others. They make us curious about the mechanism by which cognitive skills affect wages, net of years of education and experience. One possible mechanism is the use by some firms of written tests to decide whether applicants qualify for any—or more skilled and better-paying—jobs. Another possible mechanism is that interviewers may make rough assessments of cognitive skills, using cues such as grammar, vocabulary, comprehension of questions, and logical relevance of answers.

Other mechanisms for the effects may involve firms' use of personal networks to recruit job applicants, combined with some degree of homogeneity of personal networks on variables that predict test scores. An example of such a variable might be whether the youth went to high school in an inner-city or suburban area, or at a private or public school. Employers with high-wage jobs may trust that their "better-than-average" workers will bring in workers more skilled than they could have predicted from easily measured qualities such as years of education and experience. Of course, segregation of personal networks by ethnicity and gender is quite pronounced as well, and thus the use of networks can be discriminatory. But while segregated networks may contribute to the origin of group differences in cognitive skills, ethnic and gender segregation cannot account for the *effects* of cognitive skills on wages we have observed, since we estimated them *within* race/gender groups. However, there is ample reason to expect homogeneity on other variables related to cognitive skills; the principle of homophily is central to theorizing about social networks, and similarity of those with network connections is a central empirical finding (Blau 1977; McPherson and Smith-Lovin 1987; Marsden 1988). Thus, firms and occupations may recruit workers with similar cognitive skills even when they have no direct measure of these.

Research by Neckerman and Kirschenman (1991) suggests that all of the above mechanisms are at work. These researchers interviewed 185 employers in Chicago and the surrounding Cook County, with inner-city firms oversampled. Their questionnaire focused on the firm's modal entry-level job from one of the following categories: sales, clerical, skilled, semi-skilled, unskilled, and service jobs. They report that by far the most widely used recruitment mechanism is to ask current employees for referrals. They also report that 40 percent of employers have no formal job prerequisites, 40 percent have an educational level requirement, and 40 percent give a formal skills test (within the latter group, half have an educational requirement in addition to the skills test). Virtually, all employers stated that they require personal interviews, and all use these interviews to judge the skill and personal characteristics, such as dependability, of prospective employees. Thus, attention to social networks, basic cognitive skills, and employer perceptions of worker habits are all justified by the data. Each of these must play a role in any full understanding of ethnic differences in employment and earnings.

What are the policy implications of the finding that a relatively high proportion of ethnic inequality in wages is explained by differences in measured cognitive skills? It does not imply that equal opportunity between ethnic groups prevails in the socioeconomic attainment process. For one thing, some portion of ethnic differences was not explained by group differences in cognitive skills, and some of this may reflect discrimination by employers. (Although it was not our focus, we also note that these individual cognitive skills explain virtually none of the gender gap in wages; indeed, women have higher cognitive-skill scores than do men within both minority groups, and white women's scores lag those of white men by a very small amount.) Our findings suggest the need for attention to a kind of inequality of opportunity coming not from employers, but from other social and political processes: inequality of opportunity to attain cognitive skills. The processes by which unequal schooling outcomes occur are the subject of the remainder of this volume. These processes take on great policy importance in light of this chapter's finding of the high returns to cognitive skills in labor markets.

It is important to remember that our data occur relatively early in the job life cycle—sample members were twenty-six to thirty-two years of age in 1991. Wage differences between groups are smaller in this age group than among older adults. If this is entirely a cohort effect, then the patterns we observe will hold as young cohorts age. If it is not, increasing ethnic inequality as careers progress may occur, either from direct discrimination, or from the use of internal labor markets so that those who start behind fall further and further behind in wages and skill development. Future research should attend to this.

Our discussion has proceeded under the assumption that measured cognitive skills are real descriptors of potential work performance. A skeptic might argue that test scores have no link to real productivity on the job, but are a measure of cultural capital valued by elites, especially for higher-level positions. It is difficult to separate these effects, since knowledge and behavior that help one to communicate with and gain the respect of supervisors, coworkers, and customers thereby affect performance even where they would not have had others not valued this cultural capital. In a case where there was *no* demonstrable link between test scores (or their proxies) and productivity, federal courts would probably rule the use of such screening devices discriminatory under the Griggs doctrine of disparate impact (Burstein and Pitchford 1990). Our strong suspicion is that cognitive skills, as measured by test scores, have some effects on productivity that would be found to persist under a variety of cultural constellations.

In summary, we have found that the "skill dimension" is an important one for worker attainment of employment and earnings. This is demonstrated by three findings: First, individuals' cognitive skills strongly affect the skill level of the jobs they attain, and their wages. Second, the skill demands of jobs affect the wages they offer. And, finally, sizable portions of ethnic differences in the skill level of jobs held and in wages attained are explained by group differences in cognitive skills. The balance of this volume focuses on the processes by which group differences in such skills are created, and interventions by which such differences can hopefully be reduced.

NOTE

1. These tests should only be regarded as approximate "rules of thumb." The approximation used to assess whether the coefficient on a variable differed between two groups is $t = b_1 - b_2/(se_1^2 + se_2^2)^{1/2}$, where b is slope, and se is standard error. Two-tailed t-tests are used since we have no predictions about group differences in slopes.

PART II

The Determinants of Achievement in School

Chapter 5

The Dallas Research Setting, Data, Methods

Any attempt to empirically assess the roles played by basic skills, habits, and styles in the determination of schooling outcomes across poverty and ethnic groups makes great demands on data. I was fortunate in having access to the computerized student record database of the Dallas Independent School District (DISD), and in being able to further supplement these data with a questionnaire administered to the teachers of a subset of these students. The resulting database is used in Chapters 5–9 to provide a picture of the determinants of schooling achievement that is unprecedented in detail. This chapter introduces this study by describing the Dallas research setting, the data, and the statistical models and methods used.

THE RESEARCH SETTING

The DISD is a central-city school district whose experiences appear to be typical of the forces shaping inner-city schools in our largest cities. Perhaps the most important of these, and one that has been unusually strong within Dallas, is white flight: between 1968 and the beginning of our study period in 1986, the proportion of Anglos in the Dallas schools declined by 40 percent. During the study period, from 1986 to 1995, this proportion declined by an additional 25 percent. These changes have been accompanied by substantial increases in the proportion of Hispanic, black, and Asian students. As shown in Table 5.1, Dallas's experience is the most extreme example of this pattern, yet the pattern itself is strongly observed in cities as diverse as Houston, Los Angeles, Detroit, and San Diego, among others.

During the 1986–87 school year, the DISD average daily membership of 128,405 students was 20.5 percent Anglo, 49.2 percent black, 28.0 percent Hispanic (almost entirely Mexican-American, with relatively few Mexican-African-Americans), 0.4 percent American Indian, and 1.9 percent Asian. Approximately half of these students signaled their poverty status by qualifying for free or reduced lunch.

Table 5.1.   The Shifting Student Population: Percentage Change, 1968–1986, at Some of the Largest School Districts

District	White	Black	Hispanic	Asian
Baltimore	−16	15	0	0
Broward County, FL	−10	2	5	1
Chicago	−24	5	17	2
Dade County, FL	−34	9	25	1
Dallas	**−40**	**19**	**20**	**2**
Detroit	−30	31	1	0
Houston	−36	10	24	3
Los Angeles	−36	−4	36	4
Memphis	−22	24	0	1
New York	−22	8	11	5
Philadelphia	−14	5	7	3
San Diego	−32	7	9	15

Source: New York Times, June 23, 1988, citing a study by Gary Orfield and Franklin Wilson, University of Chicago.

The racial diversity of the DISD was also reflected, although not quite as strongly, among the 7,315 DISD teachers during 1986–87. Of these, 55 percent were Anglo, 37 percent were African-American, and 7 percent were Hispanic. These teachers were an experienced and well-educated group. Seventy-two percent had more than six years of experience; the median was eleven years. Fifty-one percent had bachelors degrees; almost all of the remainder had masters. At least as measured by absenteeism, morale was reasonably high among these teachers. During 1986–87 their median absenteeism was 2.5 days. Among students, average daily attendance was 93.2 percent.[1]

Performance on the Iowa Test of Basic Skills (ITBS) was also reasonably typical of large-city patterns. The 15,000 seventh- and eighth-grade students tested in 1987 scored a median large-city percentile of 49 in reading, 62 in language, and 59 in mathematics. As shown in Table 5.2, where percentiles are based on national (rather than large-city) norms, African-Americans invariably scored lowest and Anglos highest, with the African-American/Anglo gap in the 20–30 point range. Districtwide summaries for Asians and American Indians were not reported due to the relatively small size of these populations. The relatively poor performance of African-American and Mexican-American students has become a major issue for the Dallas schools. Indeed, the schools, particularly their performance and funding, have been one of the major local news stories over this time period. Perhaps the other has been citywide racial politics. It is thus not surprising that racial politics *within* the DISD has also been a subject of intense local activity, concern, and reporting. A brief chronology of events provides a useful backdrop for the present investigation.

Table 5.2.   Dallas ITBS Scores: Median National Percentile, Grades 7 and 8 (1986)

	Reading	Language	Mathematics
Anglo	53	65	58
African-American	31	44	30
Mexican-American	31	47	37
Total	36	48	37
N	15,844	15,597	15,653

Source: Department of Planning, Evaluation, and Testing, DISD.

In 1984, the Texas legislature passed a major school reform bill. Sometimes referred to as the "Ross Perot Bill" (after the local businessman and political figure closely identified with it), this reform aimed to increase school performance and accountability. To the average citizen, however, it was largely associated with its most discussed feature: a "no pass, no play" provision, in which high school football players who were not passing their courses were barred from playing. Eventually, this long-running newspaper story took a racial turn, when the state champion team, from an all-black DISD school, victorious in the championship game over an all-white team, was disqualified for allegedly playing a student with failing grades. One year later the story took a bizarre twist when several players from the team were arrested and convicted of committing a series of armed robberies. The story occasioned front-page news on an almost daily basis.

By the mid 1980s, African-Americans, allied with Hispanics, finally achieved a majority on the DISD board. The push for a black school superintendent became overwhelming, and the first one in Dallas's history was appointed in 1988. His appointment came at the end of a period in which minority standardized test scores had generally risen within the DISD (Haley n.d.). Yet by 1991, test scores were down and the Texas Education Agency, after conducting an "educational audit" (including in-person interviews with administrators and teachers at each DISD campus), gave an "unsatisfactory" rating to the district, threatening to downgrade its accreditation. Meanwhile, school board racial politics continued to be featured in the newspapers. The superintendent reorganized the administration so as to divide the district into subareas. An experiment in school-based management was begun. A board-appointed Commission for Educational Excellence recommended a sweeping program of reform, built upon an accountability system in which teachers and administrators would be judged by the standardized test score improvement (current scores, statistically adjusted for prior scores) of their students. Meanwhile, the district had been under tremendous financial pressure as a consequence of court-ordered, statewide equalization of funding for public ed-

Table 5.3. Black and Hispanic Populations of Major Metropolitan areas on April 1, 1990, and April 1, 1980, as Calculated by the Census Bureau

Metropolitan area	Black			Metropolitan area	Hispanic		
	1990	*1980*	*Change (%)*		*1990*	*1980*	*Change (%)*
New York-Northern New Jersey-Long Island	3,289,465	2,825,102	16.4	Los Angeles-Anaheim-Riverside	4,779,118	2,755,914	73.4
Chicago-Gary-Lake Co.	1,547,725	1,557,287	−0.6	New York-Northern New Jersey-Long Island	2,777,951	2,050,998	35.4
Los Angeles-Anaheim-Riverside	1,229,809	1,059,124	16.1	Miami-Fort Lauderdale	1,061,846	621,309	70.9
Philadelphia-Wilmington-Trenton	1,100,347	1,032,882	6.5	San Francisco-Oakland-San Jose	970,403	660,190	47.0
Washington	1,041,934	870,657	19.7	Chicago-Gary-Lake Co.	893,422	632,443	41.3
Detroit-Ann Arbor	975,199	921,168	5.9	Houston-Galveston-Brazoria	772,295	448,460	72.2
Atlanta	736,153	525,676	40.0	San Antonio	620,290	481,511	28.8
Houston-Galveston-Brazoria Co.	665,378	564,838	17.8	**Dallas-Fort Worth**	**518,917**	**247,823**	**109.4**
Baltimore	616,065	560,952	9.8	San Diego	510,781	275,177	85.6
Miami-Fort Lauderdale	591,440	394,042	50.1	El Paso	411,619	297,001	38.6
Dallas-Fort Worth	**554,616**	**419,030**	**32.4**	Phoenix	345,498	199,003	73.6

Area			
San Francisco-Oakland-San Jose	537,753	468,477	14.8
Cleveland-Akron-Lorain	441,940	425,861	3.8
New Orleans	430,470	409,076	5.2
St. Louis	423,182	407,918	3.7
Memphis	399,011	364,253	9.5
Norfolk-Virginia Beach-Newport News	398,093	326,102	22.1
Richmond-Petersburg	252,340	221,456	13.9
Birmingham	245,726	240,271	2.3
Boston-Lawrence-Salem	239,059	176,265	35.6
Charlotte-Gastonia	231,654	194,056	19.4
Milwaukee-Racine	214,182	164,571	30.1
Cincinnati-Hamilton	203,607	185,728	9.6
Kansas City	200,508	180,161	11.3
Tampa-St. Petersburg-Clearwater	185,503	148,465	24.9
Raleigh-Durham	183,447	146,624	25.1
Greensboro-Winston Salem	182,284	162,134	12.4
Jacksonville	181,265	156,025	16.2
Pittsburgh-Beaver Valley	178,857	181,644	-1.5
Indianapolis	172,326	157,254	9.6
McAllen-Edinburg-Mission, Tex.	326,972	230,212	42.0
Fresno	236,634	150,790	56.9
Denver-Boulder	226,200	173,687	30.2
Philadelphia-Wilmington-Trenton	225,868	147,902	52.7
Washington	224,786	94,968	136.7
Brownsville-Harlingen	212,995	161,654	31.8
Boston-Lawrence-Salem	193,199	92,463	108.9
Corpus Christi	181,860	158,119	15.0
Albuquerque	178,310	154,620	15.3
Sacramento	172,374	105,665	63.1
Tucson	163,262	111,418	46.5
Austin	159,942	94,367	69.5
Bakersfield	151,995	87,026	74.7
Tampa-St. Petersburg-Clearwater	139,248	80,265	73.5
Laredo, TX	125,069	90,842	37.7
Visalia-Tulane-Porterville, CA	120,893	73,298	64.9
Salinas-Seaside-Monterey, CA	119,570	75,129	59.2
Stockton, CA	112,673	66,565	69.3
San Barbara-S. Maria-Lompoc	98,199	55,356	77.4

Source: New York Times, July 6, 1991.

ucation. The result was significantly increased Dallas property tax rates for the support of education, accompanied by much discussion and strife.

As they move through the 1990s, Dallas in general and the DISD in particular continue to be involved in racial conflict. Court-ordered, citywide redistricting for city council elections has been hotly contested on a racial basis. After court cases, much city council debate, a public referendum, and more court cases and debate, a highly gerrymandered plan, providing five "African-American districts," two "Mexican-American districts," and seven "white districts" was implemented. Crimes of violence and police-citizen interaction continue to be focal points for concerns centered on race. The DISD continued to function under court supervision to enforce desegregation rulings until finally succeeding in having the court terminate this oversight in 1994. During the spring of 1995, a group of minority school board members walked out of a board meeting to protest "racist control" by the "white majority" (which included one Mexican-American). This issue was later smoothed over, however. During the fall of 1995, surreptitiously taped telephone conversations, released to the press, revealed that a white school board member routinely referred to other members, and DISD students and staff, by the vilest of racial epithets. He resigned amid national news coverage and a renewed effort by some black officials and community organizers to "reassert minority control" over the school district. At every election or appointment of a local official, that person's race and ethnicity are an issue. This focus on race is likely to strengthen rather than diminish in the years ahead. For one thing, much of the conflict to date has focused on the African-American/Anglo split. This is not surprising, since among major metropolitan areas, Dallas ranks eleventh in the size of its black population, and this population also shows one of the highest growth rates (Table 5.3). Yet Dallas also ranks eighth in Hispanic population, and has the second most rapidly growing Hispanic population (Table 5.3). This group too is beginning to make its voice heard.

THE FAMILY BACKGROUND OF DALLAS
PUBLIC SCHOOL CHILDREN

Of course, family support is a key determinant of children's school success. It is therefore useful to examine the household type (married couple, female-only household, male-only household, or nonfamily household), and the educational and income level of the parents of Dallas public school children. Although the district does not collect these data, the 1990 census did so. For our purposes, the best source of this information is the special tabulation from the census focusing only on households who report having children enrolled in public school. (These data are available on CD from the National Center for Education Statistics, United States Department of Education.) However, after examining these data, we found one problem. The number of Hispanic children reported to be attending the DISD is significantly below the district's own count of these children. This is not surprising, since census undercounting of Hispanic (and other) in-migrants is well-known. To minimize the distortion this undercount represents, we report the tabulations separately by ethnic group. These are shown in Table 5.4.

We see that among white households reporting children in the Dallas public schools, 72 percent are husband-wife. An even higher percentage—76 percent—of Hispanic households with children in the public schools are husband-wife. However, the situation is quite different for African-American households. Within this group, only 40 percent of households are husband-wife, whereas fully 53 percent are female-headed. Since raising a family as a single adult puts tremendous strain on both personal and financial resources, I expect that many of the children from female-headed households are less than ideally provided for.

Table 5.4. Socioeconomic Characteristics of Households with Children Enrolled in the Dallas Public Schools, Based on a Special Tabulation from the 1990 Census[a]

Household type	White (%)	Black (%)	Hispanic (%)
Married couple	71.8	40.1	75.8
Female only	21.0	52.9	16.5
Male only	5.4	6.2	6.9
Nonfamily	1.8	0.8	0.8
Total	100.0	100.0	100.0
Mother's education			
< high school	20.3	24.7	70.7
High school graduate	30.6	38.1	18.4
Some college	29.7	30.2	8.7
≥ college graduate	19.4	7.0	2.2
Total	100.0	100.0	100.0
Household income			
< $10,000	6.1	28.0	15.5
$10,000–$25,000	23.0	32.7	38.8
$25,000–$35,000	19.9	15.0	19.8
$35,000–$50,000	20.1	13.5	16.6
≥ $50,000	30.9	10.8	9.3
Total	100.0	100.0	100.0

[a] Prepared by the Mesa Group for the NCES, U.S. Department of Education.

Where the mother's education is concerned, high school graduation is at least minimally necessary if the parent is to have the skills and confidence necessary to adequately participate in and assist with the child's schooling. Among whites, 20 percent of mothers are below this educational level; among blacks the figure is 25 percent. But among Hispanics, fully 71 percent of mothers have less than a high school education. This relatively low educational level, combined with the fact that many of these parents speak only Spanish (see below), poses a serious challenge as the district seeks to educate these children in English.

Finally, Table 5.4 shows the distribution of household income. By comparison with the other groups, white household income is skewed toward the high end of the distribution. African-American and Hispanic incomes are skewed toward the lower end of the distribution, with the main difference between them being that African-American incomes are more heavily concentrated in the below $10,000 category, whereas Hispanic household incomes are more heavily concentrated in the $10,000–25,000 category. This difference is no doubt due to the much greater concentration of female-only households among blacks.

Table 5.5 uses district data to show the growth of Limited English Proficient (LEP) students between 1984 and 1995. We see that the number of these children doubled over this time period, reaching 36,385 by 1995.

Table 5.5.   Limited English Proficient Students in the Dallas Public Schools, 1984–95

School year	Limited English proficient[a]	Bilingual education	English as a second language	Post-transitional[b]
1984–85	18,058	4,963	11,394	N/A
1985–86	17,670	5,826	10,371	N/A
1986–87	16,907	5,599	10,637	N/A
1987–88	14,431	7,322	7,109	N/A
1988–89	16,597	8,053	7,860	120
1989–90	17,928	8,273	8,126	526
1990–91	19,108	8,926	8,385	658
1991–92	20,491	9,731	8,387	1,006
1992–93	22,032	10,314	9,085	1,432
1993–94	32,504	11,788	14,503	4,346
1994–95	36,385	13,473	16,208	4,530

[a] The number of limited-English-proficient students is greater than total of other columns because some parents decline special language classes and some students are assigned to special education classes.
[b] Posttransitional students have left special language programs but cannot reach the test score required to move into regular classes.
Source: Dallas Morning News, October 31, 1995.

Among these, 13,473 were being educated in "bilingual" classes, which involve extensive use of and instruction in the student's native language (almost exclusively Spanish). An additional 16,209 were placed in English-as-a-second language classes, where the focus is largely on using English to learn English. Finally, 4,530 children were defined as "posttransitional," because they have left special language programs but have been unable to reach the test score required to move into regular classes. Clearly, this large and continuously growing population of (largely Mexican-American) students whose parents speak little or no English represents a special difficulty for the district. Later results will show what sorts of educational outcomes have been achieved by these children.

STATISTICAL DATA, MODEL, AND METHODS

Data

The statistical study of schooling achievement focuses on data collected for the fall 1986 semester. At the close of this semester, in collaboration with Daniel Sheehan and Robert Grobe, members of the Office of Research, Evaluation, and Testing within the DISD, I was able to administer a "Student Work-Ethic" Questionnaire (Figure 5.1) to teachers of a stratified random sample of students. Although the full student record database was available to us, absenteeism is the only measure of "habits and styles" provided there. In order to supplement this measure, teachers were asked to rate their students on nontest performance (homework and class participation), work habits (effort, organization), and demeanor (disruptiveness, assertiveness, appearance, and dress).

Permission to field this survey was difficult to obtain, and the scope of the effort was necessarily limited. We focused on students enrolled in the seventh and eighth grade social studies curriculum. This represents two courses: Texas History/Geography (seventh grade) and American History/Citizenship (eighth grade). These were selected because (a) they are required of all students, thus minimizing self-selection, (b) they are aimed at conveying a body of substantive information distinct from language and mathematics basic skills (that is, course mastery test scores for these subjects are conceptually distinct from basic skills test scores), (c) students in these courses have recently taken the Iowa Test of Basic Skills (ITBS) as a measure of their basic skills (students in higher grade levels take a different test, which would make it difficult to compare their scores with those of seventh and eighth graders), and (d) the social studies course mastery tests are longer and more reliable than those for many of the other subjects.

The sample for each course was stratified by ethnicity. The sampling fraction for Asian students was 1. That is, all of the Asian students in each social studies course were selected. The sampling fractions for blacks, Anglos, and Hispanics were set so that the sample size for each of these three ethnic groups would be approximately twice the size of the Asian group.[2] Random samples were selected based on the size of each sampling fraction.

Measures of student habits and styles were collected from the teachers of the sampled students via the Student Work-Ethic Characteristics Questionnaire displayed in Figure 5.1. The names and identification numbers of

Figure 5.1. Student work-ethic characteristics questionnaire.

School _____   Subject ___**Texas History/Geog (407)**_____

Teacher _____   Period _____

STUDENT WORK-ETHIC CHARACTERISTICS
QUESTIONNAIRE

Directions: For each student listed indicate the percentage that completes the statement. For example, if a student does very poorly on homework, you might say that he/she does better than only 5% of the students that you have taught. If a student does very well on homework, you might say that he/she does better than 95% of the students that your have taught.

	WRITE REQUESTED PERCENTAGES FOR THE STUDENTS LISTED BELOW THAT ARE IN YOUR CLASS. (Draw a line through a student if he/she is not in your class.)					
1. This student does better on homework than ____ percent of the students that I have taught.						
2. This student does better on class participation than ____ percent of the students that I have taught.						
3. This student wants to do well and tries harder than ____ percent of the students that I have taught.						
4. This student is better organized than ____ percent of the students that I have taught.						
5. This student is more disruptive than ____ percent of the students that I have taught.						
6. This student is more assertive than ____ percent of the students that I have taught.						
7. This student's appearance and dress are better than ____ percent of the students that I have taught.						

sampled students for each teacher were written across the top of a questionnaire, which was sent to the teacher. For each student, the teacher wrote the percentage of students she or he has taught who were exceeded by that student on the particular behavior. For example, on the first item the teacher might write 95. This would mean that the student did better on homework than 95 percent of the students that the teacher had taught.

The final sample has 486 students, enrolled in twenty-two middle schools and evenly divided between the seventh and eighth grades (Table 5.6). With the exception of racial composition—the sample stratification variable—the sample means closely resemble values for the total population of seventh- and eighth-grade students. (These means and standard deviations, as well as all other reported statistics, are unweighted.) All regressions reported in this study include a dummy variable for the eighth-grade course, but its coefficient is not reported since it is of no substantive interest.

The variables collected fall into the following categories: student background characteristics, teacher characteristics, basic skills measures, student habits and styles measures, coursework mastery measures, and course grades. With the exception of the teacher questionnaire data on stu-

Table 5.6. Means and Standard Deviations for Variables in the Combined Seventh- and Eighth-Grade Social Studies Sample ($N = 486$) and the Population from which it was Drawn

Variable	Sample mean	Sample standard deviation	Population mean
8th-grade course	.51	.50	.48
Male	.51	.50	.51
Low-income	.40	.49	.44
Asian	.12	.33	.01
African-American	.33	.47	.53
Hispanic	.27	.44	.25
Female teacher	.54	.50	.55
Teacher experience (years)	14.71	7.95	13.66
African-American teacher	.42	.49	.43
Basic skills	74.58	15.34	74.42
Days absent	3.08	4.01	3.47
Work habits	57.42	30.81	NA
Disruptiveness	22.09	30.51	NA
Appearance and dress	64.24	27.19	NA
Coursework mastery	36.85	13.45	33.38
Course grades	78.45	11.04	76.71

dent habits and styles, these were collected from the DISD computerized database. I discuss each of these variable groups in turn.

Student Background Characteristics

The key student background characteristics are ethnicity and poverty. Ethnicity is measured by separate dummy variables for African-American, Mexican-American, and Asian-American youths (Anglo/white is the omitted category). A student is coded 1 on the income measure if he or she qualifies for a free lunch based on the federally specified poverty line. The district determines eligibility based on information supplied by parents at the beginning of the school year. This measure has two key weaknesses as a proxy for social class: (a) it introduces considerable measurement error into a social-class construct that is intrinsically continuous, and (b) white flight has left this central-city school district concentrated at the low end of the social-class distribution. Both deficiencies should tend to bias any estimated poverty effects downward.

All analyses control for the student's gender, which is measured by a dummy variable, with males coded 1, females 0. Thus, the statistical results are as fully informative for male and female differentials as for those associated with ethnicity or poverty. However, the gender results will not be emphasized because they generally have little to say regarding the human capital/cultural-capital causal mechanisms that are our primary focus.

Teacher Characteristics

The teacher's gender, race (African-American or white) and years of total teaching experience were extracted from teacher files.[3]

Student Basic Skills

Basic skills are measured by the Iowa Test of Basic Skills (ITBS). This includes (a) the Language total and the subtest scores—vocabulary, reading comprehension, spelling, capitalization, punctuation, and usage and expression, and (b) the Mathematics total and the subtest scores—mathematics concepts, mathematics problem solving, and mathematics computation. Each test and subtest is measured in grade-equivalent form, so that, for example, 70.00 indicates the beginning seventh-grade level. Test scores were collected during the middle of the spring 1986 term.

Student Habits and Styles

Absenteeism is measured by the number of days the student had an unexcused absence during the semester. Student work habits are measured using teacher judgments on four performance dimensions: homework, class participation, effort, and organization. These were averaged into a single variable, since the pairwise correlations between the variables are between .80 and .95. Style and demeanor are measured by teacher judgments of the student's disruptiveness and the student's appearance and dress. These have been kept as distinct variables in the analysis, since their correlations with one another and with work habits are modest (Table 5.7). One of the variables—student assertiveness—showed little relationship with key independent and dependent variables, and so has been omitted from most analyses. However, it does occasionally appear as a predictor variable when the habits and styles are entered as separate variables to predict coursework mastery and course grades in Chapters 8 and 9.

Coursework Mastery

Coursework mastery tests, centrally created and uniformly administered across the DISD, were one of the district's responses to the Texas Educational Reform Act of 1984. These tests represent an attempt to provide reliable and valid curriculum-referenced test (CRT) score measures of coursework mastery, independent of teacher-assigned course grades. To ensure the content and instructional validity of these tests, panels of teachers selected lists of "essential course elements" for each subject. Test items were then matched to these elements. Where possible, items were selected

Table 5.7. Correlations of Cognitive Variables, Noncognitive Variables, and Course Grades ($N = 486$)

Variable	Basic skills	Days absent	Work habits	Disruptiveness	Appearance & dress	Coursework mastery	Course grades
Basic skills	1.00	−0.09	0.43	−0.13	0.25	0.62	0.58
Days absent		1.00	−0.20	0.03	−0.07	−0.16	−0.32
Work habits			1.00	−0.26	0.57	0.49	0.77
Disruptiveness				1.00	−0.01	−0.19	−0.31
Appearance & dress					1.00	0.22	0.37
Coursework mastery						1.00	0.63
Course grades							1.00

from existing test item banks. However, when an appropriate item could not be found, a new item was written. Textbooks and curricular materials were used to judge the appropriateness of the items. Tests generally contain many items and are quite reliable. The alpha reliability for the Texas History/Geography test was .86; that for American History/Citizenship was .91.

Course Grades

The teacher-assigned course grade is based on a 100-point system, with 49 being the lowest grade assigned. Systemwide policy stipulates that individual teachers and/or schools are free to determine their own system of measuring and rewarding performance. Course grades are for the end of the fall 1986 term.

Statistical Model and Methods

In this study I analyze unique data collected from the DISD. These data contain distinct measures of basic academic skills and mastery of assigned coursework, as well as objective and teacher judgment measures of student habits and styles. The measures are used to estimate a block-recursive model of the course grade assignment process, in which student and teacher background characteristics affect student skills, habits, and styles, which in turn affect student coursework mastery and the course grade (Figure 5.2).

I estimate this model with no preconceptions about the magnitude or extent of teacher bias in course grade assignment. Indeed, the cultural-resources/social-interaction model suggests that any such bias operates through a subtle, longitudinal process involving multiple feedbacks between both teacher and student behavior as these are embedded within the

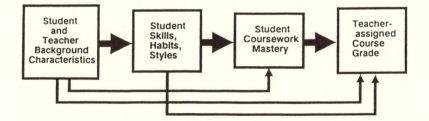

Figure 5.2.   Path diagram of the course-grade attainment process.

culture of the school, home, and neighborhood. Since most of the statistical data refer to a single school term, and teacher judgments provide the measures of student habits and styles, we are unable to statistically isolate bias occurring via such a process. Yet, estimation of the model in Figure 5.2 is still of great interest because the teacher assigns the course grade, so that teacher judgments define the reward system, whose implicit rules determine stratification outcomes. If teacher judgments of student habits and styles influence course grades net of cognitive performance, and do so in a way that at least partially explains the differential success of poverty and ethnic groups, the result would argue for modifying the dominant paradigm within this portion of sociology, sometimes referred to as the "Wisconsin model" of status attainment (Sewell and Hauser 1975; Featherman and Hauser 1978; Jencks et al. 1979, 1983). The modification entails inclusion of and greater focus on the sort of culture-linked measures of behavior and perception utilized in the present study.

The analysis plan for Chapters 6–9 follows the path model shown in Figure 5.2. Chapter 6 reports basic skills differences across ethnicity, income, and gender groups. These are presented via multiple regression analysis. Chapter 7 repeats this analysis for teacher judgments of student habits and styles. These are estimated both as additive and interactive outcomes of student and teacher characteristics. Thus, we test for the possibility that, for example, the effect of the student's race on the teacher's judgment of a student's behavior differs according to the race of the teacher.

Chapter 8 reports the analysis of student coursework mastery. In Chapter 9, course grades become the dependent variable for the analysis. For both coursework mastery and course grades we proceed in stages, beginning with the exogenous independent variables (ethnicity, poverty, race) and then adding endogenous predictors, moving toward the dependent variable through the causal paths shown in Figure 5.2. This provides a path-analytic decomposition of intergroup (exogenous) differentials into direct and indirect effects (Alwin and Hauser 1975).

NOTES

1.   This refers to *unexcused* absences. If *excused* absences are included, absenteeism is significantly higher.

2.   There were too few Native Americans for meaningful comparison with other groups, so this group was excluded.

3.   Because there are few Hispanic teachers in this data set, they have been combined with Anglos to form the "white" category.

Chapter 6

Basic Skills

We find evidence of substantial disadvantages in cognitive development among young children in chronically poor families in the United States. Deficits appear in a variety of indices of cognitive or socioemotional development, including verbal memory, vocabulary, math and reading achievement and an index of behavior problems.

—Sanders Korenman, Jane Miller, and John Sjaastad, "Long-term Poverty and Child Development in the United States: Results from the NLSY."

THE SOCIOLOGY OF BASIC SKILLS ACQUISITION

Sociologists are trained to focus on group membership, and its implications both for individual biography and for the structure of society. Yet in so doing, they typically slight one of the central mechanisms by which group membership affects individual life chances: differential skill acquisition across social groups. In this section we review what *has* been done in a nascent field, which might be called the *sociology of basic skills acquisition*. This begins the task of providing an interpretive framework for the empirical results provided in this chapter.

As noted in Chapter 2, sociologists like Bernstein and Bourdieu, as well as the Marxist economists Bowles and Gintis, began the task of describing the differential socialization provided by family and school to children of different social-class backgrounds. Melvin Kohn and his associates (Kohn 1969; Kohn et al. 1983) have, over an extended series of studies, examined the effect of workplace autonomy on child-rearing practices across the occupational stratification system. More recently, Willis (1977), Mehan (1992), Cicourel and Mehan (1985), Lareau (1989), and many other sociologists have built on this tradition of what might be called the *social psychology of class location* (see, for example, Sennett and Cobb 1972) to describe how the accident of an individual's birth determines the parental and social-institutional (in particular, school) treatment that molds individual social psychology. Such differential class cultures are made a building block of an integrative conflict sociology by Collins (1975).

Most recently, the availability of detailed information on child rearing and child cognitive and behavioral outcomes within the NLSY data (Center for Human Resources Research, various years) has made possible an unprecedented outpouring of detailed empirical research on the early cognitive development of children from low-income and/or African-American or Hispanic families. In particular, the studies of Moore and Snyder (1991), Korenman, Miller, and Sjaastad (1994), Parcel and Menaghan (1994), Hill and O'Neill (1994), Crane (1995), and Brooks-Gunn et al. (1995) have utilized these and other data to demonstrate the following with preschool and school-age children:

1.   Children from low-income households show lower cognitive development; the more chronic the family's poverty, the lower the development.
2.   African-American and Hispanic children also show lower cognitive development.
3.   These differentials in cognitive development are largely explained by characteristics of the home situation and of the mother. In particular, the mother's own education and cognitive development, as well as home support for the child's cognitive development (how much time the mother spends reading to her child, and similar variables), strongly predict that development.

These studies have largely focused on very young children, and have emphasized the child's cognitive growth prior to and independent of the causal mechanisms operating within the school. They demonstrate that low-income and minority group children come to school at a double disadvantage: first, their cognitive development is already behind that of middle-class and white children, and second, their families are less able to strongly support additional learning during the progress of their schooling. In this chapter, we carry the story forward to examine the basic skills performance of seventh and eighth graders. We examine this in two ways. First, the following section provides across-group comparisons at one point in time. The succeeding section then examines each group over time. That is, we study how these skills develop across time within each group. This latter study shows how much each group loses or gains in relative terms as its education evolves. It also shows which students within the groups lose or gain the most.

GROUP DIFFERENCES IN BASIC SKILLS ACQUISITION

Worldwide, subordinated groups occupy work roles that are dishonored and underpaid. This situation is maintained across extended time periods in part by the failure of group members to gain access to the skills necessary to advance to better positions. Overwhelmingly, this failure can be traced to their performance within the educational system. As noted above, many studies have documented that low-income and minority youths begin school with weaker skills than white middle-class children, and are also less strongly supported in school than white middle-class children. Thus, as low-income and minority youths move through grades one to six, we expect to find the performance gap widening. By middle school this gap should be substantial.

This expectation is borne out by the results in Table 6.1. In this table, basic skills are measured by the average of the Language and Mathematics total scores from the ITBS. These scores are in grade-equivalent (instructional year) form, so that, for example, 70.00 indicates the beginning sev-

Table 6.1. Regression Analysis[a,b] of Basic Skills ($N = 486$)

Independent variable	Basic skills	
	(1)	(2)
Constant	76.08	75.62
Male	−1.00	−0.09
	(0.8)	(0.0)
Low-income	−5.13	−6.19
	(3.9)	(1.9)
Asian	5.21	7.67
	(2.4)	(2.1)
African-American	−8.11	−9.36
	(5.0)	(3.7)
Hispanic	−4.70	−3.51
	(2.7)	(1.2)
Male Asian		0.55
		(0.1)
Male African-American		0.72
		(0.2)
Male Hispanic		−4.30
		(1.3)
Low-income Asian		−5.61
		(1.2)
Low-income African-American		2.82
		(0.7)
Low-income Hispanic		2.45
		(0.6)
R^2	.247	.260

[a] Unstandardized coefficients. All regressions include a dummy variable for the 8th-grade course.
[b] The absolute value of the t-statistic is in parentheses.

enth-grade level. We find that gender is nonsignificant, but both poverty and ethnicity are quite significant (column 1). Low-income students score lower on basic skills than do higher income students, Asians score higher than whites, while African-Americans and Hispanics score lower than Anglos. Since 10 points on the ITBS scale correspond to one grade level, these (unstandardized) regression coefficients indicate that the poor are 0.5 grades below the less poor, and Asians are 0.5 grades above Anglos. Mexican-Americans are 0.5 grades below Anglos, and African-Americans are 0.8 grades below Anglos. Adding gender/ethnicity and poverty/ethnicity interactions to the equation (column 2) shows that neither is statistically significant, and the increment to R^2 is negligible.

What do these scores mean in practical terms? Recall that the sample is approximately equally divided into seventh and eighth graders and that the exam is administered near the close of the spring term. Being on grade level at this time requires a score of 7.9 for seventh graders, and 8.9 for eighth graders. The average of these two scores is 8.4. This is the level, expressed as 84 in the metric of our calculations, that should be attained if the students are making acceptable progress.

By comparison, the second column of Table 6.1 permits us to see the average scores attained by subgroups of students. Consider male students from low-income households who are African-American. Their average score is computed by taking the coefficients in column 2 and adding together the constant term, and the coefficients for male, low-income, African-American, male African-American, and low-income African American. We get $75.6 - 6.2 - 9.4 + 0.7 + 2.8 = 63.5$. This is two full grade-equivalents below the expected level. And note that this is the mean for this group: we expect that approximately half of the group is below this level. It is difficult to see how children performing at this level can participate in an instructional program whose level of difficulty is so much higher than their current level of skill. Little wonder that such children are reported to be disaffected from school!

Table 6.2 shows these results broken down by the ITBS subtests whose scores have been aggregated in the previous analysis. These are the Language Total, with subtests in Vocabulary, Reading Comprehension, Spelling, Capitalization, Punctuation, and Usage and Expression, and the Mathematics Total, with subtests in Math Concepts, Math Problem Solving, and Math Computation.

Males, who showed no significant difference from females overall, are revealed to score modestly (and statistically significantly) below them on Language, and only slightly (and not significantly) above them on Mathematics. However, this male Language decrement is largely attributable to Spelling, Punctuation, and Usage and Expression. Perhaps the two most important skills—Vocabulary and Reading Comprehension—do not show

Table 6.2. Regression Analysis[a,b] of Detailed Basic Skills: Additive Specification ($N = 486$)

	Language Total	Vocabulary	Reading Comprehension	Spelling	Capitalization	Punctuation	Usage and Expression	Math Total	Math Concepts	Math Problem Solving	Math Computation
Constant	79.61	70.50	71.44	72.71	82.49	85.09	78.26	72.55	73.85	71.08	72.80
Male	-3.26	1.69	-1.48	-3.38	-0.72	-5.35	-3.61	1.26	2.41	1.88	-0.54
	(2.2)	(1.3)	(1.1)	(2.1)	(0.4)	(3.1)	(2.1)	(1.1)	(1.8)	(1.3)	(0.4)
Poor	-6.97	-7.66	-6.04	-6.84	-6.86	-6.10	-8.11	-3.29	-3.80	-4.86	-1.16
	(4.4)	(5.4)	(4.2)	(3.9)	(3.7)	(3.3)	(4.3)	(2.6)	(2.7)	(3.2)	(0.9)
Asian	4.57	-9.30	-1.16	10.42	3.86	7.91	-3.87	5.84	5.93	0.20	11.15
	(1.8)	(4.1)	(0.5)	(3.7)	(1.3)	(2.7)	(1.3)	(2.9)	(2.6)	(0.1)	(5.2)
Black	-7.51	-11.26	-10.41	-1.10	-7.04	-10.22	-11.82	-8.72	-9.44	-13.76	-3.07
	(3.9)	(6.6)	(5.9)	(0.5)	(3.2)	(4.6)	(5.2)	(5.7)	(5.4)	(7.5)	(1.9)
Hispanic	-3.64	-10.69	-6.81	-0.45	-2.42	-4.31	-7.48	-5.77	-7.60	-7.84	-1.94
	(1.8)	(5.8)	(3.6)	(0.2)	(1.0)	(1.8)	(3.0)	(3.4)	(4.0)	(3.9)	(1.1)
R^2	.206	.278	.234	.181	.144	.186	.185	.256	.251	.262	.167
Dep. var. mean	76.83	64.80	67.41	74.61	81.43	80.13	71.15	72.34	73.59	68.24	75.20

[a] Unstandardized coefficients. All regressions include a dummy variable for the 8th-grade course.
[b] The absolute value of the t-statistic is in parentheses.

such large negative effects for males. The male Mathematics advantage is strongest in Math Concepts. This is consistent with the finding that even before the stage in their school career in which males gain an advantage by taking more mathematics courses, they are performing better than females (Benbow and Stanley 1980). However, the effects of gender cultures—females skewed toward language performance, males toward mathematics—are rather modest in size.

A much larger magnitude is observed for the effect of family income on student language skill. For the Language Total, youths from low-income households score 7 points—7/10 of a grade-equivalent—lower than youths not residing in poverty households. This is a large effect, particularly since it is likely an underestimate of the true effect. (The estimate is likely biased downward due to measurement error in our use of receipt of a free lunch as a proxy for family income.) This language decrement suffered by poor youths is across the board; all of their language subtest effects vary between −6/10 and −8/10 of a grade-equivalent. This result is, of course, consistent with the many researchers (Bernstein 1977; Bourdieu 1977; Cicourel and Mehan 1985; Entwisle and Alexander 1994; among others) who have emphasized language skills as key cultural capital variables in the social stratification system.

Youths from low-income households also suffer a Mathematics decrement, but it is only half as large as that for Language. This Mathematics deficit is concentrated in the Concepts and Problem Solving subtest areas.

Asian-Americans score higher than Anglos on the Language Total. This is surprising, since these students have been largely reared by families in which at least the parents are not native English speakers. A closer look shows that these students *do* score below Anglos on Vocabulary, Reading Comprehension, and Usage and Expression. In fact, the Vocabulary deficit is almost a full grade-equivalent. Yet they outscore Anglos on Spelling, Capitalization, and Punctuation. This Asian-American Spelling effect is in excess of a grade-equivalent. And the Punctuation effect is almost 8/10 of a grade-equivalent. Apparently a great deal can be accomplished via hard work (probably on the part of both parents and children).

Asian-Americans also outscore Anglos on Mathematics. The total effect is almost 6/10 of a grade-equivalent. This results from an effect of this size for Math Concepts, essentially no effect for Math Problem Solving, and an effect of 1.1 grade-equivalents for Math Computation. This enormous Math Computation effect is also consistent with the diligence and attention to detail interpretation discussed above.

African-American students score dramatically below Euro-Americans on both Language and Mathematics Skills. For the Language Total, the deficit is 7.5 points, or 3/4 of a grade-equivalent. Even more dramatically, the difference is more than a grade-equivalent for the two central skills of

Vocabulary and Reading Comprehension. The mathematics total shows an African-American deficit of 8.7 points. This is concentrated in Math Concepts and Math Problem Solving. The latter score is 13.8 points, or 1.4 grade-equivalents below Euro-Americans.

The Mexican-American pattern resembles that for African-Americans, with significantly lower scores than Euro-Americans in both the Language and Mathematics totals. However, these deficits are not as large as for African-Americans, totaling 3.6 points in Language and 5.8 points in Mathematics. As for African-Americans, large negative effects are observed for Vocabulary, Reading Comprehension, Math Concepts, and Math Problem Solving, but in each case the Mexican-American deficit is smaller than that for African-Americans.

This analysis has been based on an additive specification: the statistical model is simplified to assume that, for example, the effect of being both African-American and male can be approximated by the sum of effects for each of these characteristics. The possibility that this is not the case—that certain combinations of characteristics "interact" to lead to outcomes different than a simple summation—is tested in Table 6.3.

The overall impression is that such interactions are not terribly important. This conclusion follows from the R^2 values in Table 6.3, which are not dramatically improved over those of the additive model in Table 6.2. If we scan the individual coefficients and t-statistics, only one group stands out. Low-income Asian-Americans have large and often statistically significant negative effects in Vocabulary, Reading Comprehension, and Usage and Expression. These language skills are far below the levels expected by simply adding together the Poverty and Asian-American effects. It will be interesting to see what, if any, consequences these language difficulties have for the coursework mastery and course grades achieved by these students. A further observation concerns the absence of large and significant negative interaction effects for black or Hispanic males. These groups are often singled out as being particularly at-risk for gang membership and other activities associated with low school performance and dropping out. Yet the skills of poor blacks and Hispanics are no worse than expected for their gender and ethnicity. Here, too, it will be interesting to see how their coursework mastery and course grades are affected.

Let us use Table 6.3 to replicate the calculation undertaken with Table 6.1, showing the magnitude of the grade-equivalent performance deficit for males from low-income households who are African-American. For reading comprehension, we get $70.35 + 0.15 - 5.25 - 10.47 - 1.32 + 1.26 = 54.72$. The reading skill of these children averages 3 grade-equivalents below the expected level for the curriculum they are being presented with. Repeating the calculation for math problem solving, we get $70.48 + 2.91 - 4.76 - 12.79 - 1.59 - 0.35 = 53.90$. The same three-year deficit! The impli-

Table 6.3. Regression Analysis[a,b] of Detailed Basic Skills: Interactive Specification (N = 486)

	Language Total	Vocabulary	Reading Comprehension	Spelling	Capitalization	Punctuation	Usage and Expression	Math Total	Math Concepts	Math Problem Solving	Math Computation
Constant	79.18	70.74	70.35	72.91	81.72	84.50	77.70	72.06	72.90	70.48	72.84
Male	-2.35	0.82	0.15	-3.04	1.08	-3.88	-3.44	2.18	4.16	2.91	-0.52
	(0.9)	(0.3)	(0.1)	(1.0)	(0.3)	(1.2)	(1.1)	(1.0)	(1.7)	(1.1)	(0.2)
Poor	-8.42	-7.08	-5.25	-9.73	-9.10	-8.83	-6.52	-3.97	-4.36	-4.76	-2.62
	(2.2)	(2.1)	(1.5)	(2.3)	(2.1)	(2.0)	(1.5)	(1.3)	(1.3)	(1.3)	(0.8)
Asian	8.45	-5.42	6.66	11.95	9.21	9.41	-3.76	6.90	7.41	2.50	10.68
	(1.9)	(1.4)	(1.7)	(2.5)	(1.8)	(1.8)	(0.7)	(2.0)	(1.9)	(0.6)	(2.9)
Black	-9.62	-12.51	-10.47	-2.46	-9.48	-12.66	-14.04	-9.09	-9.35	-12.79	-5.03
	(3.2)	(4.7)	(3.8)	(0.7)	(2.7)	(3.6)	(4.0)	(3.8)	(3.5)	(4.4)	(2.0)
Hispanic	-2.23	-12.64	-6.57	-1.18	0.23	-1.39	-6.95	-4.79	-5.63	-8.29	-0.64
	(0.7)	(4.2)	(2.1)	(0.3)	(0.1)	(0.4)	(1.8)	(1.8)	(1.9)	(2.6)	(0.2)
Male Asian	0.11	-0.01	-3.82	2.02	-2.43	1.54	-1.54	0.98	1.19	0.34	1.33
	(0.0)	(0.0)	(0.8)	(0.4)	(0.4)	(0.3)	(0.3)	(0.2)	(0.3)	(0.1)	(0.3)
Male Black	1.11	2.40	-1.32	-0.41	0.26	1.83	2.52	0.34	-0.82	-1.59	3.22
	(0.3)	(0.7)	(0.4)	(0.1)	(0.1)	(0.4)	(0.6)	(0.1)	(0.2)	(0.4)	(1.0)
Male Hispanic	-4.50	0.27	-2.88	-1.22	-5.57	-7.89	-3.11	-4.11	-5.87	-2.05	-4.30
	(1.2)	(0.1)	(0.8)	(0.3)	(1.2)	(1.7)	(0.7)	(1.3)	(1.7)	(0.5)	(1.3)
Poor Asian	-7.94	-8.97	-13.28	-4.12	-7.58	-3.68	-16.14	-3.27	-4.62	-5.71	0.29
	(1.4)	(1.8)	(2.6)	(0.7)	(1.2)	(0.6)	(2.4)	(0.7)	(0.9)	(1.0)	(0.1)
Poor Black	4.63	-0.26	1.26	5.50	6.91	5.41	1.26	1.01	1.27	-0.35	1.84
	(1.0)	(0.1)	(0.3)	(1.1)	(1.3)	(1.0)	(0.2)	(0.3)	(0.3)	(0.1)	(0.5)
Poor Hispanic	2.54	2.72	1.58	4.46	1.94	3.79	0.65	2.36	2.10	2.51	2.50
	(0.5)	(0.6)	(0.4)	(0.8)	(0.4)	(0.7)	(0.1)	(0.6)	(0.5)	(0.6)	(0.6)
R^2	.221	.290	.254	.188	.159	.200	.204	.264	.261	.267	.179

[a] Unstandardized coefficients. All regressions include a dummy variable for the 8th-grade course.
[b] The absolute value of the t-statistic is in parentheses.

cations of these skills deficits for coursework mastery and course grades are explored in Chapters 8 and 9.

BASIC SKILLS DEVELOPMENT OVER TIME

Table 6.4 shows the development of these basic skills over time. That is, current (1986) skill level is regressed against background characteristics and the individual's past year (1985) skill level. The first column presents these calculations for overall basic skill (Language and Mathematics averaged together), while Language and Mathematics skills are examined separately in columns 2 and 3.

As other researchers have found, these skills are very highly correlated over time. In column 1, last year's score predicts this year's score with a coefficient of .962 and a *t*-statistic of 40. Fully 84.5 percent of the variance in the dependent variable is explained. Knowledge of last year's test score is the principal piece of information needed in order to predict current ba-

Table 6.4. Regression Analysis[a,b] of Basic Skills, Controlling For Previous-Year Scores ($N = 448$)

	Basic Skill	*Language Total*	*Math Total*
Constant	8.21	5.88	9.69
Male	0.30	−1.21	1.60
	(0.5)	(1.6)	(2.3)
Poor	0.12	−0.56	0.69
	(0.2)	(0.7)	(0.9)
Asian	2.43	1.86	2.99
	(2.4)	(1.4)	(2.5)
Black	−2.17	−1.65	−2.45
	(2.8)	(1.6)	(2.6)
Hispanic	−0.72	0.56	−1.87
	(0.9)	(0.5)	(1.9)
Basic Skills 1985	0.962		
	(40.3)		
Language Total 1985		0.769	0.132
		(20.4)	(3.8)
Math Total 1985		0.253	0.787
		(5.3)	(18.0)
R^2	.845	.808	.776

[a] Unstandardized coefficients. All regressions include a dummy variable for the 8th-grade course.

[b] The absolute value of the *t*-statistic is in parentheses.

sic skill performance. Further, once last year's score is taken into account, males show little difference from females, and the poor show little difference from the nonpoor. That is, neither males nor the poor show any systematic loss in their skill level relative to that of females and the nonpoor. In other words, the lower scores they do show—1/10 of a grade-equivalent for males, and 5/10 of a grade-equivalent for the poor—are stable over time. Of course, only that of the poor is a substantial disadvantage. We conclude that this disadvantage occurred at earlier grades, and has stabilized by middle school. [See the work discussed above—Korenman et al. (1994), Parcel and Menaghan (1994), and so on—for the sources of this disadvantage in the early years.]

Asians and blacks, however, do show a trend over time. For Asians, there is a statistically significant gain of 2/10 of a grade-equivalent over the level predicted from their prior-year achievement. For blacks, there is a statistically significant loss of 2/10 of a grade-equivalent over the level predicted from their prior-year achievement. Hispanics also show a loss, but it is smaller and not statistically significant.

Columns 2 and 3 repeat these calculations, separately for Language and Mathematics skills. We find the expected patterns: Language skill is largely predicted by previous language skill, and Mathematics skill is largely predicted by previous Mathematics skill. In each case prior-year skill in the other variable (math when predicting language, language when predicting math) also positively affects performance. Most interestingly, these calculations reveal deeper structure to the subgroup trends in column 1. The absence of a male effect is now seen to be the average of a relative decline (versus females) in Language skill, and a relative gain (versus females) in Mathematics skill. Here is the creation of gender differentiation on these skills!

The absence of a trend in overall skill among children from poor families is seen to be an average of a small relative decline in Language and a small relative gain in Mathematics. However, neither of these effects is statistically significant. The Asian overall skill gain (versus whites) occurs for both Language and Mathematics, but that for Mathematics is larger. Here, too, we see the statistical trend underlying much commonplace observation. For African-Americans, their skill decline versus Anglos occurs in both Language and Mathematics, with the latter being larger. A similar trend is in evidence for Hispanics, where the (relative) decline is entirely due to Mathematics.

Table 6.5 takes this skill decomposition to its conclusion in the six separate Language and three separate Mathematics skill measures. In each case, the skill in question as measured in 1986 is regressed against background characteristics and the full set of nine detailed skills as measured in 1985. As in the previous table, we observe a "diagonal-effects" pattern—the strongest predictor of each skill measure is the identical skill measure from the previous year. We also find "off-diagonal" effects—within each column, other skills besides the one being predicted often show significance. However, there is no meaningful pattern to these.

More important, this detailed modeling of distinct skills and their evolution over time permits the clearest picture yet of the trends over time in the skills of the population subgroups defined by gender, poverty, and ethnicity. For males, their relative decline (versus females) in language skill is due to Reading Comprehension, Punctuation, and Usage and Expression, particularly the latter two. The largest male math gains occur in Math Concepts, with smaller gains in Math Problem Solving and Math Computation.

For the poor/nonpoor contrast, none of the separate effects is significant. Little is occurring here. However, much more distinctive effects are in evidence among ethnic groups. Asians show their largest relative gains (versus Anglos) in Spelling and Punctuation, followed by Math Concepts and Math Computation. Note that these skills are particularly subject to improvement by diligent practice. And these effects are quite large: on the order of 1/2 of a grade-equivalent in one year! At this rate of gain, a rather large gap would be created over several years.

Blacks show their largest loss (versus Anglos) in Math Problem Solving. This loss is also approximately 1/2 of a grade-equivalent. Other significant losses for blacks include Vocabulary, Reading Comprehension, Punctuation, Usage and Expression, and Math Concepts. That is, this group shows the most widespread pattern of relative skill loss (compared to Anglos). Hispanics have a somewhat different pattern, with a relatively large loss (4/10 of a grade-equivalent) in Vocabulary, no doubt due to continued difficulties from coping with English as a second language, and one that is often not spoken at home. Like blacks, Hispanics also show losses in Math Concepts and Math Problem Solving. Surprisingly, they show relative gains in Spelling.

Table 6.6 takes this analysis one final step, allowing differentiation for subgroups defined by gender/ethnicity and poverty/ethnicity interactions. However, only a few of these are statistically significant. These are large negative effects for black males in Math Concepts and Math Problem Solving, and for low-income Asians in Usage and Expression.

SUMMARY

When a single basic skills measure is constructed from the average of middle-school Language and Mathematics ITBS scores, we find that the poor are 1/2 of a grade level below the less poor, Asians are 1/2 of a grade

Table 6.5. Regression Analysis[a,b] of Detailed Basic Skills: Controlling for Previous-Year Scores, Additive Specification ($N = 448$)

	Vocabulary	Reading Comprehension	Spelling	Capitalization	Punctuation	Usage & Expression	Math Concepts	Math Problem Solving	Math Computation
Constant	17.68	9.58	4.11	6.06	3.34	1.14	7.56	4.40	12.77
Male	1.10	-1.53	-0.67	0.89	-3.46	-2.62	2.42	1.05	1.01
	(1.2)	(1.8)	(0.7)	(0.8)	(3.2)	(2.3)	(2.7)	(1.1)	(1.1)
Poor	-0.75	0.89	-1.43	0.94	0.92	-0.04	0.92	-0.40	1.53
	(0.8)	(0.9)	(1.3)	(0.8)	(0.8)	(0.0)	(0.9)	(0.4)	(1.6)
Asian	-1.80	2.87	5.39	-0.19	5.71	1.07	4.81	-0.08	4.33
	(1.1)	(1.8)	(2.8)	(0.1)	(2.8)	(0.5)	(2.8)	(0.0)	(2.6)
Black	-2.89	-2.21	0.58	-0.61	-2.96	-2.19	-2.31	-4.77	0.14
	(2.2)	(1.8)	(0.4)	(0.4)	(1.9)	(1.3)	(1.8)	(3.6)	(0.1)
Hispanic	-4.42	-0.74	3.83	0.68	0.54	0.63	-2.54	-2.01	-0.18
	(3.3)	(0.6)	(2.6)	(0.4)	(0.3)	(0.4)	(1.9)	(1.5)	(0.1)
Vocabulary 1985	0.476	0.184	0.100	0.271	0.053	0.281	0.144	0.139	-0.036
	(8.6)	(3.5)	(1.6)	(5.0)	(0.8)	(4.0)	(2.6)	(2.5)	(0.7)

Reading Compr 1985	0.175	0.419	-0.039	0.094	0.141	0.154	0.022	0.034	-0.126
	(3.3)	(8.2)	(0.7)	(1.6)	(2.2)	(2.3)	(0.4)	(0.6)	(2.4)
Spelling 1985	0.004	0.035	0.706	-0.119	0.144	0.022	0.034	0.008	0.111
	(0.1)	(1.0)	(16.4)	(1.9)	(3.2)	(0.5)	(0.9)	(0.2)	(3.0)
Capitalization 1985	0.044	0.045	-0.119	0.322	0.050	0.050	0.004	-0.048	0.010
	(1.0)	(1.1)	(2.5)	(6.0)	(1.0)	(0.9)	(0.1)	(1.1)	(0.2)
Punctuation 1985	-0.039	-0.029	0.049	0.206	0.367	0.136	0.075	-0.010	0.120
	(0.9)	(0.7)	(1.0)	(3.6)	(6.8)	(2.4)	(1.6)	(0.2)	(2.7)
Usage & Expr 1985	0.091	0.088	0.103	0.050	0.123	0.286	-0.049	0.011	-0.001
	(2.1)	(2.1)	(2.1)	(0.9)	(2.4)	(5.2)	(1.1)	(0.3)	(0.0)
Math Concepts 1985	0.118	0.059	0.139	0.198	0.128	0.163	0.320	0.262	0.138
	(2.1)	(1.1)	(2.1)	(2.7)	(1.9)	(2.2)	(5.6)	(4.5)	(2.5)
Math Prob Solv 1985	0.023	0.011	-0.046	0.050	-0.004	0.029	0.227	0.476	0.111
	(0.4)	(2.0)	(0.7)	(0.7)	(0.1)	(0.4)	(3.8)	(7.9)	(1.9)
Math Comp 1985	-0.099	0.016	0.137	-0.044	0.141	-0.019	0.198	0.140	0.534
	(1.7)	(0.3)	(2.1)	(0.6)	(2.0)	(0.3)	(3.4)	(2.4)	(9.4)
R^2	.698	.726	.722	.663	.716	.689	.703	.734	.636

[a] Unstandardized coefficients. All regressions include a dummy variable for the 8th-grade course.
[b] The absolute value of the t-statistic is in parentheses.

Table 6.6 Regression Analysis[a,b] of Detailed Basic Skills: Controlling for Previous-Year Scores, Interactive Specification ($N = 448$)

	Vocabulary	Reading Comprehension	Spelling	Capitalization	Punctuation	Usage & Expression	Math Concepts	Math Problem Solving	Math Computation
Constant	19.22	9.10	4.26	4.49	2.95	1.64	5.82	2.53	12.64
Male	-1.42	-0.94	-1.59	1.06	-1.92	-3.94	5.23	2.70	1.52
	(0.8)	(0.6)	(0.8)	(0.5)	(0.9)	(1.8)	(3.1)	(1.6)	(0.9)
Poor	-1.51	0.53	-3.84	1.78	-1.24	-2.84	-1.04	-1.28	1.37
	(0.6)	(0.2)	(1.4)	(0.6)	(0.4)	(0.9)	(0.4)	(0.5)	(0.6)
Asian	-3.07	5.04	5.10	-2.85	3.56	3.53	4.54	-0.26	4.52
	(1.1)	(1.9)	(1.7)	(0.8)	(1.1)	(1.0)	(1.7)	(0.1)	(1.7)
Black	-4.25	-1.77	0.86	-0.25	-2.04	-2.89	0.52	-1.23	0.58
	(2.2)	(0.9)	(0.4)	(0.1)	(0.9)	(1.2)	(0.3)	(0.6)	(0.3)
Hispanic	-8.21	-1.65	-0.21	2.77	1.77	-0.91	-1.62	-3.83	0.03
	(4.0)	(0.8)	(0.1)	(1.0)	(0.7)	(0.3)	(0.8)	(1.8)	(0.0)
Male Asian	2.902	-0.914	0.73	0.609	3.005	1.276	-0.375	-1.075	-0.11
	(0.9)	(0.3)	(0.2)	(0.2)	(0.8)	(0.3)	(0.1)	(0.3)	(0.0)
Male black	3.291	-1.763	-0.62	-2.611	-2.401	1.376	-5.539	-5.416	-0.60
	(1.4)	(0.8)	(0.2)	(0.9)	(0.9)	(0.5)	(2.4)	(2.3)	(0.3)
Male Hispanic	4.047	0.547	4.15	1.133	-3.714	2.353	-3.110	1.095	-1.08
	(1.7)	(0.2)	(1.5)	(0.4)	(1.3)	(0.8)	(1.3)	(0.5)	(0.5)
Poor Asian	-0.217	-3.957	1.09	-3.910	2.224	-9.422	1.942	0.771	-0.27
	(0.1)	(1.2)	(0.3)	(0.9)	(0.5)	(2.1)	(0.5)	(0.2)	(0.1)
Poor black	-0.433	1.057	1.64	1.094	2.388	-2.489	1.666	-0.868	-0.16
	(0.2)	(0.4)	(0.5)	(0.3)	(0.7)	(0.7)	(0.6)	(0.3)	(0.1)

Poor Hispanic	3.529	1.201	5.16	-3.188	2.686	-1.859	2.629	2.964	-0.68
	(1.2)	(0.4)	(1.5)	(0.8)	(0.8)	(0.5)	(0.9)	(1.0)	(0.2)
Vocabulary 1985	0.477	0.183	0.105	0.133	0.040	0.282	0.140	0.147	-0.039
	(8.6)	(3.4)	(1.7)	(1.9)	(0.6)	(4.0)	(2.5)	(2.6)	(0.7)
Read Compr 1985	0.169	0.413	-0.049	0.036	0.160	0.140	0.030	0.023	-0.125
	(3.1)	(7.9)	(0.8)	(0.5)	(2.5)	(2.0)	(0.6)	(0.4)	(2.4)
Spelling 1985	0.009	0.032	0.707	0.052	0.138	0.021	0.027	0.004	0.111
	(0.2)	(0.9)	(16.4)	(1.0)	(3.0)	(0.4)	(0.7)	(0.1)	(3.0)
Capitalization 1985	0.042	0.047	-0.122	0.298	0.054	0.058	0.004	-0.051	0.009
	(1.0)	(1.1)	(2.5)	(5.3)	(1.0)	(1.1)	(0.1)	(1.2)	(0.2)
Punctuation 1985	-0.034	-0.024	0.063	0.215	0.368	0.135	0.084	0.007	0.122
	(0.7)	(0.5)	(1.2)	(3.6)	(6.7)	(2.3)	(1.8)	(0.1)	(2.7)
Usage & Expr 1985	0.092	0.084	0.100	0.053	0.123	0.284	-0.052	0.007	-0.002
	(2.1)	(2.0)	(2.0)	(0.9)	(2.4)	(5.2)	(1.2)	(0.2)	(0.0)
Math Concepts 1985	0.121	0.060	0.139	0.237	0.109	0.173	0.304	0.257	0.135
	(2.1)	(1.1)	(2.1)	(3.2)	(1.6)	(2.4)	(5.3)	(4.4)	(2.4)
Math Prob Solv 1985	0.021	0.103	-0.051	0.009	0.003	0.015	0.233	0.477	0.115
	(0.4)	(1.8)	(0.8)	(0.1)	(0.0)	(0.2)	(3.9)	(7.9)	(2.0)
Math Comp 1985	-0.107	0.032	0.147	0.040	0.146	-0.010	0.213	0.157	0.534
	(1.8)	(0.6)	(2.2)	(0.5)	(2.1)	(0.1)	(3.6)	(2.6)	(9.2)
R^2	.702	.729	.727	.650	.720	.690	.708	.741	.636

[a] Unstandardized coefficients. All regressions include a dummy variable for the 8th-grade course.

[b] The absolute value of the t-statistic is in parentheses.

level above Anglos, Mexican-Americans are 1/2 grade level below Anglos, and African-Americans are 8/10 of a grade level below Anglos. Disaggregating into separate skills, we find important patterns and more extreme differences for population subgroups. Youths from low-income households score 7/10 of a grade-equivalent lower on Language than youths not residing in poverty households. These negative effects are largest for Usage and Expression and for Vocabulary, but they are also consistently large for the other detailed language skills. By contrast, the negative Mathematics effects for low-income children are only half as large as these Language effects.

African-American children average almost 8/10 of a grade-equivalent below Anglos in Language, and for the particularly important skills of Vocabulary and Reading Comprehension, their decrement increases to 1.0–1.1 grade-equivalents. The Mathematics decrement for this group is 9/10 of a grade-equivalent, with the Math Problem Solving effect being 1.4 of a grade-equivalent. Significant negative effects are also observed for Hispanics, although they are generally somewhat smaller than these African-American effects.

These negative effects for being low-income and either African-American or Hispanic are approximately additive. Thus, the Reading Comprehension of African-American males from low-income homes averages 3 grade-equivalents below the expected level for the curriculum they are being presented with.

By contrast with these negative basic skills effects for low-income, African-American, and Hispanic students, the picture for Asians is mixed. Even though their English Vocabulary is 9/10 of a grade-equivalent below Anglos, and their Reading Comprehension and Usage and Expression are (smaller amounts) below Anglos, their Spelling, Capitalization, and Punctuation skills are significantly *above* those of Anglos. The result is that the Language Total for Asians is above that for Anglos. A related pattern is observed for the relative Mathematics scores of Asians. For Mathematics Problem Solving—where Language skill is important—Asians do no better than Anglos. But they are so much stronger on Math Concepts and Math Computation that their Mathematics Total averages well above that of Anglos.

These results are important. They show the significant Language deficits experienced by low-income, African-American, and Hispanic children, as well as the more mixed picture for Asian children. As we shall see, these deficits strongly determine the Coursework Mastery and Course Grade outcomes for these children. As we shall also see, interventions to raise these language skills—particularly Vocabulary and Reading Comprehension—for at-risk elementary school students, provide the greatest promise of reducing the inheritance-of-poverty problem.

Chapter 7

Habits and Styles

Superlative performance is really a confluence of dozens of small skills or activities, each one learned or stumbled upon, which have been carefully drilled into habit and then are fitted together in a synthesized whole. There is nothing extraordinary or super-human in any one of these actions; only the fact that they are done consistently and correctly, and all together, produce excellence.
—Daniel Chambliss, "The Mundanity of Excellence: An Ethnographic Report on Stratification and Olympic Swimmers"

What often does strike me as a black basketball player in a pick-up game hits his shot and I miss mine is the thought: "He's taken that shot maybe five million times in his life, and I've taken it maybe five thousand."
—Gregg Easterbrook, "Blacktop Basketball and *The Bell Curve*"

HABITS AND STYLES DEVELOP SKILLS

It is a commonplace observation that being successful at almost anything is due largely to hard work. The implication for "human capital production functions" (Hanushek 1986, 1987) is clear: holding ability constant, cognitive-skill progress is determined by time-on-task multiplied by the quality of this time spent by the student, that is, the concentration or efficiency with which the time is spent. More formally, skill at time t equals that at time $t - 1$ plus the gain during the elapsed time interval, and this gain equals the time-on-task during this interval times the intensity of effort (or quality of concentration) during this effort. That is, conditional on student ability and the quality of teaching,

$$\text{achieved skill}(t) = \text{achieved skill}(t - 1) + \text{gain}(t, t - 1), \qquad (1)$$

and

$$\text{gain}(t, t - 1) = \text{time-on-task}(t, t - 1) \times \text{concentration}(t, t - 1). \qquad (2)$$

It would seem natural, then, that researchers would seek to measure these key inputs—time-on-task and concentration—separately for population subgroups. Surprisingly, however, this has not been the case, and this despite the fact that anecdotes abound regarding the schoolwork diligence shown by Asians, as well as the schoolwork carelessness shown by African-Americans. No doubt one explanation is the relative difficulty in collecting such information. Few researchers have been able to ask students to report the time they spend on schoolwork, even if the results could be credible. And those who have typically lacked any measure of the quality of that time, including the most important aspect of such quality—the student's ability to concentrate in class.

My solution to this data collection problem was to ask the teachers of our students to report on the student's skills, habits, and styles. Combined with the district's measures of the student's absenteeism, these variables provide a view of the differential effort toward schoolwork manifested by different population subgroups. These variables have two key weaknesses: (1) they combine, rather than separately measure, time-on-task and concentration; and (2) they are teacher reports rather than objective measures. Nevertheless, they remain quite useful. Regarding the former issue, it is not only difficult to separate time-on-task and concentration, it is not really necessary for our purposes here. Instead, by collecting teacher judgments of the student's homework, class participation, effort, and organization—which turn out to be highly correlated with one another—we achieve a picture of "work habits" that measures the most important time and quality inputs during school and home time, as they manifest themselves to the individual charged with creating and managing the student's progress. Of course, there could be potential bias due to the use of teacher's judgments. However, even when biased, these judgments are of interest since it is the teacher who assigns the student's grade. Further, we control some teacher characteristics—in particular, race and gender—so we can study the likely occurrence and consequences of the most commonly hypothesized such bias: that of white teachers against students of color.

ABSENTEEISM

Attendance is measured by the number of unexcused absences recorded by the student's teacher. A student's total of unexcused absences results, of course, from a variety of causes. But this variable does represent at least one measure of student time-on-task, as well as likely being correlated with other measures of the family's commitment to schooling.

Table 7.1 shows a regression analysis of the determinants of days absent. The first column regresses this variable against gender, poverty, and ethnicity variables. The second column adds interactions for gender × ethnicity and poverty × ethnicity to the regression. Finally, column 3 replaces these with variables for the teacher's years of experience, his or her ethnicity, and interactions between the teacher and student's ethnicity. (The interaction variables in columns 2 and 3 cannot be added simultaneously because of multicollinearity.)

Table 7.1. Regression Analysis[a,b] of Days Absent ($N = 486$)

	(1)	(2)	(3)
Constant	3.56	3.97	2.99
Male	−0.45	−1.23	−0.45
	(1.2)	(1.8)	(1.2)
Poor	0.01	−0.11	−0.03
	(0.0)	(0.1)	(0.1)
Asian	−1.93	−1.38	−1.54
	(3.0)	(1.3)	(1.7)
Black	−0.56	−1.62	0.29
	(1.2)	(2.2)	(0.5)
Hispanic	0.33	−0.18	0.37
	(0.6)	(0.2)	(0.6)
Male Asian		−0.36	
		(0.3)	
Male black		1.38	
		(1.5)	
Male Hispanic		1.42	
		(1.5)	
Poor Asian		−0.62	
		(0.4)	
Poor black		0.86	
		(0.8)	
Poor Hispanic		−0.26	
		(0.2)	
Female teacher			0.48
			(1.2)
Teacher experience			−0.00
			(0.2)
Black teacher			1.15
			(1.6)
Black teacher × Asian student			−1.15
			(0.9)
Black teacher × Black student			−2.08
			(2.2)
Black teacher × Hispanic student			−0.31
			(0.3)
R^2	.033	.046	.049

[a] Unstandardized coefficients. All regressions include a dummy variable for the 8th-grade course.
[b] The absolute value of the *t*-statistic is in parentheses.

Column 1 shows one statistically significant effect: Asians are less likely than Anglos to be absent. The effect is large in relative terms: the (non-poor white female) base category averages 3.56 days absent, and being Asian reduces this by 1.93 days, or 54.2 percent. We also find African-Americans less likely to be absent, but the effect does not achieve statistical significance.

When gender × ethnicity and poverty × ethnicity interactions are added to the equation (column 2), none are statistically significant. However, higher absences for African- American and Mexican-American males almost attain significance.

The third column of this table adds teacher variables and teacher/ student ethnicity interactions to the equation. One significant finding emerges: African-American students who have African-American teachers are less likely to be absent. The effect of 2.08 is large in relative terms—even larger than the reduced absenteeism of Asians shown in column 1. This suggests positive gains from the hiring and assignment of black teachers to black students. Whether these gains are due to the better bonding with and increased concerns of black teachers for black students or to some other cause, they are quite interesting. In the following chapter we will be able to see whether or not this effect translates into the better performance of these students in learning the assigned coursework.

WORK HABITS

Table 7.2 examines the determinants of the teacher's judgment of the student's work habits, defined as the average of the teacher's judgment of the student's homework, class participation, effort, and organization. Recall that these judgments are responses to the question, "This student does better than __% of all the students I have taught on __." The four items have been combined into a single measure since they are very highly correlated with one another.

Column 1 shows a simply enormous Asian effect—the fact that a student is Asian increases his or her work habits rating by 25 percentage points! This is 41 percent of the score of 61 percent for the base category (nonpoor female Anglos). The "model minority" certainly performs as such according to its teachers.

The other significant effect is for males: they are judged to be 7.5 percentage points below females in their work habits. African-Americans and Mexican-Americans are also judged to have worse work habits than Anglos, but the effects are not statistically significant. There is no significant effect of coming from a low-income household.

Table 7.2. Regression Analysis^{a,b} of Work Habits

	(1)	(2)	(3)
Constant	60.79	58.88	58.45
Male	−7.48	−4.71	−7.56
	(2.8)	(0.9)	(2.8)
Poor	−0.60	1.24	−0.07
	(0.2)	(0.2)	(0.0)
Asian	24.79	21.72	18.98
	(5.2)	(2.7)	(2.8)
Black	−2.60	1.26	−6.22
	(0.7)	(0.2)	(1.4)
Hispanic	−3.06	−0.88	−6.37
	(0.8)	(0.1)	(1.4)
Male Asian		9.41	
		(1.0)	
Male black		−3.55	
		(0.5)	
Male Hispanic		−10.19	
		(1.4)	
Poor Asian		−6.57	
		(0.6)	
Poor black		−5.64	
		(0.7)	
Poor Hispanic		3.67	
		(0.4)	
Female teacher			5.23
			(1.8)
Teacher			0.25
experience			(1.4)
Black teacher			−10.87
			(2.0)
Black teacher ×			12.11
Asian student			(1.3)
Black teacher ×			9.68
black student			(1.4)
Black teacher ×			8.00
Hispanic student			(1.1)
R^2	.091	.105	.112

^{a} Unstandardized coefficients. All regressions include a dummy variable for the 8th-grade course.
^{b} The absolute value of the *t*-statistic is in parentheses.

The second column of this table adds gender × ethnicity and poverty × ethnicity interactions to the equation. None of these achieve statistical significance. However, there are hints that male Asians have particularly strong work habits, while Asians, blacks, and Hispanics from low-income households have weaker work habits.

The final column of this table adds teacher variables to the equation. More experienced teachers rate the students somewhat higher than do less experienced teachers. African-American teachers rate the work habits of Anglo students significantly lower relative to Asian, black, and Hispanic students than do Anglo teachers. (This is the overall effect of a negative co-efficient on the black teacher variables combined with positive effects of similar magnitude on the black teacher interaction with each of the Asian, black, and Hispanic student variables.) There are at least two possible explanations for this effect. First, race-based conflict between African-American teachers and Anglo students may be occurring. There has been little to no discussion of such a possibility in the literature. Instead, studies such as Kochman (1981) have focused on conflict between black students and white teachers and students. However, there are plausible bases for such discussion. In particular, there is much anecdotal and some scholarly evidence that African-American adults impose harsher discipline on children than do Anglo adults (Hampton 1987). This apparently extends to black schoolteachers: I have heard some say, "White teachers do not know how to discipline black students. They let them walk all over them!" It may be that the harsher discipline routinely meted out by black teachers—to black and white students—is difficult for the white students to accept, and they respond by showing poorer work habits. It may also be that white students are prejudiced against black teachers and so will not do good work for them. A third possibility is that black teachers are disproportionately assigned those white students with poor work habits.

Table 7.3 disaggregates work habits into its four constituents: homework, class participation, effort, and organization. These are analyzed with a specification that allows for interactions between the student's poverty and ethnicity.

Reading across the second row of this table, we see that the 7 percentage point deficit for males in Table 7.2 is the average of even larger negative effects on three of the variables, combined with one smaller effect. Teachers judge male students to be most deficient, relative to females, on their organization. This is almost a 12 percentage point deficit. As we shall see, within this table, this effect magnitude is second only to the effects for Asians (row 4). Boys are also reported to be significantly below girls on homework (9 percentage points) and effort (8 percentage points). However, their class participation is a (not statistically significant) 4 percentage points below that of girls. This picture of seventh- and eighth-grade boys will be familiar to many parents: disorganized schoolwork, poor homework, low effort, but a willingness to jump into classroom participation anyway! [Sadker and Sadker (1986) report that boys are as much as 8 times more likely than girls to call out and demand the teacher's attention.]

The third row of this table shows that the absence of a work habits effect

Table 7.3. Regression Analysis[a,b] of Detailed Work Habits ($N = 465$)

	Homework	Class participation	Effort	Organization
Constant	63.37	62.57	64.22	63.65
Male	−9.08	−3.77	−8.28	−11.78
	(3.0)	(1.3)	(2.8)	(4.0)
Poor	−2.70	−0.61	5.59	2.38
	(0.3)	(0.1)	(0.7)	(0.3)
Asian	24.84	20.08	26.22	26.79
	(3.9)	(3.2)	(4.2)	(4.3)
Black	3.50	−5.00	−2.74	−2.24
	(0.7)	(1.1)	(0.6)	(0.5)
Hispanic	−9.53	−6.45	−9.42	−8.61
	(1.8)	(1.2)	(1.8)	(1.6)
Poor Asian	0.83	−10.23	−7.15	−4.27
	(0.1)	(0.9)	(0.6)	(0.4)
Poor black	−1.90	−4.32	−6.75	−7.81
	(0.2)	(0.4)	(0.7)	(0.8)
Poor Hispanic	9.78	2.00	1.01	4.00
	(1.0)	(0.2)	(0.1)	(0.4)
R^2	.097	.054	.099	.115
Dep. var. mean	57.62	56.77	59.15	56.31

[a] Unstandardized coefficients. All regressions include a dummy variable for the 8th-grade course.
[b] The absolute value of the *t*-statistic is in parentheses.

for children from low-income households is relatively uniform across the four detailed measures—that is, none are statistically significant. The small nonsignificant difference is in the direction suggesting that these children try harder than do those from nonpoor homes.

The fourth row shows detailed effects for Asians. These are uniformly high. The only one below the 25–27 percentage point range is that for class participation, which nevertheless achieves the 20 percentage point level. According to their teachers, Asian students are exemplary at all aspects of work habits.

None of the effects are either large or approach statistical significance for African-Americans (row 5). However, the negative effects for Mexican-Americans are larger and do achieve statistical significance (at the 5 percent level with a one-tailed test) in two of the four cases.

Not a single one of the poverty × ethnicity interactions achieves statistical significance. There is a tendency, however, for low-income Asians and blacks to do worse than the higher-income members of these groups, while the opposite is true for Hispanics.

DISRUPTIVENESS

Table 7.4 shows the determinants of teacher judgments of student disruptiveness. This measure speaks directly to the sorts of concerns that are the daily material of newspaper stories: early adolescents who are already sufficiently disaffected from school to be disruptive within it.

The first column of this table shows, not surprisingly, that boys are considered to be significantly more disruptive than girls—the differential is 6 percentage points. There is also a significant 6 point differential for students from low-income households, but they are less likely to be disruptive than students from nonpoor households. This may be because poverty makes children shy and withdrawn in demeanor rather than overly aggressive. Calculations (not shown) with the assertiveness variable further support this notion.

The largest effects are for Asians and African-Americans. Asians are rated 11 percentage points less disruptive than Anglos. African-Americans are rated 14 percentage points more disruptive than Anglos. To appropriately interpret these findings it is useful to decompose them according to the teacher's ethnicity. Since this is done in column 3, we momentarily defer interpreting these effects.

The second column of this table includes interactions between gender and ethnicity and between poverty and ethnicity. None are statistically significant, so that little is added to the picture presented by column 1.

The third column of this table includes teacher gender, experience, ethnicity, and interactions between teacher and student ethnicity. The only one of these effects that attains statistical significance is that between black teachers and black students. This effect is enormous: 19 percentage points. It shows that the greater disruptiveness reported for African-American students in column 1 is almost entirely due to the judgments of African-American teachers! (Notice that the black student variable in column 3, row 5, is reduced to a statistically insignificant 4.5 percentage points. This represents the judgment of white teachers. By contrast, the black teachers judge these students to be 4.5 (black student) − 1.6 (black teacher) + 19.4 (black teacher/black student) = 22 percentage points more disruptive than white students.)

What causal mechanisms underlie this startling finding? We have seen that African-American students show lower absenteeism and are reported to have better work habits when they have an African-American teacher, suggesting a particularly positive classroom interaction. Yet African-American teachers consider African-American students to be much more disruptive than do white teachers. One possibility is that this higher disruptiveness rating is a natural concomitant of a more intense interaction pattern. A second possibility is that African-American teachers have par-

Table 7.4. Regression Analysis[a,b] of Student
Disruptiveness ($N = 486$)

	(1)	(2)	(3)
Constant	14.54	13.94	10.33
Male	5.94	6.38	5.67
	(2.2)	(1.3)	(2.1)
Poor	−6.39	−3.83	−5.05
	(7.2)	(0.5)	(1.7)
Asian	−11.23	−8.22	−17.75
	(2.4)	(1.0)	(2.7)
Black	14.06	15.27	4.53
	(4.0)	(2.7)	(1.0)
Hispanic	5.35	5.32	3.60
	(1.4)	(0.9)	(0.8)
Male Asian		−5.10	
		(0.5)	
Male black		0.30	
		(0.0)	
Male Hispanic		−0.13	
		(0.0)	
Poor Asian		−1.96	
		(0.2)	
Poor black		−4.72	
		(0.6)	
Poor Hispanic		−1.70	
		(0.2)	
Female teacher			4.39
			(1.6)
Teacher experience			0.19
			(1.1)
Black teacher			−1.59
			(0.3)
Black teacher × Asian student			10.08
			(1.1)
Black teacher × black student			19.36
			(2.8)
Black teacher × Hispanic student			2.37
			(0.3)
R^2	.085	.087	.119

[a] Unstandardized coefficients. All regressions include a dummy variable for the 8th-grade course.
[b] The absolute value of the t-statistic is in parentheses.

ticularly high aspirations for their African-American students, and thus hold them to a higher standard of conduct than do white teachers. A third possibility is that African-American teachers are disproportionately assigned to classes or schools with the most disruptive African-American students. At this point, two implications are suggested. One supports the emphasis by Alexander et al. (1987) on the effects of individual, socially structured personal background upon teacher/student interaction patterns. That is, black teachers, because of their personal biographies, interact differently with students than do white teachers. The second implication is that the greater disruptiveness reported for African-American students cannot be attributed to prejudice on the part of white teachers.

APPEARANCE AND DRESS

Table 7.5 shows the regression analysis of teacher judgments of student appearance and dress. The first column shows significantly lower scores for low-income compared to higher income students and significantly higher scores for Asians than for Anglos. Adding interactions among the student characteristics (column 2) shows particularly high scores for low-income Hispanics. The only teacher characteristic that is statistically significant is teacher experience—more experienced teachers report that their students have a more pleasing appearance and dress (column 3). Overall, the reports of less attractive appearance and dress for low-income students and more attractive appearance and dress for Asian students are what might be expected where it is the teachers who are doing the judging. That is, they can be expected to give "higher marks" for newer clothes and for a neat, clean, and groomed appearance.

SUMMARY

Where teacher judgments of student habits and styles are concerned, one group stands out from all others. The work habits of Asian students are judged to be superb, far superior to those of Anglos. This is true across all four categories: organization, effort, homework, and class participation. In addition, these students have significantly lower absenteeism than Anglos and are judged to be significantly less disruptive than Anglos. As we shall see, these Asian habits and styles play a large role in the academic success of this group.

Other group differences are not nearly as large. Nevertheless, some are significant. African-American students have lower absenteeism than other groups when their teacher is also African-American. African-American students are also judged to be more disruptive than Anglo students, but this judgment comes entirely from African-American teachers! This suggests intense interaction patterns that merit further study.

In addition, boys are judged to be more disruptive than girls, and chil-

Table 7.5. Regression Analysis[a,b] of Appearance
and Dress ($N = 486$)

	(1)	(2)	(3)
Constant	66.28	65.68	59.89
Male	−2.70	−0.62	−2.64
	(1.1)	(0.1)	(1.1)
Poor	−6.80	−11.07	−5.70
	(2.6)	(1.7)	(2.1)
Asian	13.10	9.35	7.70
	(3.0)	(1.3)	(1.3)
Black	1.46	4.72	0.27
	(0.4)	(0.9)	(0.1)
Hispanic	4.07	0.60	3.68
	(1.2)	(0.1)	(0.9)
Male Asian		10.64	
		(1.3)	
Male black		−3.00	
		(0.5)	
Male Hispanic		−8.14	
		(1.2)	
Poor Asian		−2.55	
		(0.3)	
Poor black		−1.00	
		(0.1)	
Poor Hispanic		16.13	
		(2.0)	
Female teacher			2.06
			(0.8)
Teacher			0.53
experience			(3.3)
Black teacher			−5.28
			(1.1)
Black teacher ×			8.26
Asian student			(1.0)
Black teacher ×			2.05
black student			(0.3)
Black teacher ×			1.39
Hispanic student			(0.2)
R^2	.031	.062	.059

[a] Unstandardized coefficients. All regressions include a dummy variable for the 8th-grade course.
[b] The absolute value of the t-statistic is in parentheses.

dren from low-income households are judged to be less disruptive than students from higher-income households. Each of these effects has consequences for learning, but as we shall see, they are relatively modest in magnitude.

Chapter 8

Coursework Mastery

For many disadvantaged students the problem with the academic program
is that the curriculum presented is too difficult for them to achieve re-
spectable grades.

> —Gary Natriello, E. McDill, and A. Pallas, *Schooling
> Disadvantaged Children: Racing Against Catastrophe*

Rutter found . . . that differences in verbal intelligence at age ten were the best
single predictor of educational attainment in the high school years.

> —James Q. Wilson, *On Character*

THE IMPORTANCE OF DIRECTLY MEASURING
COURSEWORK MASTERY

The principal goal of attending school is to learn the coursework assigned
by the teacher. This is particularly the case in middle and high school,
where basic skills are assumed and each subject has a substantive focus. It
is thus somewhat surprising that most studies of differential learning and
its determinants ("educational production functions") have utilized basic
skills measures such as ITBS and other standardized test scores instead of
measures of learning assigned coursework as their dependent variables
(Hanushek 1986, 1994; Murnane 1975; Summers and Wolfe 1977; Featherman and Hauser 1978; Jencks et al. 1979, 1983; Alexander et al. 1987; Entwisle and Alexander 1994). However, on closer examination this situation
is readily comprehensible: the desired measures are almost never available. This is because the heterogeneity of what is taught in any particular
subject at any particular grade level has precluded national data collection
efforts from seeking to measure such substantive learning. Even within individual school districts, where assigned coursework by subject and grade
level is presumably more homogeneous, few have undertaken the effort
necessary to develop and uniformly administer tests of the students' success in mastering this material.

Fortunately, the Dallas public schools did develop and uniformly administer such *curriculum-referenced* tests during the time period of this study. During the summer, teachers of each of the forty odd subject/grade levels in middle and high school were assembled in working groups. Working from the published curriculum of their subject, they assembled test items matched to each of the curricular items. While data from all subjects are available, we have chosen to concentrate on seventh- and eighth-grade social studies: Texas History/Geography and U.S. History/Citizenship. (For calculations utilizing the more extensive series of subject test scores available, see Farkas et al. 1990b; Farkas 1993.) This has two benefits. First, by focusing on social studies we avoid both language arts, which is so closely related to ITBS English skills, and mathematics/science, which is so closely related to ITBS mathematics skills. We are thus able to measure student performance on substantive tasks, which may better relate to the sorts of tasks that will recur in home and work life as the students reach adulthood. Second, by focusing on seventh and eighth grade, before most school dropping out occurs, we are able to keep the full range of students within our study, rather than restricting attention to the (better-performing) students who remain in school for the higher grades.

The following section reports on the determinants of this coursework mastery, utilizing the "main model" of predictive variables: student background, teacher characteristics, and student skills, habits, and styles. Following this we look in even more detail at these determining characteristics by using measures of the detailed ITBS basic skills as predictor variables.

THE BASIC MODEL

Table 8.1 shows that when coursework mastery is regressed against student characteristics (column 1), males score higher than females, the poor score lower than the nonpoor, Asians score higher than Anglos, and African-Americans and Hispanics score lower than Anglos. While most of these effects attain statistical significance, the largest occur for Asians and African-Americans. By comparison with the base category (female, nonpoor Anglos), who average 33.3 on this test, Asians score 10 points, or almost 1/3 higher. African-Americans score 5.4 points, or about 1/6 lower. Each of these effects is large by comparison with the standard deviation of the dependent variable, which equals 13.4.

Examining interactions among student characteristics (column 2) adds little to these findings; none of them attains statistical significance and R^2

Table 8.1.   Regression Analysis[a,b] of Coursework Mastery

	(1)	(2)	(3)	(4)	(5)	(6)	(7)	(8)
Constant	33.27	32.61	29.63	29.00	2.84	2.66	1.22	1.17
Male	2.90	4.74	3.04	5.04	4.21	5.34	4.26	5.47
	(2.7)	(2.4)	(2.9)	(2.5)	(4.8)	(3.3)	(4.9)	(3.4)
Poor	−2.00	−4.03	−1.71	−3.26	−0.58	−2.67	−0.48	−2.28
	(1.7)	(1.4)	(1.5)	(1.2)	(0.6)	(1.2)	(0.5)	(1.0)
Asian	10.34	14.11	11.28	13.99	5.21	8.53	6.47	8.54
	(5.5)	(4.4)	(4.2)	(4.4)	(3.4)	(3.3)	(3.0)	(3.3)
Black	−5.41	−4.78	−5.04	−4.59	−2.15	−1.66	−1.63	−1.56
	(3.8)	(2.2)	(2.8)	(2.1)	(1.8)	(0.9)	(1.1)	(0.9)
Hispanic	−1.72	−2.20	−1.30	−2.32	0.56	−0.83	0.78	−0.99
	(1.1)	(0.9)	(0.7)	(1.0)	(0.4)	(0.4)	(0.5)	(0.5)
Male Asian		−4.70		−4.95		−5.93		−6.00
		(1.3)		(1.3)		(2.0)		(2.0)
Male black		−1.51		−1.93		−1.16		−1.40
		(0.5)		(0.7)		(0.5)		(0.6)
Male Hispanic		−2.71		−2.99		0.04		−0.20
		(0.9)		(1.0)		(0.0)		(0.1)
Poor Asian		−1.25		−2.24		1.31		0.58
		(0.3)		(0.5)		(0.4)		(0.2)
Poor black		1.73		1.19		1.60		1.27
		(0.5)		(0.4)		(0.6)		(0.5)
Poor Hispanic		4.71		4.42		3.95		3.89
		(1.4)		(1.3)		(1.4)		(1.4)
Female teacher			2.63	2.75			2.00	2.08
			(2.3)	(2.5)			(2.2)	(2.3)
Teacher experience			0.18	−1.39			0.11	0.11
			(2.6)	(1.2)			(1.9)	(1.9)
Black teacher			−0.17	−1.39			0.50	−0.70
			(0.1)	(1.2)			(0.3)	(0.8)
Black teacher × Asian student			−3.07				−3.21	
			(0.8)				(1.1)	
Black teacher × black student			−1.38				−1.72	
			(0.5)				(0.8)	
Black teacher × Hispanic student			−1.88				−1.26	
			(0.6)				(0.5)	
Basic skills					0.33	0.33	0.33	0.33
					(9.4)	(9.3)	(9.1)	(9.2)
Days absent					−0.14	−0.14	−0.16	−0.16
					(1.3)	(1.3)	(1.5)	(1.5)
Work habits					0.14	0.14	0.14	0.14
					(7.1)	(7.2)	(6.9)	(6.9)
Disruptiveness					−0.02	−0.02	−0.02	−0.02
					(1.1)	(1.1)	(1.1)	(1.3)
Appearance & dress					−0.04	−0.04	−0.04	−0.04
					(2.0)	(2.0)	(2.1)	(2.2)
R^2	.257	.265	.282	.289	.527	.534	.538	.544

[a] Unstandardized coefficients. All regressions include a dummy variable for the 8th-grade course.
[b] The absolute value of the t-statistic is in parentheses.

barely increases. However, there is the suggestion of lower coursework mastery for male Asians and higher coursework mastery for low-income Hispanics.

Adding teacher characteristics to the regression (column 3) does not significantly alter the pattern of student effects, and the student/teacher interactions are not significant. However, both female teachers and more experienced teachers are associated with higher coursework mastery among their students. The latter finding corroborates previous results, which single out teacher experience as one of the few readily measured teacher variables that positively affects learning (Hanushek 1986; Shuan 1989; Weir 1993). However, this finding lacks robustness, since it disappears when the specification is changed to permit interactions among student characteristics (column 4). The main effects of student characteristics *are* robust to the alternative specifications of the first four columns.

Columns 5–8 add the basic skills and habits and styles variables to the equations. This shows the effects of these variables in their own right, as well as the direct effects of student characteristics, net of basic skills, habits, and styles. The indirect effects of student characteristics, operating through their effects on basic skills, habits, and styles are measured by the difference between the gross-effects coefficients for the characteristics reported in columns 1–4 and the net-effects coefficients reported in columns 5–8 (Alwin and Hauser 1975).

The effects of skills, habits, and styles on coursework mastery are essentially identical across specifications (columns 5–8). Effects are large and significant, with R^2 increasing from about .27 to about .53. The bulk of this increase is attributable to the effects of basic skills (the ITBS score) and teacher judgments of student work habits: both variables positively affect coursework mastery. Since coursework mastery and basic skills are measured objectively and independently of teacher judgments of student work habits, the significant net effect of the work habits variable provides support for the validity of the teacher judgments.

As expected, both days absent and teacher judgments of student disruptiveness are negatively related to coursework mastery, but these effects are not statistically significant. The appearance and dress variable is significant and negatively related to coursework mastery, but its magnitude is small. This effect appears to reflect a trade-off between student attention to appearance and dress and to schoolwork. Or, possibly, good students "dress down" in revolt against "middle-class values." (Alternatively, they dress like "nerds.")

When the skills, habits, and styles variables are controlled, the male effect increases in magnitude and significance. Thus, males show significantly better coursework mastery than females, an effect that becomes stronger when their basic skills, absenteeism, work habits, disruptiveness, and appearance and dress are controlled. In other words, rather than these variables explaining the male/female differential in coursework mastery, males score higher on coursework mastery despite teacher judgments regarding their inferior work habits and greater disruptiveness, as noted in Chapter 7.

On the other hand, controls for basic skills, habits, and styles reduce the negative differentials for the poor, African-American, and Mexican-American students, and the positive differentials for Asian students. In particular, approximately half of the 10-point Asian/Anglo differential in coursework mastery is explained by the skills, habits, and styles variables. These results demonstrate that, for *individual* students, learning of assigned coursework is responsive, in Swidler's (1986) terms, to the extent to which the individual's "strategy" involves a positive orientation toward schooling. Further, differential *group* learning is demonstrated to be largely explicable on the basis of group differentials in skills, habits, and styles (Swidler 1986; Ogbu 1986). That is, if ethnicity and poverty groups manifested the same "strategies" toward schooling, their group differentials in performance would narrow significantly.

Table 8.2 repeats this analysis, testing for whether the skills, habits, and styles effects on coursework mastery differ according to the student's background characteristics. Since simultaneously adding many interactions leads to multicollinearity problems, equations are presented in which interactions with skills, habits, and styles are added one at a time. The results are reported in successive columns. In each case, the dependent variable is the student's coursework mastery, and the base model is equation (5) from Table 8.1.

Looking at interactions of student characteristics with basic skills (bottom panel of column 1), we find that none are statistically significant. There is, however, a suggestion that Asians attain higher coursework mastery gains than Anglos as each group's basic skills increase, and also that African-Americans and Mexican-Americans attain lower coursework mastery gains than Anglos as each group's basic skills increase.

The second column of this table shows the extent to which the effects of absenteeism on coursework mastery vary across student groups. Here we find that the significant negative effect of absenteeism for Anglos is diminished or reversed for the other ethnicities. Absenteeism does not decrease coursework mastery for Asians, blacks, or Hispanics.

The third and fourth columns show interactions with work habits and disruptiveness. None are large or statistically significant. The final column shows interactions with appearance and dress. As noted before, the main effect of this variable is negative. However, we now see a more complex story. First, the negative effect of appearance and dress is significantly weaker for males than for females. It is also significantly weaker for blacks

Table 8.2.   Regression Analysis[a,b] of Coursework Mastery: Interactive Models for the Effects of Cognitive and Noncognitive Variables

| | Interactions with | | | | |
	Basic skills	Days absent	Work habits	Disruptiveness	Appearance & dress
Constant	0.52	4.01	3.46	3.15	7.32
Male	4.80	4.13	4.01	4.44	0.58
	(1.1)	(3.7)	(2.2)	(4.1)	(0.3)
Poor	−0.30	−0.21	1.48	−0.30	0.26
	(0.1)	(0.2)	(0.7)	(1.1)	(0.1)
Asian	−4.51	2.52	4.09	4.78	0.73
	(0.6)	(1.3)	(0.7)	(1.1)	(0.2)
Black	5.08	−4.31	−4.03	−2.30	−6.10
	(0.6)	(2.9)	(1.7)	(1.5)	(2.1)
Hispanic	4.48	−1.05	−2.01	0.44	−6.10
	(0.9)	(0.6)	(0.8)	(0.3)	(2.0)
Basic skills	0.359	0.333	0.334	0.332	0.342
	(6.0)	(9.4)	(9.3)	(9.3)	(9.5)
Days absent	−0.154	−0.566	−0.121	−0.146	−0.123
	(1.4)	(2.2)	(1.1)	(1.3)	(1.1)
Work habits	0.144	0.141	0.124	0.138	0.139
	(7.3)	(7.2)	(3.6)	(6.9)	(7.0)
Disruptiveness	−0.014	−0.018	−0.015	−0.031	−0.019
	(0.9)	(1.2)	(1.0)	(0.9)	(1.2)
Appearance and dress	−0.041	−0.037	−0.038	−0.037	−0.121
	(2.1)	(1.9)	(2.0)	(1.9)	(3.3)
Interactions between ____ (see column heading) and student characteristics					
____ × male	−0.008	0.024	0.004	−0.013	0.058
	(0.2)	(0.1)	(0.1)	(0.5)	(1.8)
____ × poor	−0.003	−0.130	−0.036	0.037	0.016
	(0.0)	(0.6)	(1.2)	(1.2)	(0.5)
____ × Asian	−0.113	1.149	0.022	0.057	0.067
	(1.2)	(2.1)	(0.3)	(0.8)	(1.1)
____ × black	−0.101	0.694	0.033	0.009	0.066
	(1.3)	(2.2)	(0.9)	(0.2)	(1.6)
____ × Hispanic	−0.052	0.479	0.047	0.008	0.110
	(0.6)	(1.6)	(1.2)	(0.2)	(2.4)
R^2	.532	.534	.529	.529	.537

[a] Unstandardized coefficients. All regressions include a dummy variable for the 8th-grade course.
[b] The absolute value of the t-statistic is in parentheses.

and Hispanics than for Anglos. In sum, it is Anglo females whose coursework mastery suffers the most from their attention to their appearance and dress. Apparently, it is within the subculture of this group that such attention indicates the strongest pull away from schoolwork.

Table 8.3. Standardized Regression Coefficients (Beta Weights) for Predicting Coursework Mastery

Independent variable	
Basic skills	.38**
Days absent	−.04
Work habits	.32**
Disruptiveness	−.05
Appearance and dress	−.08*

*, Significant at $p \leq .05$.   **, Significant at $p \leq .01$.

Table 8.3 provides additional information for interpreting the main effect determinants of coursework mastery [e.g., the results of equation (5) of Table 8.1]. It presents standardized regression coefficients for the effects of student basic skills, habits, and styles upon coursework mastery. We see that basic skills and student work habits are the principal determinants of coursework mastery. These effects are large, and show that when the other variables are held constant, each of these variables is still a prime determinant of learning assigned coursework.

MODELS WITH DETAILED SKILLS, HABITS, AND STYLES

Table 8.4 repeats the calculations of Table 8.1, but using the detailed basic skill measures available on the ITBS as independent variables, instead of one summary measure of basic skills as in the previous tables. The first two columns use the Language and Mathematics Total scores, while columns 3 and 4 use all six separate Language subtests, and three Mathematics subtests.

Column 1 shows that both Language and Mathematics skill are positively related to learning the assigned coursework, but the effect for Language is dominant—almost three times that for Mathematics skill. This is not surprising, since social studies coursework relies heavily on reading and writing ability. The other variables in this calculation have effects essentially unchanged from the prior specification, in which Language and Mathematics skill were combined (Table 8.1, column 5). Column 2 repeats this calculation utilizing a specification with gender/ethnicity and poverty/ethnicity interactions. The results are essentially unchanged—the skills effects are the same as column 1, and the interactions are the same as found in Table 8.1, column 6.

The third and fourth columns repeat these calculations using detailed basic skills. The results are dramatic: the effects are largely attributable

Table 8.4. Regression Analysis[a,b] of Coursework Mastery Using Detailed
Basic Skills

	(1)	(2)	(3)	(4)
Constant	3.75	3.54	0.20	0.13
Male	4.54	5.68	4.07	5.04
	(5.1)	(3.5)	(4.6)	(3.2)
Poor	−0.42	−2.49	0.25	−2.19
	(0.4)	(1.1)	(0.3)	(1.0)
Asian	5.33	8.51	7.55	9.68
	(3.5)	(3.3)	(4.7)	(3.8)
Black	−2.39	−1.80	−0.57	−0.32
	(2.0)	(1.0)	(0.5)	(0.2)
Hispanic	0.32	−1.08	2.17	1.03
	(0.3)	(0.5)	(1.7)	(0.5)
Male Asian		−5.88		−5.24
		(2.0)		(1.8)
Male black		−1.20		−0.75
		(0.5)		(0.3)
Male Hispanic		0.01		−0.10
		(0.0)		(0.0)
Poor Asian		1.55		3.28
		(0.5)		(1.0)
Poor black		1.41		1.87
		(0.5)		(0.7)
Poor Hispanic		3.98		3.88
		(1.4)		(1.4)
Language Total	0.23	0.23		
	(5.8)	(5.7)		
Math Total	0.08	0.08		
	(1.7)	(1.6)		
Vocabulary			0.12	0.12
			(2.9)	(2.8)
Reading Comprehension			0.18	0.18
			(3.9)	(3.8)
Spelling			0.01	0.01
			(0.3)	(0.3)
Capitalization			0.01	0.01
			(0.3)	(0.3)
Punctuation			0.07	0.07
			(1.6)	(1.6)
Usage and Expression			−0.03	−0.03
			(0.8)	(0.7)
Math Concepts			0.09	0.09
			(1.7)	(1.8)
Math Problem Solving			−0.01	−0.01
			(0.3)	(0.3)
Math Computation			−0.06	−0.07
			(1.4)	(1.5)

(continued)

Table 8.4. (Continued)

	(1)	(2)	(3)	(4)
Days absent	−0.14	−0.14	−0.14	−0.14
	(1.3)	(1.3)	(1.3)	(1.3)
Work habits	0.14	0.14	0.14	0.15
	(7.3)	(7.4)	(7.6)	(7.7)
Disruptiveness	−0.02	−0.02	−0.02	−0.02
	(1.1)	(1.1)	(1.4)	(1.4)
Appearance and dress	−0.04	−0.04	−0.04	−0.04
	(2.0)	(2.0)	(2.3)	(2.3)
R^2	.530	.537	.572	.577

[a] Unstandardized coefficients. All regressions include a dummy variable for the 8th-grade course.
[b] The absolute value of the t-statistic is in parentheses.

to the significant positive effects of, first, Reading Comprehension, and second, Vocabulary. There is also some indication of positive effects from Punctuation and Mathematics Concepts. Also noteworthy is that as we move from the first to the third column of this table, the significant negative effect for African-Americans becomes much smaller and not statistically significant and the nonsignificant effect for Hispanics actually becomes positive and significant. That is, reading skill is the key to explaining the lower coursework mastery of these students. This is the "smoking gun" that led me to design and implement a large-scale reading intervention for at-risk children. (See Chapters 10–12. See also Farkas 1993.)

Table 8.5 shows calculations with detailed habits and styles. That is, instead of combining Homework, Class Participation, Tries Harder, and Better Organized into one "work habits" variable, these have all been kept separate so that detailed effects can be examined. We also include the "more assertive" variable. In the interests of additional detail, the calculations are undertaken separately for each ethnic group, and the following predictor variables are also included: teacher gender, ethnicity, and experience, as well as the percentage of students from each ethnicity in the student's class. Basic skills are measured as the Language and Mathematics totals from 1985 (one year earlier than the previous calculations).

The principal finding is that the determinants of coursework mastery show very different patterns across ethnic groups. For the two most powerful predictors—basic skills and work habits—there is an indication of two distinct patterns. One of these holds true for the two groups of native English speakers—Anglos and African-Americans, while the other holds true for nonnative English speakers—Asians and Mexican-Americans.

For Anglos and African-Americans, English language proficiency, but not Mathematics proficiency, is predictive of coursework mastery. The op-

Table 8.5. Regression Analysis^{a,b} of Coursework Mastery, Separately by Ethnicity, with Detailed Habits and Styles

	Anglo	Asian	African-American	Hispanic
Constant	9.75	−14.52	−4.31	−3.56
Male	5.57	−0.06	4.21	6.10
	(2.9)	(0.0)	(2.7)	(3.2)
Poor	−4.91	0.63	0.43	2.31
	(1.8)	(0.2)	(0.3)	(1.3)
Female teacher	−1.18	1.08	3.40	−2.30
	(0.6)	(0.3)	(2.1)	(1.0)
Teacher experience	−0.04	0.47	0.28	−0.02
	(0.3)	(2.3)	(2.6)	(0.2)
Black teacher	−0.84	0.86	−1.69	−1.20
	(0.4)	(0.2)	(1.0)	(0.6)
Language total 1985	0.29	0.02	0.22	0.08
	(2.6)	(0.2)	(3.0)	(0.8)
Math total 1985	−0.01	0.47	−0.00	0.24
	(0.0)	(2.6)	(0.0)	(1.7)
Days absent	−0.58	0.21	−0.00	−0.25
	(2.6)	(0.4)	(0.0)	(1.2)
Homework	0.23	−0.33	0.11	0.01
	(3.4)	(1.6)	(2.0)	(0.1)
Class participation	0.16	−0.05	0.17	−0.01
	(1.8)	(0.4)	(2.8)	(0.3)
Tries harder	−0.19	0.27	−0.21	0.07
	(1.6)	(1.0)	(2.7)	(0.8)
Better organized	−0.10	0.13	0.12	0.04
	(1.1)	(0.5)	(2.1)	(0.6)
Disruptive	−0.10	0.00	−0.03	−0.01
	(2.1)	(0.0)	(1.2)	(0.2)
Assertive	0.14	0.03	−0.04	0.04
	(3.0)	(0.3)	(1.3)	(1.2)
Appearance and dress	−0.08	0.03	−0.04	0.08
	(1.5)	(0.4)	(1.0)	(2.1)
Percentage black	−17.83	−5.78	7.14	2.53
	(1.4)	(0.4)	(1.7)	(0.3)
Percentage Hispanic	9.03	13.65	20.13	3.27
	(0.8)	(1.4)	(2.9)	(0.5)
Percentage Asian	11.07	9.11	11.42	29.23
	(0.8)	(0.5)	(1.2)	(2.4)
R^2	.594	.732	.531	.480
Dep. var. mean	38.12	48.58	31.79	34.63
N	128	59	156	127

^{a} Unstandardized coefficients. All regressions include a dummy variable for the 8th-grade course.

^{b} The absolute value of the t-statistic is in parentheses.

posite is the case for Asians and Mexican-Americans. Further, for Anglos and African-Americans, homework and class participation are significantly and positively associated with mastery, whereas effort ("tries harder") is negatively associated with such achievement. By contrast, for Asians and Hispanics these effects are reversed or nonexistent.

What interpretation is suggested by these findings? Among students who begin as native English speakers, those who put the greatest effort and concentration into their schoolwork develop quite strong reading, vocabulary, and related language skills, and these skills allow their coursework mastery to forge ahead. For these students, homework and class participation follow naturally, and in turn serve to further boost coursework mastery.

The situation is very different for the Asians and Hispanics. Perhaps surprisingly for these groups of nonnative speakers, it is mathematics rather than English language skill which is associated with higher coursework mastery. In search of an explanation, I speculate as follows. Perhaps English language is such a difficult problem for all these students that it does not differentiate among them very well. Instead, it may be that those who try really hard at schoolwork show the greatest progress in mathematics, so that this variable becomes the best predictor of coursework mastery. This would be consistent with the finding that "tries harder" is the habit that best predicts mastery for these students. However, this interpretation must be regarded as highly speculative.

Finally, note that the findings in Table 8.5 are less reliable than those presented in previous tables of this chapter. This is because splitting the sample by ethnicity greatly reduced sample sizes. When this situation is combined with the relatively high correlations among many of the independent variables, and the relatively large numbers of these variables, inferences from regression become more fragile.

SUMMARY

Using a direct test score measure of how well students have learned assigned social studies coursework, we find that Asians score significantly above Anglos, and African-Americans score significantly below Anglos. Smaller negative effects are observed for Hispanics and females. Student basic skills and work habits are found to exert very large positive effects on learning assigned coursework. In addition, these variables explain large portions of the coursework mastery differentials observed for Asians, African-Americans, Mexican-Americans, and the poor. Among Anglos and African-Americans, both of whom are native English speakers, excellence in homework, class participation, and English language skill are the most important predictors of social studies mastery. By contrast, among Hispanics and Asians, excellence in mathematics is the most important predictor of social studies mastery. These different patterns across ethnic groups suggest the existence of a finer level of detail by which skills and habits determine coursework success.

Chapter 9

Course Grades

We have placed considerable emphasis on socialization practices within the home and the way that universal modes of processing associated with acquisition of language and cognitive skills are embedded in sociocultural contexts. We have also insisted on the central role played by school personnel who interpret students' characteristics, academic performance, and educational policies in shaping and changing students' educational careers.
—Aaron V. Cicourel and Hugh Mehan "Universal Development, Stratifying Practices, and Status Attainment"

How shall we explain the fact that the Japanese pupils in Los Angeles have about the same IQ as the average pupil and score about the same on educational tests but obtain strikingly better grades? It may be that they possess to a greater degree than whites those qualities which endear pupils to a teacher; that is, they are more docile, occasion less disciplinary trouble, and give the appearance of being busy and striving to do their best.
—Edward K. Strong, *The Second Generation Japanese Problem*

COURSE GRADES AS A REWARD SYSTEM

The teacher assigns the course grade, so that teacher judgments define the reward system whose implicit rules determine outcomes within the school's stratification system. Grades are, of course, the chief stratifying variable within schools. Since past grades affect both the student's interest in trying hard in the future, and the student's placement within tracking systems that determine the quantity and quality of material and instruction he or she will be presented with, they are central determinants of the student's eventual cognitive skill, and thus of the student's eventual placement within society's occupational hierarchy. (For the role of cognitive skill in determining occupational and earnings outcomes, see Chapter 4.)

Because we have measures of student background variables, teacher variables, and student skills, habits, styles, and coursework mastery, we have a unique opportunity to directly measure the effect of each of these

119

on course grades. That is, we can, for the first time at this level of detail, discover the implicit rules that teachers use to determine outcomes within the school's stratification system. This will provide the answers to a number of outstanding questions. First, is it true that, as has been believed for more than fifty years, Asians receive higher course grades than Anglos because "they are more docile, occasion less disciplinary trouble, and give the appearance of being busy and striving to do their best" (Strong 1934:2)? Or is it simply that they receive fair rewards for doing better schoolwork than Anglos? Second, how does this issue of rewards for habits and styles versus coursework mastery play out for blacks and Hispanics versus Anglos? And if African-American and Mexican-American students *are* penalized for habits and styles that are unattractive to teachers, does this differ between black and white teachers? Finally, with and without accounting for such habits, styles, and coursework mastery, are boys or girls discriminated against in course grade assignment? These and related questions will be answered by the calculations presented in this chapter.

THE BASIC MODEL

Table 9.1 presents regressions in which student characteristics, teacher characteristics, interactions among these, skills, habits, styles, and coursework mastery are sequentially added to the equation to predict course grades. Moving across columns 1–4, where student characteristics are entered additively, the R^2 increases from .13 to .77; in columns 5–7, where student characteristics are entered interactively, R^2 increases from .16 to .77. This indicates that the variables successively added in these columns are quite successful in accounting for individual variation in course grade attainment.

Looking at gross differentials for gender, poverty, and ethnicity groups (column 1), the strongest effect is for Asians, who score almost 10 points higher than Anglos. Statistically significant but more modest negative effects are observed for males and African-Americans. Effects for low-income and Hispanic students are not significant.

When teacher variables and teacher/student ethnicity interactions are added to the equation (column 2), the student characteristics differentials are unchanged, and the teacher/student ethnicity interactions are not significant. There is thus no evidence that white or black teachers discriminate against white or minority students when assigning course grades.

When basic skills, habits, and styles are added to the equation (column 3), R^2 increases from .15 to .74. All effects are statistically significant and in the expected direction. As measured by their t-statistics, the most important

Table 9.1. Regression Analysis[a,b] of Course Grades: Additive Models for the Effects of Cognitive and Noncognitive Variables

	(1)	(2)	(3)	(4)	(5)	(6)	(7)
Constant	80.53	80.27	54.21	53.95	79.62	54.37	54.12
Male	−2.29	−2.15	−0.43	−1.35	−0.71	−0.15	−1.33
	(2.4)	(2.3)	(0.8)	(2.6)	(0.4)	(0.2)	(1.4)
Poor	−0.75	−0.64	0.12	0.23	−1.39	−1.07	−0.58
	(0.7)	(0.6)	(0.2)	(0.4)	(0.6)	(0.8)	(0.4)
Asian	9.90	9.96	3.47	2.07	9.37	2.28	0.43
	(6.0)	(4.2)	(2.6)	(1.6)	(3.3)	(1.4)	(0.3)
Black	−2.84	−2.91	0.45	0.81	−0.84	0.89	1.23
	(2.3)	(1.8)	(0.5)	(0.9)	(0.4)	(0.8)	(1.2)
Hispanic	−1.82	−1.01	1.45	1.29	−1.50	−0.35	−0.13
	(1.3)	(0.6)	(1.6)	(1.5)	(0.7)	(0.3)	(0.1)
Male Asian					1.99	−0.09	1.20
					(0.6)	(0.1)	(0.7)
Male black					−2.65	−1.38	−1.08
					(1.1)	(1.0)	(0.8)
Male Hispanic					−2.98	0.65	0.69
					(1.2)	(0.5)	(0.5)
Poor Asian					−0.39	2.40	2.27
					(0.1)	(1.2)	(1.2)
Poor black					−0.59	0.45	0.17
					(0.2)	(0.3)	(0.1)
Poor Hispanic					3.10	2.30	1.45
					(1.0)	(1.3)	(0.9)
Female teacher		−0.93	−1.77	−2.21	−0.93	−1.85	−1.36
		(0.9)	(3.1)	(4.1)	(0.9)	(3.3)	(2.5)
Teacher experience		0.12	0.04	0.01	0.12	0.04	0.01
		(1.9)	(1.1)	(0.4)	(2.0)	(1.1)	(0.4)
Black teacher		−2.40	−0.28	−0.39	−2.65	−1.51	−1.36
		(1.3)	(0.3)	(0.4)	(2.6)	(2.6)	(2.5)
Black teacher × Asian student			0.30	−1.44	−0.75		
			(0.1)	(0.8)	(0.4)		
Black teacher × black student			0.44	−1.33	−0.96		
			(0.2)	(0.9)	(0.7)		
Black teacher × Hispanic student			−1.47	−2.05	−1.78		
			(0.6)	(1.4)	(1.3)		
Basic skills			0.23	0.16		0.24	0.17
			(10.6)	(7.3)		(10.9)	(7.5)
Days absent			−0.44	−0.41		−0.43	−0.40
			(6.5)	(6.3)		(6.3)	(6.2)
Work habits			0.22	0.19		0.22	0.19
			(17.9)	(15.7)		(17.9)	(15.7)
Disruptiveness			−0.03	−0.02		−0.03	−0.02
			(2.9)	(2.7)		(3.0)	(2.7)
Appearance and dress			−0.04	−0.03		−0.04	−0.03
			(2.9)	(2.3)		(3.0)	(2.4)
Coursework mastery				0.22			0.22
				(8.0)			(8.0)
R^2	.131	.150	.737	.769	.160	.739	771

[a] Unstandardized coefficients. All regressions include a dummy variable for the 8th-grade course.
[b] The absolute value of the t-statistic is in parentheses.

are the positive effects of work habits and basic skills, followed by the negative effect of absenteeism. These results provide powerful evidence for the importance of basic skills, student behavior, and teacher judgments of student habits and styles as predictors of school success. In addition, with these variables in the equation, most student characteristic variables are reduced to statistical insignificance. The only exception is the positive effect for Asians, and it is reduced by approximately two-thirds, from 9.9 points to 3.5 points.

Of course, skills, habits, and styles likely affect course grades via their impact on the student's coursework mastery. However, adding coursework mastery to the equation (column 4), produces only a modest increase in R^2. While coursework mastery exerts a strong, positive, significant effect on course grades, the basic skills, work habits, and styles variables remain significant. Thus, although the magnitudes and significance of these variables are somewhat diminished, they are still relatively large, significant, and in the expected directions, indicating that these variables operate only partially via their effect on coursework mastery, but show persistent net effects in their own right. Apparently teachers directly reward students with these traits, over and above the relationship of these traits with coursework mastery.[1]

In this specification of the equation, income, African-American, and Mexican-American effects remain insignificant, indicating that the differential course grades received by these groups are explained by their differential performance on the intermediate variables. The Asian effect is further reduced and is no longer significant, indicating that this group's higher course grades can also be explained by group members' performance on the intermediate variables. A notable exception to these trends is that a significant negative male effect reappears. This was to be expected, since males show both higher coursework mastery and lower course grades than females. However, the effect is quite modest, being only 1.35 grade points. Nevertheless, this significant net effect for males is consistent with previous research reporting that, particularly in the seventh and eighth grades, teachers find boys difficult to deal with and grade them down accordingly.

Columns 5–7 repeat these calculations with the set of student-characteristic interactions added to the equation. These interactions are not statistically significant, affirming the robustness of the findings already reported.

Next, we follow Alexander et al. (1987) in testing whether the skills, habits, styles, and coursework mastery effects on course grades differ according to the student's background characteristics, and the interaction between these and the teacher's background characteristics. Tests for interactions with student characteristics are shown in Table 9.2; those for higher-order interactions, including both student and teacher characteristics, are shown in Table 9.3. Since simultaneously adding many interactions leads to multicollinearity problems, equations are presented in which interactions with skills, habits, styles, and coursework mastery are added one at a time. The results are reported in successive columns. In each case, the dependent variable is the student's course grade.

Looking at interactions of student characteristics with basic skills (the bottom panel of column 1), we find that only one is significant: Hispanics receive a much higher course grade return to basic skills performance than do Anglos. Since this effect is positive and the others are not significant, these results provide no evidence that teachers are biased toward Anglos in course grade assignment. We also find that neither absenteeism (column 2) nor perceived work habits (column 3) interacts significantly with the background variables. Once again, there is no evidence of teacher bias.

For disruptiveness, there is only one significant effect: boys are penalized for being disruptive, whereas girls are not. With these interactions in the equation, the main effect of perceived disruptiveness falls to zero. Thus, the disruptiveness effect observed in Table 9.1 is shown to be entirely concentrated among males. This is, of course, consistent with previous findings that teachers are particularly disturbed by the behavior of twelve- and thirteen-year-old boys. Although this effect is significant, it is small in magnitude.

The only significant interaction for appearance and dress occurs for African-Americans. Better appearance and dress are associated with lower course grades for this group. However, the effect is small. For coursework mastery there is also a single significant interaction: Hispanic students receive greater returns to coursework mastery than do Anglo students. This effect is of reasonable size. For cognitive performance, either basic skills (column 1) or coursework mastery, Hispanics receive greater rewards than do any other group. The reasons for this are not known, although we may speculate that because many of these students must master English as a second language, teachers are particularly impressed and provide particularly strong rewards when they do so.

In the hope of better understanding these effects, Table 9.3 reestimates these effects, including higher-order interactions among student and teacher ethnicity and the variables in Table 9.2. Looking across the bottom rows of Table 9.3 we see that only one of the added interactions achieves statistical significance: the negative association between black teachers and Hispanic students in the column for interactions with student disruptiveness. There is also a (smaller and not significant) negative effect for black teachers and black students in this column. That is, the negative effect of disruptiveness on course grades is particularly strong when black teachers are judging Hispanic or black students.

Other aspects of this table are unchanged from Table 9.2. In particular,

Table 9.2. Regression Analysis[a,b] of Course Grades: Interactive Models for the Effects of Cognitive and Noncognitive Variables

| | Interactions with | | | | | | |
	Basic skills	Days absent	Work habits	Disruptiveness	Appearance and dress	Coursework mastery	No interactions
Constant	55.29	52.48	52.96	52.13	52.91	53.97	52.80
Male	0.71	-1.20	-1.63	-0.67	-2.95	-0.49	-1.42
	(0.3)	(1.8)	(1.5)	(1.0)	(2.2)	(0.3)	(2.7)
Poor	-2.49	0.15	-0.45	0.26	-1.09	-1.48	0.32
	(0.9)	(0.2)	(0.4)	(0.4)	(0.8)	(0.9)	(0.6)
Asian	1.13	1.63	-1.27	1.45	2.40	2.93	1.43
	(0.2)	(1.4)	(0.4)	(1.4)	(0.9)	(0.9)	(1.6)
Black	-3.11	0.75	1.24	0.50	3.09	-0.79	0.35
	(0.9)	(0.8)	(0.9)	(0.6)	(1.8)	(0.4)	(0.5)
Hispanic	-8.00	0.73	0.48	0.76	1.97	-4.78	0.30
	(2.0)	(0.8)	(0.3)	(0.8)	(1.1)	(2.1)	(0.4)
Basic skills	0.14	0.17	0.17	0.17	0.17	0.18	0.17
	(3.9)	(7.5)	(7.4)	(7.6)	(7.1)	(8.0)	(7.6)
Days absent	-0.42	-0.34	-0.43	-0.42	-0.43	-0.42	-0.43
	(6.6)	(2.2)	(6.6)	(6.5)	(6.6)	(6.4)	(6.6)
Work habits	0.18	0.18	0.18	0.18	0.19	0.18	0.18
	(14.8)	(14.9)	(8.8)	(15.0)	(15.1)	(14.9)	(15.2)

	Interaction variable[a]					
Disruptiveness	−0.03	−0.03	−0.00	−0.03	−0.03	−0.03
	(3.4)	(3.2)	(0.2)	(3.1)	(3.4)	(3.3)
Appearance and dress	−0.02	−0.02	−0.02	−0.02	−0.02	−0.02
	(1.8)	(1.9)	(1.9)	(0.9)	(2.0)	(2.0)
Coursework mastery	0.21	0.21	0.21	0.21	0.16	0.21
	(7.9)	(7.7)	(7.7)	(7.7)	(3.8)	(7.7)
Interactions between ____ (see column heading) and student characteristics						
____ × male	−0.03	−0.00	−0.03	0.02	−0.03	
	(0.8)	(0.2)	(2.1)	(1.2)	(0.7)	
____ × poor	0.04	0.01	0.01	0.02	0.05	
	(1.0)	(0.8)	(0.3)	(1.1)	(1.2)	
____ × Asian	0.01	0.03	0.01	−0.02	−0.02	
	(0.1)	(0.8)	(0.2)	(0.5)	(0.3)	
____ × black	0.04	−0.02	−0.01	−0.04	0.03	
	(1.0)	(0.7)	(0.4)	(1.8)	(0.6)	
____ × Hispanic	0.11	−0.00	−0.02	−0.03	0.14	
	(2.1)	(0.1)	(0.9)	(1.0)	(2.4)	
R^2	.763	.759	.761	.761	.765	.758

[a] Unstandardized coefficients. All regressions include a dummy variable for the 8th-grade course.

[b] The absolute value of the t-statistiic is in parentheses.

Table 9.3. Regression Analysis[a,b] of Course Grades: Complex Interactive Models for the Effects of Cognitive and Noncognitive Variables

	Interactions with					
	Basic skills	Days absent	Work habits	Disruptiveness	Appearance and dress	Coursework mastery
Constant	57.30	53.82	53.80	54.03	54.02	55.95
Male	0.40	−1.19	−1.47	−0.69	−3.10	−0.83
	(0.2)	(1.8)	(1.3)	(1.1)	(2.3)	(0.6)
Poor	−2.17	−0.02	−0.46	−0.14	−1.40	−1.47
	(0.7)	(0.0)	(0.4)	(0.2)	(1.0)	(0.9)
Asian	1.40	2.11	−0.93	1.96	2.94	3.28
	(0.3)	(1.9)	(0.3)	(1.9)	(1.1)	(1.0)
Black	−3.56	−0.99	1.04	0.46	2.59	−0.90
	(1.0)	(1.1)	(0.8)	(0.5)	(1.5)	(0.5)
Hispanic	−7.37	1.14	0.49	1.14	1.91	−4.48
	(1.8)	(1.2)	(0.3)	(1.3)	(1.1)	(2.0)
Female teacher	−2.18	−2.26	−0.32	−2.25	−2.38	−2.25
	(4.1)	(4.2)	(0.3)	(4.2)	(4.4)	(4.2)
Teacher experience	0.02	0.02	0.02	0.01	0.01	0.01
	(0.5)	(0.4)	(0.5)	(0.2)	(0.4)	(0.4)
Black teacher	−2.23	−1.03	−0.32	−1.58	0.01	−1.97
	(0.8)	(1.5)	(0.3)	(2.4)	(0.0)	(1.2)
Basic skills	0.12	0.16	0.16	0.17	0.16	0.18
	(3.1)	(7.2)	(7.2)	(7.4)	(6.9)	(7.7)
Days absent	−0.40	−0.28	−0.40	−0.40	−0.41	−0.40
	(6.2)	(1.5)	(6.2)	(6.2)	(6.3)	(6.2)
Work habits	0.19	0.19	0.19	0.19	0.19	0.19
	(15.2)	(15.3)	(8.6)	(15.2)	(15.5)	(15.3)
Disruptiveness	−0.03	−0.03	−0.02	−0.02	−0.02	−0.03
	(3.0)	(2.8)	(2.5)	(1.0)	(2.6)	(2.9)

Appearance and dress	-0.02 (2.1)	-0.03 (2.3)	-0.02 (1.9)	-0.02 (2.1)	-0.02 (.7)	-0.03 (2.3)
Coursework mastery	0.22 (8.2)	0.22 (8.0)	0.22 (8.0)	0.21 (7.9)	0.22 (8.0)	0.15 (3.3)
Interactions between ____ (see column heading) and student and teacher characteristics						
____ × male	-0.02 (0.7)	-0.05 (0.3)	0.00 (0.1)	-0.03 (1.7)	0.03 (1.5)	-0.01 (0.4)
____ × poor	0.03 (0.9)	0.09 (0.7)	0.01 (0.7)	0.01 (0.4)	0.03 (1.3)	0.05 (1.1)
____ × Asian	0.01 (0.1)	0.02 (0.0)	0.03 (0.7)	-0.03 (0.3)	-0.02 (0.4)	-0.02 (0.3)
____ × black	0.05 (1.2)	-0.20 (0.9)	-0.01 (0.4)	0.01 (0.4)	-0.04 (1.3)	0.04 (0.8)
____ × Hispanic	0.11 (2.1)	-0.08 (0.4)	0.00 (0.1)	0.00 (0.1)	-0.02 (0.6)	0.15 (2.5)
____ × black teacher	0.02 (0.5)	-0.06 (0.3)	-0.02 (0.8)	0.05 (1.6)	-0.02 (0.8)	0.03 (0.6)
____ × Asian student × black teacher	-0.00 (0.2)	-0.15 (0.3)	0.01 (0.5)	0.02 (0.2)	-0.00 (0.1)	-0.00 (0.1)
____ × black student × black teacher	-0.00 (0.1)	0.06 (0.2)	-0.00 (0.1)	-0.04 (1.2)	0.00 (0.2)	-0.01 (0.2)
____ × Hispanic student × black teacher	-0.01 (0.6)	-0.15 (0.6)	0.00 (0.1)	-0.08 (1.9)	-0.01 (0.5)	-0.01 (0.5)
R^2	.773	.770	.770	.773	.772	.775

[a] Unstandardized coefficients. All regressions include a dummy variable for the 8th-grade course.

[b] The absolute value of the t-statistic is in parentheses.

the large, positive returns to basic skills and coursework mastery for Hispanic students are still in evidence and are found to occur whether the
teacher is African-American or white.

With interactions somewhat scattered and small in magnitude compared to the main effects of Table 9.1, we summarize these main effects using standardized regression coefficients (beta weights) in Table 9.4. We see
that even with coursework mastery controlled, each of the remaining variables significantly affects course grades. The work habits variable exerts by
far the largest effect: the standardized coefficient is approximately twice
the magnitude of that for coursework mastery, its closest competitor. The
effect for basic skills, the other cognitive performance indicator, is similar
to coursework mastery, followed by absenteeism, with disruptiveness and
appearance and dress having the smallest effects. *Most striking is the powerful effect of student work habits upon course grades. This confirms the notion
that, as alleged by cultural-capital sociologists, but neglected by human capital
economists, teacher judgments of student habits and styles are powerful determinants of course grades, even when student cognitive performance is controlled.*
Habits and styles, as well as cognitive performance determine school
success, and the effects of cognitive performance are approximately
equally divided between coursework mastery and basic skills. That is, although coursework mastery is a significant determinant of schooling
achievement, teachers' grading systems cause final grades to be determined by much more than coursework mastery alone. (See note 1 for further discussion.)

The differential course grade attainment of gender, ethnicity, and poverty groups is almost entirely accounted for by the cognitive and noncognitive (that is, habits and styles) performance variables, the only exception
being the small but statistically significant deficit suffered by males. Overall, Asian course grades are 10 points—a full letter grade—higher than
those for Anglos. Yet, after controls for cognitive and noncognitive vari-

Table 9.4. Standardized Regression Coefficients
(Beta Weights) for Predicting Course Grades

Independent variable	
Basic skills	.22**
Days absent	−.15**
Work habits	.53**
Disruptiveness	−.05**
Appearance and dress	−.07*
Coursework mastery	.27**

*, Significant at $p \leq .05$.   **, Significant at $p \leq .01$.

ables, this differential declines 80 percent to a statistically insignificant 2 points. Although Asian students outscore non-Asians on basic skills and coursework mastery, and this cognitive performance contributes significantly to their higher course grades, Asian student noncognitive performance as reflected in teacher judgments of their work habits contributes an even greater amount to the school success of this group.

These results provide a corrective to prior discussions, which have emphasized the threat of student disruptiveness as the key noncognitive variable in teachers' reward systems (see the quotation from Strong at the beginning of this chapter). Thus, although Asians are viewed as less disruptive than Anglos, this variable explains little of the substantial Asian/Anglo course grade differential. Instead, Asian students achieve higher course grades than Anglos by outperforming them on basic skills, coursework mastery, and—most important—work habits, as measured by the teacher's perceptions of the student's homework, class participation, effort, and organization.

Thus, both functionalist and cultural-capital sociologists are correct to believe that teachers reward "citizenship" over and above cognitive (test score) performance. But to be rewarded, this citizenship must move beyond an absence of threat and into the realm of performance as indicated by school attendance and by work habits. When this occurs, a double reward is generated. First, coursework mastery increases and is rewarded. Second, net of this effect, school attendance and work habits are rewarded as performance variables in their own right (as shown in Table 9.4).

The chain of effects operating through basic skills to test scores has a similar double payoff reward structure. That is, good basic skills performance generates a course grade reward both in and of itself, as well as for the increase it produces in the student's coursework mastery test score. Thus, any individual or group possessing strong basic skill performance as well as a reputation for good citizenship can achieve unusually high course grades. As measured by the Dallas school data, Asian students have done just this. (For a discussion that is at least partially complementary, see Dornbusch, Ritter, and Steinberg 1991.)

The differentials observed for other groups are more modest. The perceived poor work habits and greater disruptiveness of males lower their course grades below those received by females, but the effect is small. African-American students show modestly lower course grades than Anglos, an effect almost entirely attributable to their lower basic skills and coursework mastery test scores. Thus, although these students are perceived (although only by African-American teachers) to be more disruptive than Anglos, this has almost no effect on their course grades. The course grades of low-income students and of Hispanic students are not significantly different from those of nonpoor Anglos.

MODELS WITH DETAILED SKILLS, HABITS, AND STYLES

Table 9.5 repeats the calculations of Table 9.1, but utilizes the detailed basic skills subtests of the ITBS. Columns 1, 2, 5, and 6 use the Language and Mathematics Totals in place of a single basic skills measure; columns 3, 4, 7, and 8 use all nine distinct subtests.

Table 9.5. Regression Analysis[a,b] of Course Grades Using Detailed Basic Skills

	(1)	(2)	(3)	(4)	(5)	(6)	(7)	(8)
Constant	53.55	53.52	52.35	52.23	52.77	52.78	52.31	52.21
Male	−0.49	−0.18	−0.49	−0.10	−1.44	−1.36	−1.34	−1.14
	(0.9)	(0.2)	(0.9)	(0.1)	(2.7)	(1.4)	(2.4)	(1.2)
Poor	0.22	−1.08	0.40	−1.15	0.31	−0.57	0.34	−0.70
	(0.4)	(0.8)	(0.7)	(0.8)	(0.6)	(0.4)	(0.6)	(0.5)
Asian	2.54	1.99	3.46	2.47	1.42	0.22	1.88	0.46
	(2.6)	(1.2)	(3.3)	(1.5)	(1.5)	(0.1)	(1.9)	(0.3)
Black	−0.14	0.63	0.42	1.20	0.36	1.01	0.54	1.27
	(0.2)	(0.6)	(0.5)	(1.0)	(0.5)	(0.9)	(0.7)	(1.2)
Hispanic	0.38	−0.78	0.89	−0.07	0.31	−0.56	0.44	−0.28
	(0.5)	(0.6)	(1.1)	(0.1)	(0.4)	(0.5)	(0.6)	(0.2)
Male Asian		−0.16		0.15		1.06		1.24
		(0.1)		(0.1)		(0.6)		(0.7)
Male black		−1.25		−1.38		−1.00		−1.23
		(0.9)		(1.0)		(0.8)		(0.9)
Male Hispanic		0.64		0.40		0.64		0.42
		(0.4)		(0.3)		(0.5)		(0.3)
Poor Asian		2.30		3.09		1.98		2.40
		(1.1)		(1.5)		(1.0)		(1.2)
Poor black		0.57		0.87		0.28		0.48
		(0.3)		(0.5)		(0.2)		(0.3)
Poor Hispanic		2.45		2.50		1.62		1.70
		(1.4)		(1.4)		(1.0)		(1.0)
Language total	0.13	0.13			0.08	0.09		
	(5.3)	(5.4)			(3.5)	(3.6)		
Math Total	0.11	0.10			0.09	0.09		
	(3.4)	(3.3)			(3.0)	(2.9)		
Vocabulary			0.04	0.04			0.01	0.01
			(1.4)	(1.4)			(0.5)	(0.5)
Reading comprehension			0.05	0.05			0.01	0.02
			(1.7)	(1.7)			(0.4)	(0.5)
Spelling			0.01	0.01			0.01	0.01
			(0.5)	(0.3)			(0.4)	(0.3)
Capitalization			0.01	0.01			0.01	0.01
			(0.5)	(0.6)			(0.4)	(0.5)
Punctuation			0.02	0.02			0.00	0.00
			(0.6)	(0.6)			(0.1)	(0.1)

(*continued*)

Table 9.5. (*Continued*)

	(1)	(2)	(3)	(4)	(5)	(6)	(7)	(8)
Usage and			0.05	0.05			0.05	0.06
Expression			(1.9)	(2.1)			(2.3)	(2.4)
Math Concepts			−0.01	−0.01			−0.02	−0.03
			(0.2)	(0.2)			(0.8)	(0.8)
Math Problem			0.04	0.04			0.04	0.04
Solving			(1.3)	(1.2)			(1.5)	(1.3)
Math Computation			0.05	0.06			0.07	0.07
			(1.8)	(1.9)			(2.4)	(2.5)
Days absent	−0.46	−0.45	−0.46	−0.45	−0.43	−0.42	−0.43	−0.42
	(6.7)	(6.5)	(6.7)	(6.5)	(6.6)	(6.5)	(6.6)	(6.4)
Work habits	0.21	0.21	0.21	0.22	0.18	0.18	0.18	0.18
	(17.4)	(17.4)	(17.3)	(17.3)	(15.1)	(15.0)	(14.8)	(14.8)
Disruptiveness	−0.03	−0.03	−0.03	−0.03	−0.03	−0.03	−0.03	−0.03
	(3.5)	(3.4)	(3.6)	(3.6)	(3.3)	(3.2)	(3.4)	(3.3)
Appearance	−0.03	−0.03	−0.03	−0.04	−0.02	−0.02	−0.02	−0.03
and dress	(2.6)	(2.7)	(2.7)	(2.8)	(2.0)	(2.1)	(2.1)	(2.2)
Coursework					0.21	0.21	0.21	0.21
mastery					(7.7)	(7.6)	(7.3)	(7.3)
R^2	.728	.730	.734	.737	.758	.760	.761	.764

[a] Unstandardized coefficients. All regressions include a dummy variable for the 8th-grade course.
[b] The absolute value of the *t*-statistic is in parentheses.

The Language and Mathematics totals are found to have roughly equal effects on course grades. This justifies averaging them together into a single score in the prior analysis. The effects of other variables are essentially unchanged from those reported in Table 9.1.

The detailed ITBS subtests show an interesting pattern. Vocabulary and Reading Comprehension are important for course grades when coursework mastery is not held constant (columns 3 and 4), but become statistically insignificant when it is held constant. That is, these variables affect coursework mastery only *via* their effect on coursework mastery. By contrast, Usage and Expression and Mathematics Computation are significant even after coursework mastery is held constant. That is, teachers give higher social studies grades to students with better usage and expression and mathematics computation, even when their social studies coursework mastery is identical.

Table 9.6 repeats these calculations, separately by ethnicity, using the full detail on habits and styles. Basic skills are measured by Language and Mathematics Totals, and both teacher variables and school ethnic composition are controlled. For each group, the first column shows the determinants of course grades without coursework mastery controlled; the second column adds coursework mastery to the equation.

Table 9.6. Regression Analysis[a,b] of Course Grades, Separately by Ethnicity, with Detailed Habits and Styles

	Anglo		Asian		African-American		Hispanic	
	(1)	(2)	(1)	(2)	(1)	(2)	(1)	(2)
Constant	42.90	40.06	18.20	36.21	49.99	50.54	59.50	60.02
Male	2.42	0.79	−5.78	−5.70	−0.80	−1.33	0.70	−0.20
	(0.8)	(0.3)	(0.9)	(1.0)	(0.5)	(0.7)	(0.2)	(0.1)
Poor	0.78	2.21	5.96	5.18	0.10	0.05	−1.68	−2.02
	(0.2)	(0.5)	(0.8)	(0.8)	(0.1)	(0.0)	(0.5)	(0.6)
Female teacher	−4.39	−4.04	3.07	1.73	−3.05	−3.48	5.10	5.44
	(1.3)	(1.2)	(0.4)	(0.3)	(1.7)	(1.9)	(1.3)	(1.4)
Teacher experience	0.22	0.23	0.44	−0.14	0.18	0.14	0.17	0.17
	(1.1)	(1.2)	(0.9)	(0.3)	(1.5)	(1.2)	(0.7)	(0.7)
Black teacher	−9.95	−9.70	11.01	9.94	−3.37	−3.15	1.39	1.57
	(2.9)	(2.8)	(1.3)	(1.3)	(1.8)	(1.6)	(0.4)	(0.4)
Language total 1985	−0.01	−0.10	0.47	0.45	0.23	0.20	−0.09	−0.10
	(0.1)	(0.6)	(1.5)	(1.6)	(2.9)	(2.5)	(0.5)	(0.6)
Math total 1985	0.41	0.41	−0.28	−0.87	−0.10	−0.09	0.43	0.40
	(2.1)	(2.1)	(0.6)	(2.1)	(1.0)	(1.0)	(1.8)	(1.6)
Days absent	−0.79	−0.62	−0.90	−1.15	−0.83	−0.83	−1.44	−1.40
	(2.3)	(1.8)	(0.7)	(1.0)	(3.9)	(3.9)	(4.0)	(3.9)
Homework	0.15	0.08	−0.73	−0.33	0.12	0.11	0.08	0.08
	(1.4)	(0.8)	(1.4)	(0.7)	(2.0)	(1.7)	(0.9)	(0.9)
Class participation	0.12	0.07	0.02	0.09	0.09	0.07	−0.05	−0.05
	(0.8)	(0.5)	(0.1)	(0.3)	(1.3)	(1.0)	(0.6)	(0.6)
Tries harder	−0.11	−0.05	1.21	0.88	−0.04	−0.01	0.04	0.03
	(0.6)	(0.3)	(1.8)	(1.5)	(0.4)	(0.1)	(0.3)	(0.2)
Better organized	0.05	0.08	−0.05	−0.20	0.11	0.09	0.06	0.06
	(0.3)	(0.6)	(0.1)	(0.4)	(1.7)	(1.5)	(0.5)	(0.5)
Disruptive	0.01	0.03	−0.18	−0.19	−0.05	−0.04	−0.04	−0.04
	(0.1)	(0.5)	(0.8)	(0.9)	(1.7)	(1.5)	(0.6)	(0.6)
Assertive	0.01	−0.03	−0.06	−0.09	−0.02	−0.02	−0.01	−0.02
	(0.1)	(0.4)	(0.3)	(0.6)	(0.6)	(0.4)	(0.2)	(0.3)
Appearance and dress	−0.05	−0.02	0.06	0.02	−0.07	−0.06	0.07	0.06
	(0.6)	(0.3)	(0.3)	(0.1)	(1.7)	(1.5)	(1.1)	(0.9)
Percentage black	−11.84	−6.63	8.03	15.19	10.24	9.34	−19.06	−19.43
	(0.6)	(0.3)	(0.2)	(0.5)	(2.1)	(1.9)	(1.4)	(1.4)
Percentage Hispanic	5.76	3.13	3.68	−13.25	22.31	19.77	−18.67	−19.15
	(0.3)	(0.2)	(0.2)	(0.6)	(2.9)	(2.5)	(1.6)	(1.6)
Percentage Asian	6.14	2.91	−45.26	−56.56	26.80	25.35	0.92	−3.41
	(0.3)	(0.1)	(1.1)	(1.6)	(2.4)	(2.3)	(0.0)	(0.2)
Coursework mastery		0.29		1.24		0.13		0.15
		(2.0)		(3.6)		(1.3)		(0.9)
R^2	.409	.431	.438	.583	.588	.593	.447	.452
Dep. var. mean	75.67	75.67	83.75	83.75	74.90	74.90	73.76	73.76
N	128	128	59	59	156	156	127	127

[a] Unstandardized coefficients. All regressions include a dummy variable for the 8th-grade course.

[b] The absolute value of the t-statistic is in parentheses.

The major surprise in this table is that Asians receive extraordinarily high returns to coursework mastery. For this group the coefficient on this variable is more than four times that of Anglos, the group with the next highest return. In addition to this very high return to coursework mastery, Asians also receive positive returns to English Language skill and to student effort. The "frog pond effect" (grading on a curve) lowers the course grades of Asians in classes with a large percentage of Asian students. (For a general treatment of the frog pond phenomenon, see Farkas et al. 1990b.)

Anglos also receive above-average returns to coursework mastery. That is, their coefficient for this variable in Table 9.6 is above the overall average of this coefficient in Table 9.1.

SUMMARY

The findings in this chapter confirm the premise of this volume, that student skills, habits, and styles explain the differential schooling success of groups defined by gender, ethnicity, and poverty status.

The largest course grade differential is for Asians, who score almost 10 points, or one full letter grade, above Anglos. Significant negative effects are observed for African-Americans and for males, but these are smaller in magnitude. Effects for Hispanic and for low-income students are not significant.

When student basic skills, and teacher judgment of student habits and styles are added to the equation, the ability to predict course grades increases immensely. The most important predictors are student basic skills and work habits. Further, with these variables controlled, intergroup differentials are enormously reduced.

When coursework mastery is added as a predictor, it is found to positively and significantly affect course grades, but the skills, habits, and styles variables also remain significant. That is, teachers grade directly on these traits, over and above their relation to coursework mastery. (However, this does not necessarily imply that teachers' grading systems are nonmeritocratic. See note 1 and the discussion below.) With these control variables in the equation, intergroup differentials are even smaller.

Thus, groups such as Asians receive a double payoff for their positive basic skills and work habits. First, these increase course grades via their effect in increasing coursework mastery. Then, these variables are rewarded a second time in their own right, over and above their effect on coursework mastery. This "double-payoff reward structure" has enabled Asians to gain school success far in excess of that achieved by Anglos. It has also depressed the course grades received by African-Americans and Hispanics.

What is the detailed mechanism of these effects? Most schoolteachers arrive at a final grade by averaging weekly assignments and several test scores from throughout the term. It is likely that, even holding constant a student's coursework mastery test score from the end of the term, those students with better work habits were more careful and complete in turning in weekly assignments, and scored somewhat higher on tests. Thus, the higher course grades received by these students may well have been "earned" within a meritocratic grading system, even though such students may not have scored any higher on the end-of-term coursework mastery test than did a student with weaker work habits. That is, the double payoff for good work habits noted above should not necessarily be viewed as antimeritocratic. This reward structure has the effect, however, of widening the course grade achievement gaps separating Asians and Anglos on the one hand, and that separating Anglos and African-Americans or Hispanics, on the other.

NOTE

1.   That is, teacher's grades are affected by these traits, over and above their relationship with our *end-of-term test score* measure of coursework mastery. If, as seems likely, net of this measure of coursework mastery, students with better skills and better teacher-judged habits and styles receive higher grades because they scored higher on weekly assignments and during-term tests, these higher grades do not indicate that teachers are failing to use a meritocratic grading system. That is, the system may be meritocratic, but still possess the property that students with identical (tested) coursework mastery at the end of the term receive very different grades because of their very different basic skills and work habits.

PART III

Intervention

Chapter 10

Intervening to Affect the Skills, Habits, and Styles of At-Risk Students

[L]earning deficits must be prevented in a comprehensive approach emphasizing early education, improvement in instruction and curriculum, and intensive intervention at the earliest possible stage when deficiencies first begin to appear. The goal is to prevent remediation at all costs: Once students have fallen seriously behind, they are unlikely to ever catch up to their agemates because the experience of failure introduces problems of poor motivation, self-esteem, and behavior that undermine the effectiveness of even the best remedial or special-education approaches.

> —Nancy A. Madden, Robert E. Slavin, Nancy L. Karweit,
> and Barbara A. Wasik, "Success for All:
> Longitudinal Effects of a Restructuring Program for
> Inner-City Elementary Schools."

THE PROBLEM

The previous chapters have demonstrated that the skills, habits, and styles of African-American and Mexican-American children from low-income households place them at severe risk of school failure. These skills, habits, and styles constitute a negative feedback loop, so that by eighth grade, for example, African-American males from low-income households read, on average, three grade levels below the assigned textbooks (Chapter 6). Similar results are found for Hispanic children. And this reading deficit largely explains the low coursework mastery of these students (Chapter 8). *Thus, for much of their school career, few to none of these students are able to read the assigned textbooks.*[1]

Since reading is largely taught in elementary school and reading skill essentially defines students' success during these early years, it is useful to examine the extent to which these students fall behind in reading during these years. Below, I present such data for Dallas during 1994–95. Doing so, however, requires attention to the fact that, by Texas regulations, the majority of English as a Second Language (ESL) children are excluded from testing in English during these early years. Accordingly, I begin the analysis by showing reading comprehension scores for *tested* students. However, we will then examine the imputed full distribution for all students, utilizing test scores the Reading One-One program (described in Chapter 11) collected for students not tested by the district.

Table 10.1 shows the distribution of end-of-year reading scores for *tested* first- through third-grade students. The categories represent 10-percentile groupings of the national distribution of ITBS scores. (Thus, for example, among first graders, the lowest tenth of scores within the national percentile are those below a grade-equivalent of 1.2, interpreted as "mastering the material taught in the second month of first grade.") We see that among the 8,122 Dallas first graders tested near the close of spring 1995, 52 percent ended the year below the national average grade-level score of 1.8. Among the 7,759 tested second graders, 54 percent ended the year below the average grade-level score of 2.8. Among the 7,812 tested third graders, 66 percent ended the year below the national average grade-level score of 3.8.

However, because of state regulations, these tested students are many fewer than those actually enrolled in these grades. Yet untested students are real students and are typically the ones most likely to read below grade level. They seek a future, they occupy teachers, and, if their reading skills are well below grade level, they have difficulty profiting from the instruction offered and are prone to drop out. Accordingly, it is important that they be counted and included in any attempt to bring all children up to grade level.

Table 10.2 shows the result when estimated scores for these untested students are added to the (Table 10.1) distribution of tested students. (For the methodology underlying Table 10.2, see the Appendix.) Not surprisingly, the great majority of untested students are Hispanic. In spring 1995, these untested Hispanic students in Dallas numbered 4,504 first graders, 3,502 second graders, and 3,422 third graders.

When all students are counted, we get the following results. Among 13,391 first graders, 64 percent ended the year reading below grade level. Among 12,081 second graders, 70 percent ended the year reading below grade level. Among 12,172 third graders, 78 percent ended the year reading below grade level.

As these children move to higher grades, an increasing share fall below grade level in reading. And yet, teachers have no choice but to work with the assigned textbooks, each constituting hundreds of pages of grade level reading material in social studies, science, English, and other subjects. Children lack the basic skills needed to cope with this material, yet beyond third grade, instruction in these skills is neither part of the teacher's training nor of her teaching assignment. Little wonder that, as reported in

Chapters 6–9, these students are alienated from school and perform poorly there.

Closely related to skills, habits, and styles, the student's self-esteem and ability to concentrate are key predictors of school success. As we shall see in Chapter 11, tutors in the Reading One-One program rated the attentiveness of each child during each tutoring session. Each student's average attentiveness was then computed across all of the tutoring sessions he or she received, and used as a predictor variable (along with other variables) to estimate the student's reading gains. Not surprisingly, student attentiveness was found to be one of the most important predictors of achievement. Further evidence comes from the qualitative information contained in tutor reports and teacher comments. These overwhelmingly support the notion that self-esteem, time-on-task, attentiveness, and support from and bonding with an adult constitute a feedback loop that is strongly determinative of student success or failure. In the inner city, the result is usually failure. The process typically evolves as follows.

Children from low-income households begin first grade less than reading-ready.[2] Consequently, they cannot meet the curricular demand of learning to read by the end of the first semester. As a result, they reach the end of first grade seriously behind in their schoolwork, and already well into a cycle of failure in which their skills are below the level demanded by the curriculum, and their self-esteem, willingness to try, and time-on-task are inadequate to succeed at the assigned tasks.

By second grade, the situation of children who are receiving negative feedback from this process, and are not progressing at grade level, worsens dramatically. The second-grade curriculum assumes that students can read acceptably, and the reading level expected increases substantially during this year. The teacher has little choice in moving the class on to higher reading levels, since many other and related skills must be mastered: spelling, capitalization, punctuation, composing and writing essays and stories, and (sometimes) cursive writing. In addition, the students must be moving forward in their mathematics, social studies, science, music, art, and other subject matter instruction. All of these skills require substantial time-on-task, and many are themselves dependent upon the student's ability to read and write.

The third-grade curriculum is the last to include large amounts of basic skills instruction. By now, the assigned reading is quite demanding in terms of sophisticated vocabulary and reading comprehension. Reading is not to be done simply line by line. Instead, students are expected to keep the main theme of the piece in mind while observing the development of individual subthemes. Reading must be fluent, as must the student's ability to compose and write essays and stories. Cursive writing must also be mastered. As noted by Madden et al., "Disadvantaged third graders who

Table 10.1. Distribution of Dallas Public School's ITBS Reading Comprehension Scores, April 1995, Tested Students

					National percentile ranges					
Grade-equivalent ranges:	1–10 K.1–1.19	10–20 1.2–1.39	20–30 1.4–1.59	30–40 1.6–1.69	40–50 1.7–1.79	50–60 1.8–1.99	60–70 2.0–2.19	70–80 2.2–2.59	80–90 2.6–2.89	90–99 2.9–4.7
First grade										
Black *N* = 5085	384	355	881	378	705	590	524	502	256	509
%	7.6	7.0	17.3	7.4	13.9	11.6	10.3	9.9	5.0	10.0
Hispanic 1590	157	126	281	150	238	156	161	144	66	111
%	9.9	7.9	17.7	9.4	15.0	9.8	10.1	9.0	4.2	7.0
White *N* = 1447	77	59	165	98	139	151	134	161	104	358
%	5.3	4.1	11.4	6.8	9.6	10.5	9.3	11.1	7.2	24.8
Total *N* = 8122	618	540	1328	626	1082	898	819	806	426	978
%	7.6	6.6	16.3	7.7	13.3	11.1	10.1	9.9	5.2	12.0
Cumulative percentage below grade level	7.6	14.3	30.6	38.3	51.6					
Grade-equivalent ranges:	K.4–1.69	1.7–1.99	2.0–2.19	2.2–2.59	2.6–2.79	2.8–3.09	3.1–3.39	3.4–3.79	3.8–4.59	4.6–7.0
Second grade										
Black *N* = 4798	598	723	440	689	444	712	451	189	343	211
%	12.5	15.1	9.2	14.4	9.3	14.8	9.4	3.9	7.1	4.4
Hispanic *N* = 1579	168	220	145	204	155	255	158	69	116	88
%	10.7	14.0	9.2	12.9	9.8	16.2	10.0	4.4	7.3	5.6

Grade-equivalent ranges:

	K.4–1.69	1.7–1.99	2.0–2.19	2.2–2.59	2.6–2.79	2.8–3.09	3.1–3.39	3.4–3.79	3.8–4.59	4.6–7.0
White										
N = 1382	60	87	85	107	85	166	145	81	222	343
%	4.4	6.3	6.2	7.8	6.1	12.0	10.5	5.9	16.1	24.8
Total										
N = 7759	827	1030	670	1000	684	1133	753	339	681	642
%	10.7	13.3	8.6	12.9	8.8	14.6	9.7	4.4	8.8	8.3
Cumulative percentage below grade level	10.7	23.9	32.6	45.5	54.3					

Grade-equivalent ranges:

	1.3–2.09	2.1–2.79	2.8–3.09	3.1–3.39	3.5–3.79	3.8–4.19	4.2–4.69	4.7–5.39	5.4–6.49	6.5–9.7
Third grade										
Black										
N = 4605	643	856	798	477	523	259	266	238	227	318
%	14.0	18.6	17.3	10.4	11.4	5.6	5.8	5.2	4.9	6.9
Hispanic										
N = 1943	212	327	326	230	270	129	128	116	110	95
%	10.9	16.8	16.8	11.8	13.9	6.6	6.6	6.0	5.7	4.9
White										
N = 1264	69	106	126	99	134	80	96	128	148	278
%	5.4	8.4	10.0	7.8	10.6	6.3	7.6	10.1	11.7	22.0
Total										
N = 7812	924	1290	1251	806	927	467	490	482	485	690
%	11.8	16.5	16.0	10.3	11.9	6.0	6.3	6.2	6.2	8.8
Cumulative percentage below grade level	11.8	28.3	44.3	54.7	66.5					

Table 10.2. Total End-of-Year Distribution, ITBS Reading Comprehension Scores for Tested DPS Students Combined with Estimated Reading Comprehension Scores for Untested DPS Students, 1994-95 School Year

Grade-equivalent ranges	K.1-1.19	1.2-1.39	1.4-1.59	1.6-1.69	1.7-1.79	1.8-1.99	2.0-2.19	2.2-2.59	2.6-2.89	2.9-4.7
First Grade										
Black										
tested: N = 5085	384	355	881	378	705	590	524	502	256	509
untested: N = 473	67	62	154	66	123					
total: N = 5558	451	417	1035	444	828	590	524	502	256	509
%	8.1	7.5	18.6	8.0	14.9	10.6	9.4	9.0	4.6	9.2
Hispanic										
tested: N = 1590	157	126	281	150	238	156	161	144	66	111
untested: N = 4504	1784	669	669	290	201	245	156	245	89	156
total: N = 6094	1941	795	950	440	439	401	317	389	155	267
%	31.8	13.0	15.6	7.2	7.2	6.6	5.2	6.4	2.5	4.4
White										
tested: N = 1447	77	59	165	98	139	151	134	161	104	358
untested: N = 292	42	32	90	53	76					
total: N = 1739	119	91	255	151	215	151	134	161	104	358
%	6.8	5.2	14.7	8.7	12.4	8.7	7.7	9.2	6.0	20.6
Total: N = 13391	2511	1303	2241	1035	1482	1143	975	1051	515	1134
%	18.7	9.7	16.7	7.7	11.1	8.5	7.3	7.9	3.8	8.5
Cumulative percent at or below grade level	18.7	28.5	45.2	52.9	64.0					

Grade-equivalent ranges	K.4-1.69	1.7-1.99	2.0-2.19	2.2-2.59	2.6-2.79	2.8-3.09	3.1-3.39	3.4-3.79	3.8-4.59	4.6-7.0
Second Grade										
Black										
tested: N = 4798	598	723	440	689	444	712	451	189	343	211
untested: N = 541	112	135	82	129	83					
total: N = 5339	710	858	522	818	527	712	451	189	343	211
%	13.3	16.1	9.8	15.3	9.9	13.3	8.4	3.5	6.4	4.0

Grade-equivalent ranges	1.3–2.09	2.1–2.79	2.8–3.09	3.1–3.39	3.5–3.79	3.8–4.19	4.2–4.69	4.7–5.39	5.4–6.49	6.5–9.7
Hispanic										
tested: N = 1579	168	220	145	204	155	255	158	69	116	88
untested: N = 3502	1666	731	544	391	102	51	17			
total: N = 5081	1834	951	689	595	257	306	175	69	116	88
%	36.1	18.7	13.6	11.7	5.1	6.0	3.4	1.4	2.3	1.7
White										
tested: N = 1382	60	87	85	107	85	166	145	81	222	343
untested: N = 279	40	57	56	71	56					
total: N = 1661	100	144	141	178	141	166	145	81	222	343
%	6.0	8.7	8.5	10.7	8.5	10.0	8.7	4.9	13.4	20.7
Total: N = 12081	2644	1953	1352	1591	925	1184	771	339	681	642
%	21.9	16.2	11.2	13.2	7.7	9.8	6.4	2.8	5.6	5.3
Cumulative percent at or below grade level	21.9	38.1	49.2	62.4	70.1					

Grade-equivalent ranges	1.3–2.09	2.1–2.79	2.8–3.09	3.1–3.39	3.5–3.79	3.8–4.19	4.2–4.69	4.7–5.39	5.4–6.49	6.5–9.7
Third grade										
Black										
tested: N = 4605	643	856	798	477	523	259	266	238	227	318
untested: N = 620	121	161	150	90	99					
total: N = 5225	764	1017	948	567	622	259	266	238	227	318
%	14.6	19.5	18.1	10.9	11.9	5.0	5.1	4.6	4.3	6.1
Hispanic										
tested: N = 1943	212	327	326	230	270	129	128	116	110	95
untested: N = 3422	805	1661	503	327	101	25				
total: N = 5365	1017	1988	829	557	371	154	128	116	110	95
%	19.0	37.1	15.5	10.4	6.9	2.9	2.4	2.2	2.1	1.8
White										
tested: N = 1264	69	106	126	99	134	80	96	128	148	278
untested: N = 318	41	63	75	59	80					
total: N = 1582	110	169	201	158	214	80	96	128	148	278
%	7.0	10.7	12.7	10.0	13.5	5.1	6.1	8.1	9.4	17.6
Total: N = 12172	1891	3174	1978	1282	1207	493	490	482	485	691
%	15.5	26.1	16.3	10.5	9.9	4.1	4.0	4.0	4.0	5.7
Cumulative percent at or below grade level	15.5	41.6	57.9	68.4	78.3					

have failed a grade or who are reading significantly below grade level are very unlikely to graduate from high school . . . and will experience difficulties throughout their school careers" (1993:125).

By fourth grade, the curriculum and teacher focus is no longer on basic skills, such as learning to read. Instead, students are now expected to be reading to learn. The focus is on detailed subject matter in science, social studies, and so on. Language arts and mathematics assume the more basic skills and advance rapidly through more sophisticated material. Yet, as shown in Table 10.2, the majority of central-city fourth graders read below grade level. At this point, where basic skills instruction is being reduced, these students become essentially "lost to the system."

The most important predictor of middle- and high-school failure and dropout is reading far below grade level. The most important predictor of reading level at the end of each grade is the reading level at which the student began the grade. In sum, reading achievement, the foundation of schooling success, is a cumulative process, in which success in the early grades is crucial. The resulting overwhelming importance of cognitive readiness at the kindergarten or first-grade level for later school success suggests that interventions occurring on or before school entry, with follow-ups in the early elementary years, are the most effective means of improving children's school achievement and preventing later academic problems (Slavin 1989; Madden et al. 1993; Slavin et al. 1995; Wasik and Slavin 1993; Reynolds 1992). It is difficult to overstate the importance of early reading capability to the student's later academic success.

WHAT CAN BE DONE?

What can be done to improve the situation faced by these students? Too many of these children enter kindergarten and first grade lacking the foundation necessary to succeed at the assigned curriculum. The best interventions attack this problem directly. Any or all of the following would make a positive impact:

1. First, increase the oral English language skills and early alphabetic skills of these children during their preschool years. Perhaps most valuable would be to improve the instruction provided by Head Start and similar programs. Presently, preschool and Head Start staff too often use the excuse that the children are "not developmentally ready" in order to avoid teaching them the very skills that middle-class parents provide as a matter of course. Appropriately providing this instruction requires strong

skills on the instructor's part; it is very hard work, but it is absolutely essential if these children are to be ready for elementary school. Other possibilities include programmatic efforts to assist parents to provide more learning experiences for their preschoolers. Such parenting programs vary from simply attempting to get low-income parents to converse more with their children, up through reading to them and teaching them their letters and sounds. All are potentially valuable.

2.   Second, it is crucial that kindergarten teachers work very hard to get their students ready to read by the beginning of first grade. Far too often I have seen a situation in which the attitude is, "It's only kindergarten, we can't expect teacher and student to get that much done." But children who do not know their letters and sounds fluently by the beginning of first grade are unlikely to end the year reading at grade level. Visiting Dallas elementary schools, I often heard first-grade teachers complain that the kindergarten teachers send them children who are not yet ready to learn to read. At the one school where I saw real success—low-income first graders reading well by Christmas—the teacher told me that this was attained under the following special circumstances. She was the lead first-grade teacher, and had undergone training in a program aimed at preparing teachers to work with learning-disabled children. The program stressed alphabetic/phonics instruction in a rigorous fashion. She not only used it with her first graders, but got the principal to back her in having the other first-grade teachers use it also. When this proved insufficient, the principal backed her in getting the kindergarten teachers to also implement the program. *Then* the students began entering first grade "reading ready," and after that success came easily.

3.   Third, teachers and parents must cooperate to increase the time-on-task that children spend working on their reading and writing skills. Homework, properly monitored and assisted by parents, is essential if the students are to get sufficient practice to attain these complex skills. Close cooperation between teachers and parents is necessary to keep the child on track. Many parents would like to help their children with schoolwork, but don't know how. Thus, parenting programs that are linked to the child's teacher and assigned schoolwork are very desirable. In addition, summer instruction is needed, since it has been well documented that when they are away from school over the summer, low-income children lose a great deal of the skills they learned during the school year (Heyns 1978; Entwisle and Alexander 1994).

4.   Fourth, teachers must adapt their curricula and instructional styles so that most children are presented material they are able to succeed with, while still increasing their English language reading and writing skills. This applies to the regular curriculum across the board. It applies even

more powerfully to certain "politically correct" instructional failures such as "bilingual instruction" in the form in which it is typically delivered in Texas (in practice, it is often monolingual instruction in Spanish, with little provision for the transition to English). Even though the failure of bilingual programs is beginning to be documented (see, for example, *New York Times*, October 20, 1994, p. A20), the program is still widely used in Dallas and other cities.

While I am fully in favor of celebrating distinctive cultural contributions, and "giving children their culture," I believe, as argued by Hollinger (1995), it is absolutely essential that multiculturalism include an element of choice for the children and their parents, and that the "bestowal of culture" by schoolteachers and administrators not come at the price of ineffective instruction and the effective lifetime consignment of the child to skills that are only marketable within the minimum-wage labor market. Yet in Dallas as well as other Texas cities, this appears to be occurring, with bilingual program students learning neither language well,[3] and a Hispanic school dropout rate around 50 percent. A Ford Foundation study showed that Hispanic immigrant parents prefer English immersion for their children, but school districts rarely provide this choice. Indeed, I well recall interviewing a Texas schoolteacher of Mexican-origin who, after speaking in favor of the bilingual curriculum she was following with her class, admitted that she sent her own daughter to Catholic school for English immersion. In the language of Hollinger, we must move beyond the present state of multiculturalism, to a multicultural cosmopolitanism, where memberships may be multiple and are voluntarily chosen, and away from the current multicultural pluralism, where individuals are forced to identify with one group alone, and ethnic membership is imposed on children so that the school employment careers and personal agendas of some adults can be advanced.[4] (For further discussion, see Lieberman 1993:184–85.)

5.   Finally, the most powerful possible intervention should be provided for those early elementary students who are already falling through the cracks in the system. When, as is currently the case, many of these children begin first grade less than reading ready, they are unlikely to be able to meet the curricular demand of successfully reading by the end of the first semester. As a result, they are seriously behind in their schoolwork and are beginning the cycle of failure in which their skills are below the level demanded by the curriculum. Related to this low skill level are self-esteem, willingness to try, and time-on-task inadequate to succeed at the assigned tasks. As we shall see, research has shown that the interventions that most successfully improve this situation typically involve one-on-one instruction.

ONE-ON-ONE INSTRUCTION

One might suppose that we would know a great deal about what works for improving the reading skills of children from low-income households during the early elementary school grades. This is because the nation has dedicated relatively large sums of money to this task for the past thirty years. In particular, there is a federal program, named Title I when it was first authorized in 1965, named Chapter 1 in recent times, and renamed Title I when it was reauthorized by Congress in 1994. This program of federal aid to local school districts is targeted on just these children and skills. Program expenditures have grown over the years to a 1995 annual level of approximately six billion dollars, about twice the size of the better-known Head Start program, which focuses on younger children.

Unfortunately, most of what we have learned from these expenditures is *what doesn't work*. That is, much of the instruction provided by this program has been ineffective (Slavin 1989; Natriello and Pallas 1990; Arroyo and Zigler 1993).

Program service delivery was structured as follows. In order to be certain that these children would, in fact, receive the special assistance they so desperately need, program regulations required that Title I expenditures be kept strictly separate from regular school district expenditures. That is, they permitted no substitution of Title I money for funds the local school district would have spent anyway. Instead, Title I was required to provide services over and above those that the district would ordinarily provide.

The result was to create a self-contained bureaucracy within the bureaucracy of our major urban school districts. The Title I director within each district controls her own budget, often involving millions of dollars, which she receives annually from Washington. With it, she hires and fires, and places Title I teachers and teacher aides in schools. Even within each school, the program has had its own separate existence. The Title I director determines each school's Title I budget, and then hires accordingly. The lead Title I teacher assigned to the school tests the children and determines which students have such low performance as to qualify them for Title I services. She and the other Title I staff typically pull these children out of their classes for special instruction in groups of five to ten students. Both within school districts as entities and also within individual schools, the program has been essentially self-contained.

It also gained a poor reputation. The lowest-performing children, with the greatest psychological and medical problems, were pulled out of their classes. Although each had a different problem and performance level, they were instructed together in groups of five to ten. The Title I teachers tended to be low skill, and to have little training or effective curriculum to address the needs of the children. Faced with an essentially impossible task, constantly getting nowhere with the most troubled children, they naturally had low morale. The children were stigmatized, the teachers were stigmatized, the entire program was stigmatized. Its failure to produce positive results for children was widely known (Slavin 1989; Arroyo and Zigler 1993; Natriello et al. 1990).

As a consequence, reform movements grew up, led by educators concerned to invent more effective and powerful interventions for these at-risk students. The best-known and apparently most effective were Reading Recovery, from the Ohio State University School of Education, and Success for All, from a federally funded research center at Johns Hopkins University. Both focus on one-on-one tutoring, using certified teachers. Both have been demonstrated to significantly raise the reading performance of at-risk children (Madden et al. 1993; Wasik and Slavin 1993; Pinnell et al. 1994, 1995; Rasinsky 1995; Slavin 1990a, 1990b; Slavin et al. 1995).

Of course, these results are not surprising. Common sense suggests that to reach, say, the five lowest performers in any particular first-grade class, the best strategy is to pull them out of the class and work intensively with each. Only in this way can instruction be focused on each student's specific starting point and instructional needs, and also be keyed to building up self-confidence and self-esteem, which are typically depressed in these students. The approach follows that of Slavin et al.: "[S]tudents receive help early on, when their problems are small. This help is intensive and effective enough to catch students up with their classmates so that they can profit from their regular classroom instruction. Instead of letting students fall further and further behind until they need special or remedial education or are retained in grade, students . . . are given whatever help they need to keep up in their basic skills" (1990:258).

Most important, research studies utilizing appropriate statistical techniques have now begun appearing on a regular basis in the major journals, demonstrating that one-on-one instructional programs are effective with low-performing children. *Over the thirty years of experience with Title I, only one-on-one instructional programs have demonstrated such a record of success with at-risk children.*

At bottom, the success of one-on-one tutoring is based on the following characteristics, which are provided by no other methodology: First, the instructional curriculum and feedback is custom tailored and fine-tuned to the student's current performance level. Second, bonding with an adult provides the encouragement necessary to maintain time-on-task and a good concentration level. And finally, the privacy of one-on-one allows the student to risk failing. At the same time, there is no other student to give the answer. The intensive personal interaction with a tutor who has bonded with the students and responds sensitively to his or her skills, personality, and moods functions as an "operating room" in which the student's skills, habits, and styles can be repaired.

Programs such as Success for All report positive experiences with cooperative learning techniques that place the students in paired-reading situations. But for the weakest students within Success for All, this supplements, rather than replaces, one-on-one tutoring. The Reading One-One Program (described in Chapter 11) has also experimented with having tutors work with two or more students at a time. Always the finding has been that a high-quality tutoring session is just not sustainable in other than a one-on-one format.

As implemented by the two most widely known tutoring programs—Reading Recovery and Success for All—the tutoring intervention employs certified teachers and is thus quite expensive. Indeed, in their review of such programs, Wasik and Slavin identify this high cost level as their chief drawback: "The major drawback to tutoring is its cost. Providing tutoring to large numbers of students across the grade span would, of course, be prohibitive" (1993:179). *Yet such delivery of intensive services to large numbers of students is exactly what is needed.*

Unfortunately, using certified teachers on the regular payroll to perform this tutoring *is* prohibitively expensive. For example, suppose that a certified teacher earns $35,000 per school year. Add on approximately 40 percent for fringes and overhead. The result is approximately $50,000 per year. Also suppose that she tutors 6 hours per day for 30 weeks during this school year. (Given the relatively large number of holidays and other disruptions, 30 weeks is realistic.) Then her cost as a tutor is $55.56/hour. Thus, providing even 60 hours of instruction per student would cost more than $3,000. Calculated another way, suppose that this teacher can tutor 8 children per day and that she does this for the entire school year. Then the annual cost per child is approximately $6,000. However calculated, the cost is so high that this service delivery mechanism will never serve the very large number of at-risk students who so desperately need assistance. It is in response to this situation that I invented Reading One-One, a tutoring program that has been able to attain results similar in magnitude to those of Reading Recovery and Success for All, but that operates at less than one-fourth the cost of these programs. This program—its history, techniques, effects, and costs—is the subject of the following chapter.

NOTES

1. If a subgroup of eighth-grade students' reading scores averages three grade-equivalents below grade level, and the distribution of these scores is approximate-

ly bell-shaped, with a standard deviation of 1.5 grade-equivalents, then approximately 95 percent of all students lie in the range of two standard deviations above and below the average. That is, 95 percent have reading levels below grade 8 and above grade 2.

2.   As implied by Table 10.2 and verified by data collected by Reading One-One tutors, thousands of Dallas students begin first grade without having mastered the names and sounds of the English alphabet.

3.   This observation is based on observation and interviews within school districts in several Texas cities.

4.   Compare the school success we observed for Asian students, who, lacking a cadre of Asian school staff to "give them their culture," receive English immersion, with that of Hispanic students, who, if their family is Spanish-speaking, are tracked into the bilingual program.

Chapter 11

Reading One-One

with Keven Vicknair

The aim . . . is to create a repertoire of genuinely bicultural skills that combine the best of what both the mainstream and underclass cultures have to offer . . . [B]ecause of the complexity of the underclass's problem, a criterion for successful programs is that educational intervention should be as radical as Wilson's proposals are for economic intervention. In particular, *these programs must go well beyond what is offered by the conventional kindergarten through twelfth grade educational system.* . . . If the place to begin is indeed an expanded Head Start program, the effort surely cannot end there.
— David Greenstone, *Culture, Rationality, and the Underclass*

SCHOOL REFORM IN DALLAS

My implementation of a tutoring intervention in the Dallas schools would never have occurred had it not been for the school reform movement and my involvement in it. The background is as follows. In 1989, the Dallas superintendent appointed an "educational excellence" commission of citizens, which held public hearings on school reform. After writing their report, rather than simply going out of business, a number of these individuals ran for the school board on a promise to implement the report. Three of them were elected (the board totals seven people), and their leader eventually became head of the school board. School reform became a central issue, and the new board, in conjunction with a new superintendent, promoted from within as a supporter of the board, undertook three important actions.

First, they decentralized the administrative structure of the district by creating ten geographically based areas, each consisting of one or two high schools, four or five of their feeder middle schools, and approximately twelve of their feeder elementary schools. This created a new management structure, with the area directors as key players. The group of area direc-

151

tors met monthly with the superintendent. They also met monthly with the principals under them. They thereby came to occupy key roles in the shaping and implementation of policy. Not unrelated to this policymaking power, area directors (themselves former principals) also assumed great decision-making power over the careers of the principals working under them. This power was increased by the practice of moving as many as 25 percent of the principals across schools (some promoted, some demoted, some moved sideways), which accompanied the installation of a test-based "accountability system" (see below).

Second, the administration instituted a form of site-based management, referred to as "school-centered education." Each school was instructed to form a committee composed of parents, teachers, and administrators, to function as an advisory-to-the-principal and decision-making body regarding matters such as goals, efforts, and expenditures. Giving substance to this organizational change was a plan to devolve greater budget authority to the schools. In particular, full authority for spending their Chapter One budgets, typically involving substantial sums of money, was given to the elementary schools.

Finally, the board and superintendent instituted an "accountability system" based on test scores. Standardized test scores, statistically adjusted for the student's test score performance the previous year, as well as student ethnicity, poverty status, gender, and other variables, were used, in conjunction with other variables (such as attendance rates) to compute a ranking of all schools, from the most to the least successful. (The procedure is quite complex, involving regression-adjusted scores for each outcome for each grade, which are then weighted and averaged.) Teachers in the schools judged most successful receive a monetary reward, and their principals are praised and often promoted. Schools judged least successful receive close scrutiny, and their principals are often demoted. The process is relatively public, with the final ranking of schools published in the newspaper, and a celebratory banquet for the "winners."

THE IMPLEMENTATION OF READING ONE-ONE

My research on student performance as determined by skills, habits, and styles was put to a practical test when, in 1990, school reformers from the business community challenged me to say what sort of intervention I would recommend. The results reported in previous chapters led me to several conclusions. First, the vocabulary and reading comprehension basic skills of far too many low-income African-American and Hispanic students are abysmally low. Second, higher skills in these areas are absolutely essential if these students are to succeed. Third, remediation to improve these skills must work directly and powerfully on the student's self-esteem and work habits, as well as on the skills themselves. Fourth, the intervention must occur in elementary school, where the skills are taught and a pattern of failure is typically established.

Surveying the professional literature in this area, it became obvious that two existing programs already accomplished these goals: Reading Recovery (Ohio State University) and Success for All (Johns Hopkins University). Accordingly, I set out to use my own university students to provide similar services within the DISD. During spring 1991, I recruited thirty University of Texas at Dallas (UTD) undergraduate and graduate students to register for course credit and participate in the project. They were told that for three hours of credit, they must tutor two hours per day, on two separate days of the week, for a total of four tutoring hours per week. For six credit hours they were required to tutor eight hours per week, preferably on at least three days, and for nine credit hours they must tutor twelve hours per week, preferably on at least four days.

With the assistance of the staff of the Reading Recovery program within the Richardson Independent School District (RISD) and of Robert Slavin and Barbara Wasik of Success for All,[1] the tutors were trained to implement half-hour one-on-one tutoring sessions with first, second, and third graders. These sessions combined whole-language and phonics approaches, and were based on maximizing the time spent by the student actively reading to the tutor. Each session included the following elements: familiar rereading of two or three little books, reading a new book (possibly with the tutor taking a "running record" (Clay 1979) for diagnostic purposes), drill of letters, sounds, and words, and a writing section in which the child dictates, writes, and reads back a short story (possibly only a sentence or two). Students worked from leveled books of the "Sunshine" series (Wright Publishing Co.), as well as from classroom-assigned basal readers and other materials provided by the teachers.

We began operating within one elementary school whose principal had invited us to implement the program. Logistics were organized as follows. School records were used to identify more than 170 first to third graders in this school who were in the bottom fortieth percentile on the ITBS reading test administered in the fall of 1990. These were sorted by classroom (each of the first to third grades was divided into four or five classes of approximately twenty-two students each) and the classroom teachers were approached as to their willingness to let these children be pulled out of class for tutoring. The teachers each gave a schedule of times when they would permit such pullout.

Schedules of availability were collected from each of the tutors, and these were matched to those provided by the teachers. This matching was something of a nightmare, but it *did* provide a kind of approximate random assignment—students were assigned to tutors (sometimes more than one) and to varying numbers of hours per week simply on the chance basis associated with our ability to make a match and work out everyone's schedule.

As noted above, tutors were trained in the reading instruction techniques pioneered by Reading Recovery (Clay 1979) and Success for All (Slavin et al. 1990a). In a two-hour period they would administer half-hour sessions to each of four students. After each session, the tutor was instructed to take a few minutes to complete a "tutoring session report form." These formed the basis of the progress file kept on each tutored student. At the end of the term, tutors wrote a term paper summarizing their experiences and observations. Tutor papers and student progress files have been retained to facilitate the research component of the project.

The program evolved from this beginning. During fall 1991, four new schools asked to join the program. The process was word of mouth among principals. But what really accelerated the process was the decentralization that had just occurred within the district, in particular, the creation of areas and area directors, and the increased authority given to individual schools to spend their Title I money, at the same time as they were pressured by the accountability system to spend the money effectively to improve test scores.

The major opportunity we were given was that during spring 1992 I was permitted to describe the program at one of the monthly meetings of the superintendent with his area directors. At this meeting, one of the area directors stood up to say that federal reform of the Chapter One guidelines permitted programs such as ours to be run with Chapter One funds. This area director invited us to speak at his next monthly meeting with his principals.

Apparently only a very iconoclastic individual, such as this man is, would speak up as he did. Indeed, he was considered a "wild man" by other district administrators and was marginalized by them. He returned this treatment with interest, regularly referring to central district headquarters as "a snake pit" in his monthly meetings with principals. Nevertheless, at least one other area director did not want this Director's schools to use our program to gain test score benefits above those of her schools, so she too invited us to address her principals.

The result of these presentations, combined with positive word-of-mouth from the principals and teachers of our operating schools, was that twelve schools signed up to use a portion of their Chapter One funds so that we could furnish them paid tutors for the 1992–93 school year. Central to this process was the establishment, via pressure from this area director, of the notion that under school-centered education, and for the first time, principals throughout the district were to have control over the way their Chapter One program moneys were spent.

By the close of the 1993 school year, word-of-mouth among pleased principals and teachers enabled us to sign up twenty-six schools for paid tutoring during the 1993–94 school year. This was repeated again during the spring of 1994, so that thirty-two schools signed up for the 1994–95 school year. During this time period, no school dropped the program due to dissatisfaction with our work. Instead, we collected twenty-five pages of (single-spaced) positive comments from the teachers and principals of the schools we were operating within. (I quote from some of these later in the chapter.)

Reading One-One curriculum and management also evolved over this time period. In curricular terms, we found that most first-graders, as well as many of the higher-grade students we tutored, did not yet know their letters and sounds and had not mastered sounding-out skills for unfamiliar words. Consequently, they required this basic instruction before they could being to progress through the curriculum of reading increasingly difficult little books. Accordingly, we created Level One (Alphabet) and Level Two (Word Families) curricula for these sets of skills, adding these to the Level Three (Reading Ready) curriculum, which itself continued to evolve. By 1994, the Reading One-One tutor's manual had evolved beyond dependence on the Johns Hopkins manual, and had become fully our own creation. By this time, the program had assumed the following form.

Tutoring Session Format

Children to be tutored are selected by their teachers and principal. Tutors have a specific curriculum to follow, which combines elements of whole language and phonics. (For a treatment of the issues between these sometimes antagonistic perspectives, see Adams 1990.) For each child, the one-on-one forty-minute[2] tutoring sessions are scheduled each day for either three or four days per week, depending on the plan selected by the individual school. Detailed records concerning the children's progress are updated each session and kept on file in the school. Teachers receive progress reports on their students twice each semester.

During tutoring sessions, tutors seek to identify the strengths and weaknesses of each student's reading performance, provide lessons that teach unused reading skills, and encourage the continuation of productive reading behavior. Tutors are taught recommended strategies to implement these actions. The goal is to give the student the reading time and guidance that is necessary for him/her to achieve grade-level academic performance.

During each session the tutor focuses on learning letter/sound relationships, using sounds to read words in connected text, and understanding what is read. These are the key elements in the reading process. These elements are addressed in the three curricula designed for students of different skill levels. Each session is made up of four parts. Skill assessments are performed every fifth session. Students are advanced to a higher curriculum once they demonstrate their readiness by scoring high marks on these assessments.

Assessment

On the first day of tutoring, each new student is given a series of tests to determine their placement. First they are presented with shuffled flash-cards containing the fifty-two upper- and lowercase letters. They are asked to name the letter and tell the sound it makes. A student who knows less than 90 percent of the letters or sounds is placed in the Level One curriculum.

If a student knows 90 percent or more of the letter names and sounds on the initial assessment, he or she is given a Word Families test (see below). The student is shown a list of words taken from each of the thirty-one word families and is asked to read them. A score below 90 percent on the Word Families test places the student in the Level Two curriculum. These students learn phonetically regular words, each associated with a "family" of words that contain a targeted sound or phonetic pattern. These word families are ordered and grouped by type of sound and difficulty level.[3]

Students are initially classified into the Level Three curriculum with Letter and Sound ID scores greater than 90 percent *and* a Word Families test score greater than 90 percent. Once students are identified as Level Three students, they are given a series of "Cloze" tests to determine their actual reading level. Students read a story that has every fifth word omitted. As they read the story they are expected to fill in each blank with an appropriate word. Students are tested on different-leveled books until they score in the 60 to 80 percent range. They then begin instruction at this level book.

Tutoring Session for Level One Students

Students who cannot identify all the letters of the alphabet and who have not learned the sounds associated with single letters must be taught these skills before they can learn sounding-out and reading. The four basic parts of this lesson plan are

1. review of previous letters/sounds (five minutes),
2. introduction of new letters/sounds and/ or reteaching of previous material (fifteen minutes),

3. reading to the student (five minutes),
4. assisted writing (ten minutes).

Every fifth session the student is assessed on letter/sound identification and letter writing. They remain in the Level One Group until they master both letter identification and basic letter sounds. Letters are taught in the following order with emphasis on consonants and short vowel sounds:

1. b	11. l	21. short e
2. soft s	12. h	22. v
3. t	13. short o	23. consonant y
4. short a	14. hard c	24. soft g
5. m	15. n	25. soft c
6. f	16. p	26. z
7. r	17. short u	27. q
8. d	18. j	28. x
9. short i	19. k	29. vowel y (long e)
10. hard g	20. w	30. vowel y (long i)

A student is able to advance to the Level Two group after he/she is able to score 90 percent or higher on both Letter and Sound ID assessments.

Tutoring Session for Level Two Students

Level Two serves as a bridge from studying separate letters and sounds to reading stories. Students are taught word attack skills via thirty-one "families" of phonetically regular words, each containing a targeted sound or phonetic pattern. "Sight words" (which cannot be sounded out) are also taught. These word families are ordered and grouped by type of sound and difficulty level. The four basic parts of this lesson plan are

1. review of previous word families (five minutes),
2. teaching new word family or reteaching previous material (fifteen minutes),
3. reading to the student (five minutes),
4. writing a word family story (ten minutes).

Each part of the lesson is taught in a flexible manner so that, for example, students who are able to read at least some words themselves are encouraged to do so. Word Families are taught in the following order with the emphasis on vowel sounds, consonant combinations, and simple phonics rules such as "magic [e]". There are thirty-one total word families, subdivided into nine groups.

WORD FAMILIES

Group	Families
1: Short [a]	1–4
2: Short [e]	5–7
3: Short [o]	8–10
4: Short [u]	11–14
5: Short [i]	15–17
6: "Magic [e]"	18–19
7: Words with two different vowels together	20–23
8: Double vowels	24–26
9: [ch], [sh], and [th] Sounds	27–31

Additional decoding skills (for example, consonant combinations) are also taught. At the beginning of every fifth session the student's progress is assessed by asking the student to read a random member of each previously introduced word family. The student advances to the Level Three group when he/she is able to read randomly selected words from each of the families 1 through 31 with 90 percent or better accuracy.

Tutoring Session for Level Three Students

Students who score 90 percent or better on Letter ID and Sound ID assessments as well as 90 percent or better on the Word Families test are able to decode text and thus are ready to begin reading books. In order to facilitate and track student progress, small reading books that are ranked by difficulty level are used. We typically use books from the Wright Group Publishing Co.'s "Sunshine" series. The first level is broken down into sublevels, increasing in difficulty from A to J. After level J of the first level, there are levels 2, 3, . . . , 11. The leveled books are the preferred material for taking rudimentary running records[4] in order to better measure student achievement. The four basic parts of this lesson plan are

1.   Rereading a book the student read previously (5 minutes). The child selects and reads books that are below or at the student's identified reading level. The tutor centers instruction around a few of the strengths and weaknesses exhibited.

2.   New reading (15 minutes). The tutor introduces a new book on the

student's current reading level: (a) As the student reads the book, the tutor takes a running record and provides instruction on reading strategies, (b) The tutor checks the student's comprehension.

3. Drill (five minutes).   The tutor provides practice on identifying high-frequency words from set of forty-seven word lists.

4.   Writing (ten minutes). The tutor helps the student compose and edit through various creative writing exercises.

Assessing Reading Progress

We have developed Cloze tests for Wright Group books. These are administered at the first Level Three session and periodically thereafter to determine the student's correct reading level. A student progresses to the next level of books only after scoring in the 60–80 percent range for that level. The most informative student reading performance measure is the collection of running records tutors regularly take of their student's reading experiences. Tutors take a running record to record the number of correctly decoded words and to note the types of errors the student made. Tutors then file the results for each student at every session. In addition to the daily running record, tutors also utilize a list of comprehension questions we have developed for each book. As the student reads a new book, the tutor periodically stops and tests the student's knowledge of the material he or she is reading.

Program Management

Program management evolved significantly over time. Much of this was focused on increasing the quality of tutoring delivered. The steady-state system functions as follows. Tutor recruitment outreach is widespread, including area colleges and universities as well as community organizations and businesses. Applicants are given an English basic skills test; only those who pass fill out an application and receive a personal interview. Those selected are given a very detailed tutor's manual and are trained on it during two 3-hour sessions. These sessions culminate in a written examination. Those who pass undergo a criminal background check and are then placed in a school.

Direct supervision within each school is managed by a full-time Reading One-One coordinator. The coordinator monitors tutor attendance and performance. In addition, a central staff member circulates among the schools, sitting with each tutor during a session, grading her or his performance, and providing feedback. When the tutor's performance achieves a certain level, she or he becomes a "certified Reading One-One tutor."

As these and related curriculum and management structures evolved, the Reading One-One "niche" became clear. It is to provide student reading improvements whose magnitude of effect is similar to those achieved by Reading Recovery and Success for All, but at less than one-fourth the cost of these programs. The cost saving is due to using hourly paid tutors recruited from students and the general public, rather than certified teachers. (Tutors also include college students who receive no pay, but prepare a research paper on their experiences and receive course credit toward their degree.) The key issue thus becomes the standard program evaluation question: What *are* the effects of this intervention, and what is the mechanism by which they operate?

DATA AND METHODS FOR STUDYING PROGRAM EFFECTS

The best way to evaluate a program intervention is to randomly assign subjects to the treatment and to a comparison group. Then, the two groups are identical on all causal variables, including unmeasured ones, so that any difference in cognitive score gains can be attributed to the intervention. Unfortunately, such random assignment was not possible in this study. In such cases one must do the best possible by comparing outcomes between a group that received the treatment and an appropriately selected comparison group. But this strategy is fraught with dangers due to the likelihood that treatment and comparison groups are different on key variables other than the treatment itself. This situation is at its worst in evaluating compensatory education programs such as Reading One-One, since three danger-producing situations are present. First, students are assigned to the group receiving tutoring in a highly nonrandom manner. That is, teachers typically assign those students who "need it most." This includes students with troubled home lives, difficulty concentrating in class, and emotional/behavioral problems. These are the students who would have progressed least in the absence of the program. Second, measures of these variables that are implicitly used by teachers for program assignment are not available on the school district's database. Thus, they cannot be entered into a regression analysis and statistically controlled (adjusted for) when using the treatment and comparison group to estimate the program effect. Finally, these conditions are exacerbated by the Texas policy of excluding large numbers of (mostly ESL) students from testing in the early elementary grades. Since students are nonrandomly excluded, with the lowest performers most likely to be missing from the data set, biases introduced by the first two problems are likely to be magnified.

I have dealt with these problems as follows. First, instead of attempting to construct a (poorly matched) comparison group of students who were not tutored, I have found a "comparison group" from within the tutored students. This is accomplished by comparing outcomes for tutored students who received more sessions with those who received fewer. That is, the number of tutoring sessions the student received is the "program treatment" variable. This accomplishes the goal of comparing otherwise identical individuals who received differential program treatment by restricting attention to students all of whom are similar in having been selected by their teachers for tutoring, and by comparing students within this group who are relatively similar in most ways other than the number of tutoring sessions they received. I am confident of this last observation because students received more or fewer sessions in a "quasi-random" fashion determined by accidents of scheduling (teacher decisions about when students would be available for pullout combined with when tutors were available for tutoring) and whether or not the school contracted for three or four sessions per week. (The latter is further controlled by school dummy variables in the analysis.) But what about the possibility that for some unknown reason, the "better" students were assigned more tutoring sessions? We investigated this possibility by using regression analysis to predict the total number of tutoring sessions a student received. We found no statistically significant tendency for the "better students" (those with higher scores on reading comprehension prior to tutoring or those who were more attentive during tutoring) to receive more tutoring sessions. In fact, the opposite was the case, since LEP (Limited-English Proficient) students tended to receive more tutoring sessions. Thus, if any bias is introduced by using the number of sessions variable to estimate the program effect, it is in a conservative direction. That is, our estimates of program effect are likely to be *smaller* than the true effect.

As for the second "problem"—the nonrandom assignment of students to tutoring on the basis of unmeasured causal variables—we have largely solved it by using the number of tutoring sessions, with its "quasi-random assignment," to measure the treatment, as discussed above. However, we have been able to go one step further by creating a variable that *does* measure the student's ability to concentrate, namely, the "attentiveness during tutoring" variable. Since this is based on direct tutor observation, averaged over many sessions, it is a very accurate measure of student emotional/behavioral functioning. (As we shall see, this is supported by the strong effects it shows in Tables 11.2–11.4.) Our ability to hold this variable (which is not available on standard district databases) constant when estimating program effects further guarantees the unbiasedness and efficiency of our estimates of program effect.

Finally, we have dealt with the issue of large numbers of cases nonrandomly missing due to students being excused from ITBS testing by administering our own tests to all tutored students, both before and after tutoring. The resulting Reading Achievement Scale (Figure 11.1) is a "curriculum-referenced test" in the sense that it directly embodies Reading One-One instructional goals. The Woodcock-Johnson reading comprehension test is the most widely used instrument for evaluating reading interventions. (See, for example, Madden et al. 1993; Pinnell et al. 1994.) And we have both of these (one-on-one administered) measures for all tutored students, with none excluded from the study. Thus, this third problem, too, has been fully resolved.

In this analysis we examine program effects for children who were tutored during 1994–95, the fifth year of program operations. We restrict attention to those students who received a reasonable "dose" of the program treatment: at least twenty-five sessions. As mentioned above, program effects are estimated from a regression analysis in which the key independent variable is the number of tutoring sessions a student received. An attractive feature of this analysis is that we control for the student's attentiveness during tutoring. This is the average across all tutoring sessions of the tutor's rating (1, 2, or 3) of the student's ability to concentrate during the session. Further, for the program Reading Achievement Scale and for the Woodcock Reading Comprehension Test score, we have measures for all tutored students, both before and after tutoring. This is a much better situation than occurs for the Iowa Test of Basic Skills, since more than half of tutored elementary students are typically exempted from this test, and thus would have to be excluded from any evaluation based solely on the ITBS. This would be particularly worrisome, since these students are far from randomly chosen. Instead, they are typically concentrated among students whose families speak Spanish at home, and who thus experience the greatest difficulties in English reading comprehension.

PROGRAM EFFECTS

Table 11.1 shows the means of the variables for students who received at least twenty-five tutoring sessions. Across first, second, and third grade, these students are between 54 and 58 percent male. They are also overwhelmingly Hispanic: 75 percent among first graders, 72 percent among second graders, and 68 percent among third graders. This is largely due to political-bureaucratic features of program growth: Hispanic administra-

Table 11.1. Means of Variables for Full-time Reading One-One Students, 1994–95

	First grade	Second grade	Third grade
Male	.543	.546	.584
Hispanic	.748	.717	.684
African-American	.084	.190	.249
Number of sessions	61.40	61.39	60.52
Average attentiveness	2.59	2.67	2.71
Alternate	.054	.035	.084
Limited English proficiency	.600	.576	.540
Receives free lunch	.867	.859	.844
Receives reduced lunch	.032	.061	.058
Repeated this grade	.069	.033	.021
Reading Scale Score, before	3.27	7.65	10.29
Reading Scale Score, after	10.48	14.30	17.24
Woodcock Reading Comprehension, before	.713	1.564	2.467
Woodcock Reading Comprehension, after	1.494	2.317	3.123
N	405	538	430

tors over majority Hispanic areas of the school district seemed most open to and interested in the program. It was also influenced by the fact that Hispanic children from Spanish-speaking homes were often perceived by their teachers as being most in need of tutoring. This also varied by grade level: African-American children constituted 8 percent of tutored first-graders, 19 percent of tutored second-graders, and 25 percent of tutored third graders. (Recall that we allowed classroom teachers to select those students they wanted tutored.)

We see that for all three grades, the average student received about 61 tutoring sessions. On a scale of 1–3, the attentiveness of the average first grader was 2.6. Second and third graders averaged 2.7. Clearly, most children are quite attentive in the one-on-one format. Children who received fewer than 35 tutoring sessions were typically "alternates," who were tutored only when a regularly scheduled student was absent. We see that 5 percent of first graders, 4 percent of second graders, and 8 percent of third graders fell into this category.

We also see that tutored students are seriously at-risk of school failure. Sixty percent of tutored first graders are Limited English Proficient, as are 58 percent of second graders and 54 percent of third graders. Across all three grades, approximately 90 percent of tutored students received a free or reduced lunch (the great majority received a free lunch).

The two reading measures available for all tutored students are the

Reading Scale Score and the Woodcock Reading Comprehension score (in grade-equivalents). The program Reading Scale score is detailed in Figure 11.1. The lowest level, 1, indicates a student who knows fewer than 25 percent of his or her letters or sounds; the highest level, 25, indicates a student able to proficiently read books at approximately fifth-grade level.

Table 11.1 shows that tutored first graders began with an average Reading Scale score of 3.3 and ended with an average score of 10.5. This means that at the beginning of tutoring, the average first grader knew fewer than 75 percent of the letters and sounds. By the end of tutoring, the average first grader had learned their letters and sounds and five word family groupings, and was working on word family group 6 ["magic (e)"]. Tutored second graders began at level 7.7, word family group 3. These students ended, on average, at level 14.3, reading level 1 books, G–J. Finally,

Figure 11.1.   Reading One-One Achievement Scale, 1994–1995

Score	Reading Level
1	Knows the name of, and sound made by, less than 25% of the 52 lower- and uppercase letters.
2	Knows the name of, and sound made by, 25% to 50% of the 52 lower- and uppercase letters.
3	Knows the name of, and sound made by, 50% to 75% of the 52 lower- and uppercase letters.
4	Knows the name of, and sound made by, over 75% of the 52 lower- and uppercase letters.
5	Word Family Group 1, short [a] sound
6	Word Family Group 2, short [e] sound
7	Word Family Group 3, short [o] sound
8	Word Family Group 4, short [u] sound
9	Word Family Group 5, short [i] sound
10	Word Family Group 6, "magic [e]"
11	Word Family Group 7, words with two different vowels together
12	Reading level 1 books, sublevel A to C
13	Reading level 1 books, sublevel D to F
14	Reading level 1 books, sublevel G to J
15	Reading level 2 books
16	Reading level 3 books
17	Reading level 4 books
18	Reading level 5 books
19	Reading level 6 books
20	Reading level 7 books
21	Reading level 8 books
22	Reading level 9 books
23	Reading level 10 books
24	Reading level 11 books
25	Reading library books

tutored third graders began at level 10.3 (word family group 6) and ended at level 17.2, reading level 4 books. These are substantial average gains, particularly since they have been achieved by the very lowest performing students. However, they fall short of bringing the average student all the way up to reading at grade level.

Another view of these students' average reading abilities before and after tutoring is provided by their Woodcock Reading Comprehension scores, measured in grade-equivalents. First graders begin at 0.7 grade-equivalents, ending at 1.5 grade-equivalents. (By comparison, the "average" U.S. first grader begins at 1.0 and ends at 1.9.) Tutored second graders begin at 1.6 and end at 2.3 grade-equivalents. Tutored third graders begin at 2.5 and end at 3.1 grade-equivalents. The overall finding is similar to that indicated by the Reading Scale Scores: tutored students make substantial progress in one year, but do not on average move all the way up to grade level. Of course, the issue is the incremental gains that can be attributed to the one-on-one tutoring the students receive. That is, other things being equal, what extra gains are due to each additional tutoring session received by the typical student?

This question is answered using the Reading Achievement Scale score by the regression analyses reported in Table 11.2. Moving across the second row of this table, we see that, across each of grades one, two, and three, the effect of more tutoring sessions is positive and statistically significant. Among first graders, 100 tutoring sessions (the high end of what students typically receive) raises reading by 8.4 levels. For second graders, the gain is 5.1 levels, and for third graders it is 7.4 levels. These are very substantial gains, and show that tutoring exerts a substantial positive effect upon students' reading levels. Of course, the average student received only 60 sessions. One goal for the future is to manage our relationships with the schools so that more students can receive closer to 100 sessions during the school year. A second goal is to provide tutoring for students over the summer, too, so that, for example, with the school year and summer combined, a student might receive as many as 150 total sessions.

Other predictor variables also show interesting effects. In particular, the students' attentiveness during tutoring and their reading achievement level before tutoring began are also strong positive predictors of the final reading achievement level.

Table 11.3 repeats these calculations using the Woodcock-Johnson Reading Comprehension test score. Since we administered this instrument to all students before and after tutoring, no cases are excluded from this calculation. The Woodcock, which is administered one-on-one, is the research instrument most commonly used in published evaluations of compensatory reading programs. (See, for example, Madden et al. 1993; Pinnell et al. 1994.)

Table 11.2.   Regression Analysis[a,b] of Reading Achievement Scale

	First grade	Second grade	Third grade
Intercept	5.418	−15.765	−12.765
Number of tutoring sessions	.084**	.051**	.074**
	(6.26)	(5.19)	(6.31)
Average attentiveness	2.426**	2.372**	1.808**
	(5.11)	(5.99)	(3.43)
Reading achievement before	.980**	.573**	.526**
	(13.52)	(21.34)	(17.57)
Alternate	−.511	−.932	−.636
	(0.72)	(1.47)	(1.20)
Male	−.284	−.113	.065
	(1.02)	(0.56)	(0.26)
African-American	−.279	.615	−.204
	(0.45)	(1.32)	(0.33)
Hispanic	.400	−.053	−.950+
	(0.80)	(0.14)	(1.71)
Repeated this grade	−.768	1.512*	−1.084
	(1.13)	(2.55)	(1.25)
Limited English proficiency	−.196	−.827**	−.291
	(0.53)	(2.90)	(0.81)
Received free lunch	−.447	.749+	−.466
	(0.93)	(1.95)	(1.08)
Received reduced lunch	1.322	.826	−.707
	(1.51)	(1.55)	(1.10)
R^2	.519	.607	.618
Mean of dep. var.	10.494	14.301	17.244
N	405	538	430

[a] All regressions include dummy variables for each of the different schools and a variable for the child's age.

[b] The absolute value of the t-statistic is in parentheses.

**1% significance.   *5% significance.   +10% significance.

Looking across the second row of Table 11.3 we see that the effect of more tutoring sessions is always positive and statistically significant. The estimated effects for 100 tutoring sessions are first grade, 7.3 months of gain; second grade, 7.8 months of gain; third grade, 6.7 months of gain. These are large effects, and as we shall see, are quite competitive with those reported in published studies of Reading Recovery and Success for All. These results constitute the strongest evidence that Reading One-One is a successful intervention for tutored students.

Once again, other variables also show interesting effects. Both student attentiveness and the student's Woodcock score before tutoring began are positively related to Woodcock reading comprehension at the end of tu-

Table 11.3. Regression Analysis[a,b] of Woodcock Reading Comprehension Score

	First grade	Second grade	Third grade
Intercept	3.987	−3.063	−4.236
Number of tutoring sessions	.0073*	.0078**	.0067+
	(2.40)	(5.19)	(1.68)
Average attentiveness	.255*	.642**	.605**
	(2.37)	(5.38)	(3.38)
Woodcock comprehension, before	.317**	.643**	.674**
	(5.32)	(15.62)	(15.05)
Alternate	.062	.282	−.205
	(0.38)	(1.49)	(1.14)
Male	.008	.039	−.104
	(0.12)	(0.64)	(1.22)
African-American	−.221	.094	−.126
	(1.55)	(0.68)	(0.59)
Hispanic	−.131	−.067	.077
	(1.16)	(0.59)	(0.41)
Repeated this grade	−.183	−.107	−.250
	(1.19)	(0.60)	(0.85)
Limited English proficiency	−.219**	−.258**	−.330**
	(2.66)	(3.08)	(2.78)
Received free lunch	.108	−.102	−.107
	(0.99)	(0.88)	(0.73)
Received reduced lunch	.784**	−.113	−.328
	(3.94)	(0.71)	(1.52)
R^2	.194	.464	.469
Mean of dep. var.	1.494	2.317	3.123
N	405	538	430

[a] All regressions include dummy variables for each of the different schools and a variable for the child's age.
[b] The absolute value of the t-statistic is in parentheses.
**1% significance.   *5% significance.   +10% significance.

toring. There is also a tendency for LEP students to score lower in reading comprehension.

Table 11.4 repeats these calculations utilizing ITBS scores (scaled in grade-equivalents) administered by the district. The chief problem is the large numbers of students who must be deleted from the calculation because they were not administered the ITBS both before and after tutoring. Among first graders, so many are missing the "before" score (measured by a test administered when they would have been in kindergarten), that only eleven students have both scores. This is too few for the calculation, so the first column of this table is empty.

Table 11.4.   Regression Analysis[a,b] of ITBS Reading Comprehension Score

	First grade	*Second grade*	*Third grade*
Intercept		−5.031	−.017
Number of tutoring sessions		.0077[+]	.0080
		(1.78)	(1.42)
Average attentiveness		.563**	.333
		(3.83)	(1.42)
ITBS comprehension, before		.245	.569**
		(1.61)	(4.26)
Alternate		.450[+]	.075
		(1.79)	(0.35)
Male		.098	−.028
		(1.10)	(0.25)
African-American		−.111	−.385
		(0.75)	(1.62)
Hispanic		−.114	.087
		(0.88)	(0.37)
Repeated this grade		.369	.320
		(1.46)	(1.00)
Limited English proficiency		−.403**	.172
		(3.01)	(0.93)
Received free lunch		.295*	−.178
		(2.08)	(1.04)
Received reduced lunch		.095	.155
		(0.46)	(0.63)
R^2, adjusted		.184	.148
Mean of dep. var.		2.178	2.639
N	11	214	218

[a] All regressions include dummy variables for each of the different schools and a variable for the child's age.
[b] The absolute value of the t-statistic is in parentheses.
**1% significance.   *5% significance.   [+]10% significance.

Columns 2 and 3 report the results for second and third graders for whom the ITBS reading comprehension test score was available. Among second graders, these represent 214 of the 538 tutored students studied in Tables 11.2 and 11.3. Among third graders, they represent 218 of the 430 third graders studied in these tables.

The second row of Table 11.4 shows that even with this restricted sample, we find similar program effects to those estimated in Tables 11.2 and 11.3. One hundred tutoring sessions increase the reading comprehension of second graders by 7.7 months; that of third graders by 8.0 months. As before, positive effects are also found for student attentiveness and student reading comprehension prior to the beginning of tutoring.

In sum, all three reading comprehension measures show positive effects of Reading One-One tutoring, with magnitudes of effect on the order of seven to eight months of gain for one hundred tutoring sessions. As discussed below, these effects are of a similar order of magnitude to those reported for the more expensive programs: Reading Recovery and Success for All. Two other observations are similar to findings reported by Success for All. First, Slavin et al. (1995) report that their largest effects occur for LEP students. Since a majority of Reading One-One tutored students are LEP, this may at least partially account for the relatively large effects reported above. Second, Slavin et al. find that as a school gains experience operating the program, its annual effects increase. They attribute this to a positive learning curve. We have observed a similar phenomenon, with the effects reported above for 1994–95 being significantly larger than those observed for the previous year (Farkas et al. 1994). We attribute these gains to management activities accompanying program maturation. In particular, we instituted much stricter controls on the cognitive skills of tutors during 1994–95. To be hired they had to pass a general English skills test, and then had to pass an exam on the training they received. Further, their tutoring was monitored quite closely, and they were shown how to improve their instructional skills. Those who still did not meet the required standard were let go. Further, student assessment procedures were improved—Cloze tests were introduced to ensure that students were moved up to the next reading level only when they had fully mastered the comprehension skills required by the current level.

COMPARISON WITH OTHER PROGRAMS

Of course, the most important evidence regarding the effectiveness of hourly paid tutors is the magnitude of the gains achieved by the students they tutor. *Remarkably, during 1994–95, these attained the same level as reported by Reading Recovery and Success for All.* This is shown in Table 11.5, where we see that all three programs report gains of approximately 0.3–0.7 grade-equivalent (3–7 months of instruction) above what students would have attained without tutoring. This is particularly remarkable for Reading One-One, which achieved these gains while serving more than four times as many students as the other programs for each dollar spent. The research community is coming to realize that successful assistance for at-risk students needs to be continuous throughout the elementary years. This makes effective, low-unit-cost programs such as Reading One-One particularly attractive.

Table 11.5. School Year Gains Achievable via Quality One-on-One Tutoring (in Grade-Equivalents[a])

	Average Gain	Average Gain From	
		60 sessions	100 sessions
First grade			
Success-for-All (Madden et al. 1993)	0.2		
Success-for-All (Slavin et al. 1994)	0.3		
Reading Recovery (Pinnell et al. 1994)	0.3[b]		
Reading One-One (Table 11.3)		0.4	0.7
Second grade			
Success-for-All (Madden et al. 1993)	0.5		
Success-for-All (Slavin et al. 1994)	0.3		
Reading One-One (Table 11.3)		0.5	0.8
Third grade			
Success-for-All (Madden et al. 1993)	0.5		
Success-for-All (Slavin et al. 1994)	0.7		
Reading One-One (Table 11.3)		0.4	0.7

[a] Estimated from the Woodcock-Johnson Reading Inventory.
[b] Translated from the reported standardized effect estimates into grade-equivalents by relying on the correspondence between these reported in Slavin et al. (1994).

INSIGHTS FROM QUALITATIVE DATA

The quantitative data presented above show that Reading One-One significantly raises the reading skills of at-risk elementary school students. Qualitative data—observations of tutoring and reports from tutors—show that this occurs via improvements in the students' detailed skills, habits, and styles. In particular, the intertwined view of culture and learning put forward earlier in this volume is fully supported by our observations of student behaviors and outcomes, both prior to, during, and as a consequence of tutoring. Below, I use quotations from the term papers written by college student tutors to describe and document the process by which tutoring affects student skills, habits, and styles.

To begin with, tutor/student bonding is very powerful. The following tutor statement is typical:

> I was surprised by the swiftness with which I began to care about these kids. I found myself talking about them with my friends and thinking about them throughout the day. I developed an emotional attachment with all four of my kids. Their problems became our problems. The first time C completed a book I was so moved that I cried. The first time J talked to me about himself, I was absolutely elated. When C would let her guard down and read well I

would be amazed at her talents. . . . I was deeply proud of all four of my students and their achievements, and I am sure they were all aware of this.

Further, the children's work habits and subsequent skill attainment are reported to be highly dependent upon their confidence and self-esteem. Tutors were successful in improving student skills when they combined direct skills instruction and supervised student practice with strong support for the student's self-esteem:

> There are five variables which seem to contribute to students' progress . . . moods, attention, ability, desire, and self-confidence. These are ordered from least to most important. . . . The two students that made the most progress responded very well to the reassurance offered them. . . . S and L, after attaining the self-confidence which they previously lacked, were able to use their ability. . . . Then, they became more attentive and less moody and really made wonderful progress. So, all of the variables seem to depend upon self-confidence.

> The biggest thing I learned . . . is that these kids . . . have a need to be loved, wanted and given attention. [They] don't usually think much of themselves. They don't realize what they are capable of. . . . Half of my job was tutoring, the other half was building these kids up.

> I soon found that most of the students I saw had poor self images and very little confidence. I tried to address this and increase their feelings of self-worth.

> When I first began working with L, she lacked pieces of her foundation. She had absolutely no self-confidence. She was very quiet, and she read in a mousy voice that was barely audible. . . . I knew immediately that the key for her would be finding her self-confidence. As the weeks went by and she began to trust me, she began to transform. The nervous look on her face disappeared and she developed a loud, clear reading voice that rang with confidence. She became . . . responsible for correcting her mistakes. . . . She developed a larger vocabulary and her retention of new words was very high. . . . Her reading developed the smoothness I had hoped it would.

> My biggest challenge this semester was C. When I began to understand the scope of his problems I was very afraid for him. He could scarcely read small words like "and" and "the." For the first several weeks he did not seem to progress at all. He appeared at times to be dyslexic, which I did not know how to compensate for. His concentration ability was limited to ten or fifteen minutes. . . . He also had to relearn the long- and short-vowel sounds, because he could not recall them. Another problem is that he is two years older than his classmates. . . . When he started making progress, I was startled by the intensity of the change. I remember the look of pride on his face when he completed his first book. After that he wanted to read, and it was noticeable that he was exerting more effort. He progressed through two series of

books, which is approximately twenty books. That is an incredible feat for a boy who could not tell me what sounds the last four letters of the alphabet made four months ago. His attitude has become more positive, as has his self-concept. He has proved to himself that he can read, and because of that he finds it enjoyable and rewarding. His vocabulary has skyrocketed, as has his speed.

Similar reports were collected from the teachers of tutored students. A selection of these follows:

The children really like the tutoring program. They feel special getting attention from just one adult. Their attention is focused and the learning process is so much greater.

The fact that the tutoring sessions are structured is really beneficial for the students. They know exactly what to expect as they progress through the various levels of the program. The tutoring program has been especially beneficial for my students because they are limited in their English ability. The extra practice in writing, reading comprehension and vocabulary development has really been helpful for my ESL and bilingual students.

Back in September I was faced with the difficult task of teaching two types of curriculums. Out of 22 students, 7 had to be instructed only in English and the rest in a Bilingual setting. I set up my learning environment as an ESL classroom. Along with ESL, I used the Whole Language Approach in my instruction. My main objective was to achieve the optimum goal of reading. When I first learned that the UTD students were coming to tutor a selected group of first grade students, I decided to designate the English speakers for inclusion in the program; I hoped that they would improve their reading skills and benefit most from the program. At the same time, I continued to work with the Bilingual group on their vocabulary and reading in English. During the following months, several of my students that were involved in the tutoring program moved away. I was then asked to choose some replacements which included several Bilingual students. I am now happy to report to you that not only have the English speakers improved their reading skills, but also the children of the Bilingual group are reading in two languages.

We would like to express our heartfelt gratitude and appreciation for your efforts in working with our students this year. Your efforts were evident in many ways. Many students showed growth in reading and vocabulary. An increase in self-esteem and motivation was apparent in all tutored children. Bringing enthusiasm and encouragement to these students fostered pride and self-confidence in themselves they might not have expressed otherwise.

What I'd like to share with a principal or another teacher is my experience in the first three weeks of school where I had a room full of children with various ranges of reading skills. My biggest stress in coming to work every day was—how am I going to pull these low ones up to even first grade level. It was something I thought about all the time. What this program has done has been to help bring those children up from my lowest level children, up to where they can participate in class, up to where·they can read second grade material. It has been a wonderful help in that way. Really, at our school, if we could offer it to all of our students, all students could benefit from it. The ones who would benefit most, without a doubt, are the students whose reading skills are very low. Sometimes our students don't have support from home. There isn't a parent there reading stories to them at night; there isn't a parent there saying let me see the words you covered—in that way all of our students could benefit.

I have two students in particular where the program has made a tremendous difference. Their reading skills were very, very low. They couldn't keep up with the second grade work, they were probably very frustrated and felt very overwhelmed by what we were covering. These students now can read the second grade class work and they feel better about themselves; it's made a tremendous difference for them. There's a student who's not in the lowest group, but he's not quite where he should be. I've never seen a student so low on motivation. I don't know if it was the individual attention, or just having a one on one relationship with somebody, but there is a clear difference in his motivation from when he started going to the program.

I have been greatly impressed with the UTD Reading Program currently within our school. I have 9–10 students who receive this service and they've become excited and very motivated about reading. This program gives them the opportunity to experience individual success within their actual reading level. The progress reports given to the teacher are very informative and enables us to have yet another tool to measure progress of our students.

The kids are really learning and they enjoy spending time with the tutors. Their reading skills increase daily and that builds their self-esteem and helps them to participate in the classroom. Self-esteem is a very important quality that we help build here and the UTD tutors are helping our students every day by building their self-esteem by increasing their reading abilities. We are really, really satisfied with it.

These students need individual tutoring in the Language Arts skills to help them perform and succeed on grade level. As a classroom teacher it is often hard to give each child in need the attention. This program fills this need. Each child is given individualized instruction by patient and caring tutors. They are assessed on a regular basis and all results are given to the classroom teacher so he/she can monitor progress. Reading, phonics, language, as well as writing and vocabulary are taught to make this a well-rounded program. All seven second grade teachers have seen definite improvement in their students, not only in skills but in self-confidence *and* self-esteem. The program is operated in an efficient and professional manner. I would *highly recommend* it to any school.

It is exceptional! The students enjoy the one-on-one individualized instruction and teachers benefit from the results. The students learn strong basic foundations that enhance their reading and writing skills. The tutors are eager and enthusiastic. There is a special bond between the tutor and student that encourages learning and promotes success. This well-balanced program provides the necessary individualized instruction that the teacher cannot always provide.

The UTD tutoring program has been a success for the students I chose to participate. Their ability to attack unfamiliar words as well as their self-esteem has greatly increased. I believe the program is also good because the instruction proceeds beyond the curriculum parameters. The tutors become friends with the students! They establish a bond of trust and this helps to increase the student's desire to go and learn each day.

My students and I are thoroughly enjoying your program! This is our first year being involved in a tutoring program such as this and I think it is EXCELLENT! I really like the individualized attention/instruction that each child receives. There's a plan A, B and C designed for each child to succeed. This instruction correlates with the classroom curriculum. My students are benefiting so much and it has built up their confidence in reading! We're looking forward to future years with One-One.

The UTD program has been successful with the slower learners in my class. The program provides each learner with the basic skills that they have not mastered. My ESL students have done especially good in the program. The improvement I've seen is better English usage, sentence construction, composition writing and reading. (The tutor) is very good with the students. He serves as tutor and role model to young boys. He gives the students encouragement and verbal praise. All of the UTD tutors are excellent. I wish that all Dallas schools could have UTD tutors on their campus.

I would like to describe some of the improvements made by one of my students as a result of the UTD tutors. One student has gone from not having full recognition and even knowledge of sounds, and is now able to read! This student is significantly challenging because of his behavior and these strides are really remarkable! Finally, I would recommend the UTD program to other schools because of the flexibility and professionalism of the staff and because of the student improvements I've seen. Not only would I recommend keeping the program in our school (and Texas), but I would recommend *more funding* so these tutors can do an even better job at increasing literacy among elementary school students.

The presence of UTD in our school is recognized by faculty and staff as a vital force to the education of our students. I am very supportive of the program and its goals. (The program coordinator) is a wonderful, forceful leader of this great program and I must say, I love this program. It works for me and my kids. I hope this program will continue in our particular school!

Based upon my observations and valuable input from my second grade teachers, this program has been very successful. Perhaps the most notable and positive improvement in the school has been the creation of this new program. The influence has been seen throughout the school. The UTD Program is of great benefit to many students with individual needs, it gives them an opportunity to perform and succeed on grade level. The program has raised the educational attainment and most of all the self-esteem of these students. Each tutor demonstrates their pride in their work by being patient and caring with each individual student assigned to them. A sense of sincere interest is shown to each individual and they are consistently fair in dealing with them. All of the students like and respect each tutor and are pleased to be in their tutoring sessions.

Overall, we collected twenty-five pages of (single-spaced) comments like these from teachers and principals!

DISCUSSION

This chapter has detailed how my involvement in the Dallas school reform movement lead to the creation and implementation of Reading One-One, a tutoring program focused on reading instruction for the lowest-performing elementary school children. We have seen how the program grew from serving only one school in spring 1991, to serving thirty-two schools during the 1994–95 school year. In this latter year, approximately 2,400 students received approximately 144,000 hours of one-on-one instruction, and made reading gains comparable to those of the most nationally successful one-on-one programs, at less than one-fourth the cost of these programs. As the children's skills, habits, and styles improved, tutors, teachers, and principals reported themselves to be enormously pleased with the experience and the results.

Unfortunately, this "happy ending" is not the last word. The central bureaucracy of the school district, not at all pleased with the rapid expansion of the program, moved during spring 1995 to drastically curtail the program. However, at the same time, we were able to begin the process of disseminating the program to other cities. As these events developed, I gained a much richer appreciation for the complexity of bureaucratic politics within the school district, and for the central role played by these politics in determining the instructional and social experiences of schoolchildren. This highly consequential subject is the focus of the following chapter.

NOTES

1. I am grateful to Jane Grigsby of RISD Reading Recovery for providing written materials as well as videotape of "Behind the Glass" sessions, and for con-

ducting training sessions for my tutors and permitting me to attend the regular teacher training class meetings with "Behind the Glass" sessions. I am also grateful to Bob Slavin and Barbara Wasik of Johns Hopkins University for providing a copy of the (draft) tutor training manual that Wasik wrote. Without the assistance of these individuals this project would have been much more difficult to get underway.

2.   Each child is scheduled for a forty minute time period. "Pickup" and "return" travel times typically allow thirty to thirty-five minutes for instruction.

3.   Much additional discussion would be necessary to fully explain and justify the program details summarized here and below. Many pedagogical issues would have to be addressed, some of them controversial. Readers interested in this subject may contact the author directly. A future publication will focus on this and related material.

4.   A running record is a technique for providing a visual representation of the student's reading behavior. As the student reads, the tutor makes check marks on a blank piece of paper for each word read correctly. If a word is not read correctly, the tutor writes what the child said, then comes back later and writes next to this what the child should have read. The percent of words read correctly can then be calculated, and the pattern of errors shows what decoding strategies the child is using, and therefore the ones they are not using and should receive further instruction in (see Clay 1979).

Chapter 12

Bureaucratic Politics
and Instructional Service Delivery:
The Central Bureaucracy Strikes Back[1]

> Now that you've demonstrated program effects similar to those of Success
> for All and Reading Recovery, at less than one-fourth their cost, customers
> should be beating a path to your door. It'll be just like it was when my com-
> pany first pioneered its most famous product.
> —Paraphrase of personal remarks to the author
> by a corporate philanthropist, summer 1995

As already noted, Reading One-One expanded during 1991–95 from one
to thirty-two Dallas elementary schools. Tutored students made large
gains, and principals and teachers reported being enormously pleased.
And yet, at the close of the 1995 school year, the Dallas Public Schools took
actions that had the effect of reducing the program to only eight Dallas
schools for the 1995–96 school year. We who invented and manage Reading One-One find this to be both troubling and puzzling. We do not understand it, but we are attempting to. This chapter summarizes these
efforts. It offers a tentative explanation, along with a variety of experiences
that seem to support it. There may well be alternative explanations for and
implications of the events described. Thus, the framework we offer for understanding the behavior of Title I bureaucrats should be regarded as tentative and open to modification. However, the incidents happened as
reported.

To set the stage, observe that Reading One-One offers a type of innovation that is both very common and quite popular in the free-market side of
our economy: a valued service or good is provided at a fraction of its pri-
or cost. Whether airline tickets after deregulation, pizza delivered to your
door, low-fat ice cream in the supermarket, radial tires, or television and
computer equipment, the innovations are quickly adopted by consumers
and largely account for the nation's rising standard of living.

Given the empirical and anecdotal evidence for the success of Reading

One-One in raising children's reading skills, and the positive feedback from teachers and principals, why is it that schools whose principals and teachers praised the program withdrew their support, resulting in a drastic reduction in the number of schools and children served? And what are the implications of these actions for dissemination of this innovation and that of other cost-effective innovations, under Title I funding? The answers are difficult to know, but I speculate as follows. First, there are what might be considered legitimate reasons for being skeptical about the usefulness of the Reading One-One innovation. Second, there are specious reasons, associated with bureaucratic politics and/or self-interested behavior. I discuss each of these in turn.

On the legitimate side, the innovation is new: it is run by outsiders with little prior track record and the results discussed in the previous chapter constitute only a single study demonstrating success. However, the likelihood of this being the real reason the district moved to curtail the program is diminished by the fact that our statistical results and the opinions of principals and teachers *were* so positive, that the program functioned successfully and grew dramatically over a five-year period, and that district administrators not only failed to seek information on these matters, but in fact refused to meet with me to discuss them.[2]

To understand the alternative explanation—bureaucratic and/or self-interested behavior—we must examine the rules, incentives, and network affiliations that determine Title I decision-making at the local level. To begin with, under government monopoly supply of free schooling, there is little consumer sovereignty, particularly regarding the educational services provided to the children of low-income parents. Title I administrators within school districts exercise wide authority over how those funds will be spent, and typically do so with little or no input from parents. Nor do they encourage input from principals and teachers. A number of anecdotes make this point clear:

1.   When an iconoclastic school superintendent in Massachusetts sought to provide Title I funds to parents in the form of vouchers, so they could make their own tutoring arrangements for their children, he was opposed by the Title I bureaucracy. He says, "I understand why it's threatening to the bureaucracy. But I think it's important to be open to change" (*New York Times*, January 13, 1996, p. 6).

2.   As discussed below, within Dallas at the beginning of the 1995–96 school year, district administrators abruptly removed 80 percent of the approximately thirty million dollars of Title I funds from the elementary schools, where they had been providing add-on services to thousands of low-income, low-performing students. No credible explanation was given to principals within the district, nor was the disposition of the funds ex-

plained. When someone from our office called the Title I office to ask for a budgetary breakdown of planned Title I expenditures for the following year, they were told, "We don't release that information." I have been told that if an individual were to pursue the matter, that person would be considered "an enemy of the district." (The matter was kept so quiet that the local newspaper never even reported the story.)

3. At the same time, district administrators increased their expenditure on "Program Z," a "volunteer" tutoring program serving very few students at high cost. This is discussed in detail below.

4. In Dallas and elsewhere, it is common for Title I funds to be used to hire regular teachers to tutor children after school and sometimes during the summer. They are typically paid more than thirty dollars per hour (more than twice what Reading One-One would charge), and this is informally seen as an "income supplement" for the teachers.

5. In a different school district, the principal of a low-income school received add-on Title I funds *for the first time* this year. (The low incomes of the families of the children in her school suggest that she should have been receiving these funds to enrich their education every year.) She fears that she will not get any next year, but she is afraid to ask about it.

6. In another district, a school board member heard about Reading One-One, studied our materials and research, and came to Dallas to see the program. She was positively impressed, and told her superintendent. He invited me to make a presentation and after quizzing me sharply, said that the program sounded good and that he would like to try it. He told me to work with the administrators under him. These people dragged their feet and finally held a meeting with my local collaborator, which I was not allowed to attend. At this meeting, district reading experts claimed both (a) that the Reading One-One research results could not be true, and (b) that if they were true, they did not need Reading One-One, since they could create such a program for themselves. My collaborator suggested that they bring in Reading One-One on a small scale, to examine its effects and better copy its techniques and procedures. The administrators refused and have shown no further interest in a low-cost tutoring program.

I explain these observations by hypothesizing that the decisions of Title I administrators are guided more by the desire to maintain full program control and the continued employment of regular Title I personnel than a desire to provide cost-effective service to the children. In particular, there is a systemic conflict between the interests of central district administrators and the teachers and principals out in the buildings. This makes it difficult to introduce and maintain an innovation such as Reading One-One. Central administrators see the program, with its emphasis on low-cost service provision using nondistrict employees, as challenging their authority and leadership in the school system. On the other hand, teachers and principals see the large number of students tutored one-on-one as supplementing their efforts with these students.[3] In this chapter I attempt to document these assertions, and discuss the future of Title I service delivery in light of these observations. I begin with a brief history of program expansion and contraction in Dallas.

READING ONE-ONE EXPANSION AND CONTRACTION IN DALLAS

As far as students, teachers, and principals were concerned, Reading One-One was a great success in Dallas through the close of the 1994–95 school year. By this time it was also beginning to spread to other school districts. However, within Dallas, the program had always been opposed by the Title I bureaucracy. Title I teachers were encouraged to make things difficult for us.[4] A Title I administrator lectured these teachers about how to ingratiate themselves better with the regular classroom teachers in their schools by giving those teachers a share of the abundant supply of reading-related instructional materials they had purchased with Title I funds. (Title I teachers typically had so much money for materials that they bought far more than they could use, but they hoarded these materials since Title I regulations required them to be used only for qualifying children.) During 1992–93, Title I administrators began sending their own teachers to be trained in Reading Recovery, apparently to offset partially the perception that their skill levels had been low and their curriculum lacking.[5] Wherever possible, they opposed Reading One-One and sought to restrict program expansion to additional schools. In spring 1993, they held a "Chapter One Fair," in which a variety of service providers ran booths to inform principals about their offerings. Reading One-One was placed in an obscure room, behind a pillar (this is both humorous and true). Nevertheless, some principals spoke to program staff and gave the program a try.

The next year the Title I bureaucracy tried a different tack. They convened a committee, "to reduce the number of Chapter One service providers to those with the best results." Not surprisingly, Reading One-One was slated for phase-out.[6] This time, the area director who had originally given the program the opportunity for Chapter One funding, an iconoclastic individual who was particularly open to outside innovations and was regularly at odds with other administrators, saved it.

However, by spring of 1995 he had left the district to become a superintendent in his own right in another city. This time, top district administrators were implementing a different approach to Title I expenditures, which—whether directly intended or not—resulted in a sharp reduction of the services provided by Reading One-One. This new Title I strategy was suggested and facilitated by a typical twist in the policy process at the federal level. By the early 1990s, academics and others had noticed how stigmatizing and ineffective Title I services had been, going all the way back to the program's inception in 1966 (Slavin 1989; Natriello, McDill, and Pallas, 1970; Arroyo and Zigler 1993). Their opportunity to change this occurred when the legislation was reauthorized during the spring and summer of 1994. The result was a new law in which districts were encouraged to "mainstream" the targeted children. This was operationalized as "reducing pullout." Districts were also encouraged to distribute the money to more schools, including middle and high schools, and to make more schools into "schoolwide programs."

In a schoolwide program, expenditures that "benefit" *any* children are permitted, rather than program funds being strictly targeted as add-on services to the lowest performers. Thus, almost any and all school expenditures can, in principle, qualify for funding with Title I dollars. These might include items like copying and computers, which the district would have spent its own funds on anyway. It is because such substitution or "displacement" of funds and services is a standard concern in the management and evaluation of public programs that, prior to reauthorization, schoolwide programs were restricted to only the relatively small number of schools with the densest concentrations of low-income families.

Thus, under reauthorization, the displacement of regular funds by Title I funds can be expected to increase. Further, the purchase of services targeted exclusively on low-performing children, such as those provided by Reading One-One, can be expected to decrease. Even assuming that the Dallas schools administration desired such outcomes, how could they be made to occur within a system of "school-centered decision-making," when the principals and teachers in our schools were overwhelmingly in favor of the Reading One-One program? The answer lies in the combination of two tools still available to central administrators: (a) control of the overall budget allocation, and (b) apparent steering of principal decision-making.

First, the administration used the reauthorization of Title I to completely alter the distribution of program funds within the district. They moved most of the money out of the elementary schools where it had been concentrated, including those where we had been doing most of our work. For example, during 1994–95, one of the schools where Reading One-One operated (Fannin Elementary) received $1,000,000 in Title I funds, of which $150,000 went to Reading One-One to provide 18,400 tutoring sessions to 200 low-performing children. For the following year, this school's Title I budget was reduced to $190,000. They were also told, "As it is, you will have to lay off many Title I teachers and aides. It will be just too demoralizing if you lay them all off." Under this pressure, the principal told us that they could not have us back the following year. Similar events occurred at all our schools.

So where did the money go? A small amount was distributed to elementary schools whose enrollment of low-income children had not previously qualified them for funding. Under new federal guidelines, some also went to middle and high schools (which had previously received none). This, of course, makes little sense, since one gets much more "bang for the buck" remediating poorly reading elementary school students than attempting to work with middle and high school students whose low skill levels, psychological defenses, and teenage interests mitigate against success. Further, these middle and high school principals were completely unprepared for the funds and had few ideas about effective programs to spend them on. Nevertheless, this is where the legislation permitted the money to be sent, and this is where the district sent a portion of it. (Middle and high school principals were guided toward spending it on "Program Z," described below.) Further, as of the present writing (February 1996), no one I spoke to knew what the totality of the money had been spent on. Apparently it was simply held back, to be spent at a future time in unknown ways. The extent to which it was used to purchase goods and services that would ordinarily have been purchased with district funds is also unknown. (However, it is interesting to note that during the summer of 1995, district administrators announced that no tax rate increase would be necessary for the following year.)

The second technique used by district administrators was the steering of principal decision-making. As in most public school districts, a very hierarchical and authoritarian culture abounds. Teachers are well aware of their asymmetric power relationship with principals, who largely determine their working conditions and career advancement. Even more powerfully, principals are aware that area directors determine their career advancement, and area directors are aware that the central administration determines their promotion or demotion. And each group is correct to fear the one above it, since it is these individuals who determine the career success of lower levels. Indeed, the district is a vast array of friendship and other network connections, where every principal was once someone else's assistant principal, and most central administrators were once principals and, with a political misstep, may be so again. Overlaid on this web of personal affiliations are ethnicity-based power centers, often having their own funding streams. These include the Bilingual Education program, the Hispanic Principals' Association, and the (largely African-American dominated) Title I and "desegregation" programs.[7] With many principals and other administrators changing jobs (both up and down the hierarchy) on an annual basis, it is reasonable to be cautious and "political" in one's actions.

(The district's "test-based accountability system" has made administrators more cautious than ever, since many more individuals are being either promoted or demoted under the new system.)

It is from within this climate that top administrators steered area directors and principals away from Reading One-One. Even those principals who were enormously impressed by the program would say, "They're telling us that pullout is being de-emphasized." Yet at the same time, a private sector pullout "tutoring program" was being strongly encouraged. Let us call it Program Z.

PROGRAM Z

Two years previously, the administration brought all principals to a series of meetings with the CEO of Program Z (a private-sector company). The CEO gave the principals an aggressive sales talk in which he said, "the Administration supports this—sign up before you leave this meeting or your school will never get another chance." An educator from another part of the state has told me, "Salesmen from this company often conduct themselves as though selling used cars." This program's brochure boasts that it is recommended by the U.S. Department of Education. The program dominates Title I spending in many Texas school districts. Dallas principals who committed Title I funds to the program received all-expenses-paid out-of-town training weekends.

Program Z sells a copy of the same database management software to each school—approximately $30,000/school, plus a $5,000 annual maintenance fee. Each school is to assign a Title I teacher to the program ($30,000–45,000 plus fringes and overhead). The teacher is then supposed to type a list of the instructional materials the school has available into the program. Then, when the characteristics of a student to be tutored are entered (e.g., "low-reading fourth grader") the program prints out an individualized instructional program using these materials for the student. The teacher is supposed to recruit unpaid volunteers to do all the actual one-on-one instruction with the students. There is little provision for training or monitoring these volunteer tutors. Few volunteers will come on a steady basis (say, an entire semester) for more than one day per week, two hours per day. In order to tutor fifty children this way, four times per week, you would need sixty-seven to one hundred such tutors. And all these strangers coming and going would be absent a lot. In fact, most schools recruited no more than five tutors (many had none) and relatively few sessions were delivered, considering the relatively large program cost.[8]

It seems obvious that the program is less cost-effective than Reading

One-One. Even if one *could* recruit sixty-seven to one hundred unpaid tutors per school, the school's cost to tutor fifty children would be at least $40,000 for the teacher who manages the program each year plus the $30,000 initial cost for the computer program, plus the annual "maintenance fee." (And we have not begun to discuss the lack of continuity or bonding when the student sees a different tutor each day, the lack of training of the tutors, or the low quality of the curriculum.) Yet despite several years in which most Dallas schools that paid for the program failed to recruit many tutors and thus to deliver many tutoring sessions, many Dallas schools, at the urging of top administrators, committed their Title I funds to expand the program for the following year, using it for fourth- to sixth-grade mathematics instruction, as well as for middle and high school instruction.

By comparison, Reading One-One charged $38,500 to tutor fifty children four times per week, for twenty-three weeks during the school year. Almost all these funds go to the tutors who actually do the work. And this cost includes a Reading One-One coordinator who is present in the school full-time and sees that everything gets done. It also includes a Reading One-One central staff person who oversees her. And at this price, Reading One-One staff deliver a very high-quality service (as attested to by principals and teachers). Tutors participate because they love the kids. Thus, Reading One-One is an innovation: a volunteer/part-time job program. The pay causes tutors to perform as though it is a "real job," but it is the personal satisfaction that brings the tutors in and keeps them going. Many have said that the experience has changed their lives. Yet, as a consequence of the fact that all thirty-two schools where Reading One-One operated during 1994–95 lost most of their Title I funding, combined with "steering" by district administrators, only eight schools funded the program for 1995–96. The number of students served by Reading One-One declined from 2,400 during 1994–95, to 400 during 1995–96. At the same time, Program Z was becoming widespread.

DETERMINANTS OF SCHOOL DISTRICT DECISION-MAKING

Why does this district's administration, and that of many other districts, look so favorably on a program that is costly and yet has difficulty serving more than a relatively small number of students? At least part of the answer involves public relations. District administrators understand that volunteer (unpaid) tutors contribute relatively little to children's intellectual progress.[9] This is because they usually come only once per week, are untrained, and have no curriculum to follow. But administrators constant-

ly speak in public forums to encourage such voluntarism as a public relations aspect of "school-community ties." Indeed, the Dallas superintendent announced that such encouragement would be a hallmark of his
administration. Program Z works well with this approach. It provides a Title I teacher in every school who is reaching out to recruit volunteer tutors
from the neighborhood. By providing the rudiments of a curriculum, it
makes the most of their tutoring hours. It is done under the auspices of the
district (rather than an outside provider such as Reading One-One), so that
the "community involvement credit" accrues to district administrators.
Further, Program Z typically makes its own staff members available in the
district to work on community relations. Compared to these positives, the
negatives are substantial: Title I teachers are able to recruit relatively few
tutors, these tutors typically come only once per week so that they cannot
bond with the students, they are untrained, few students are served, and
at high unit cost. Yet the central administration appears to be unconcerned
with these negatives.

Beyond the "community public relations" motivation for administrators
to stay with Program Z, there is the "business as usual" or "standard operating procedures" behavior that is typical of bureaucratic managers.
These individuals strongly prefer to implement policies that they have
used before and that they trust and understand (Allison 1971; Hult and
Walcott 1990). This tendency is reinforced by the overlapping network of
personal affiliations between district administrators and external suppli-
ers of educational services such as Program Z. Staffers in companies such
as Program Z have typically spent much of their careers in public school
districts. They understand the expected presentational style, and know
how to package their materials to be consistent with what is currently popular. In addition, they cultivate close relationships with district personnel.
Program Z, for example, hires teachers and principals from one district to
give testimonials in other districts during sales visits. They invite principals and teachers who sign up for the program to all-expenses-paid training weekends at out-of-town hotels. They invest much time and effort in
cultivating district administrators. The payoff for these efforts is seen in the
following anecdote. A professor of education in another city heard about
Reading One-One and (with our assistance) implemented the program in
her local district. She used her teachers-in-training as Reading One-One tutors, paying them from a research and training grant she already had.[10]
These tutors were very successful with the students. However, the local Title I administration, which was already using Program Z, was unwilling to
even consider spending a portion of its own Title I budget on the Reading
One-One tutors.

Of course, school districts have always been political battlefields, and
thus hotbeds of decision-making driven by networks of personal affilia-

tion. For example, it is well-known that a variety of educational programs are funded simply because one or more school board members strongly support them. It is therefore not surprising that the educational bureaucracy uses considerations like the effect on community public relations and the desire for business as usual in support of the usual network affiliations to make their decisions regarding much more than Program Z. Indeed, whole realms of curricular choice and educational supply and equipment decisions are apparently determined by these twin considerations. Three good examples are (a) the extensive purchase of computers and computer software, (b) the "whole-language" emphasis in elementary reading instruction, and (c) bilingual education.

Computerized instruction is the current educational fad. Nationwide, billions of dollars are being spent on hardware and software. Within Dallas, millions of dollars continue to be spent on this equipment. Much of this is Title I money. And yet out in the schools one sees two things. First, some of the equipment remains in its original boxes. Second, when low-performing children *are* placed in front of these programs, they all too often doodle with them for a while, and then lose interest. This is not surprising. After all, the program, unlike a human being, cannot figure out what problem the student is having and respond in an appropriate, nuanced, warm, eye-contacting way. Yet central administrators typically show little concern for these problems. The reason seems to be that proclaiming that the district has a "high technology initiative" generates positive public relations and demonstrates that the administration is "in charge" of curriculum and instruction. Since other districts are doing this too, and the educational vendors are members of the "club," the strategy has quickly and easily become business as usual.

Where "whole language" is concerned, the debate between this approach and direct phonics instruction goes back more than forty years (Flesch 1955, 1981; Chall 1967; Adams 1990). The best scientific evidence suggests that, taken by itself, whole language without at least some phonics instruction is often ineffective in teaching at least some children to read.[11] The most effective techniques no doubt involve a combination of whole language and phonics as implemented by Success for All and Reading One-One. However, a relatively large proportion of district reading specialists are believers in the whole-language philosophy. Reading Recovery itself is based on this philosophy, which according to their publications appears to dominate the International Reading Association, the professional association of reading specialists. We have found that in many districts Reading Recovery is "business as usual." Where this is the case, we represent a low-cost competitor capable of putting the current administrations' reading experts out of business. In several cities we have found that they respond quite aggressively to this threat.[12]

One might ask why administrators do not try our lower-cost alternative anyway. I speculate that the answer lies in the fact that *they perceive that their own program control and claims to expertise are at least partially dependent upon the job security and prestige of their current staff members and their network affiliations. From this perspective, business-as-usual appears much safer than the risky strategy of allowing our program's nose inside the tent.* It is interesting to observe that Reading One-One's "niche" is halfway between that of (typically low-quality) programs using volunteer tutors and therefore delivering weak program effects and that of (typically high-quality) programs that use certified teachers as tutors, deliver strong program effects, but do so at high unit cost. The Reading One-One approach is to use hourly paid workers, carefully trained and managed, to achieve large effects at low unit cost. But the resulting outside provider/outside worker aspect of the program causes district administrators to dislike it. They prefer (a) the weak effects of volunteer tutors where their own staff maintain management control and the administrators get the "community outreach credit," (b) the weak effects of "old-style Title I" where teachers take students in groups of five to ten and administrators maintain control, or (c) the large effects and high unit costs of teacher-tutors where the administration once again maintains control. It should also be noted that the Reading One-One approach might, in fact, utilize something other than hourly paid tutors. For example, it might be used to provide at least some training for the teacher aides currently on the district's payroll. (Some principals have already commissioned Reading One-One to provide such training. The problem is that since the aides are not Reading One-One employees, they often resist or ignore the direction provided by our staff.) Or unpaid volunteers might be utilized as Reading One-One tutors. (This is currently being tried in Salt Lake City, where the Church of Latter Day Saints has provided a group of volunteers who have been trained in the Reading One-One methodology.) The concern in this case is that the volunteers will not come often enough per week or stay with the job for enough weeks to achieve strong bonding with the students. The main point, however, is that we have always been ready and anxious to work with central district administrators to try the program in any of these modes. We have discovered that while individual principals are often excited about these possibilities, central administrators typically show no interest at all.

As for bilingual education (which, in practice, is largely Spanish instruction administered in Spanish to students of Hispanic background), its implementation has typically failed to live up to its intention of easing *the transition* of students who speak Spanish in their home into speaking and reading English in school. As I have observed this program in a variety of Texas cities, it is *monolingual* instruction—Hispanic children in grades K–3 are largely taught Spanish in Spanish. Indeed, bilingual teachers often refuse permission to have a student tutored in English, because "it will con-fuse them."[13] Typically, bilingual instruction continues to be Spanish in-struction, in Spanish, through third grade. Somewhere between fourth and sixth grade, the students are typically immersed in English, with no tran-sitional curriculum and with English reading skills well below those ex-pected by the regular curriculum.

That the program has failed miserably is seen by the fact that, in Dallas, fully 89 percent of Hispanic third graders end the year with English read-ing skills below grade level (see Table 10.2). More than 50 percent of His-panic students in Dallas drop out before graduating from high school.[14] And yet, district administrators continue to strongly support the program. It is strongly supported by the Hispanic Teachers Association and seen as a Hispanic teacher employment program that "gives Hispanic children their culture." I have been told by a district administrator that it is "polit-ically untouchable." In other words, because of community public rela-tions and social network relationships, the program constitutes business as usual. That it furnishes tens of thousands of Hispanic children with such poor English-language skills that they are doomed to the low-income la-bor market is not considered relevant. Nor are the children's parents typi-cally given a real choice as to whether they wish to have their children immersed in English-language instruction in place of the "bilingual" program.

How do these programs and policies square with the district's rhetoric of reform, decentralization, and school-based management? It appears that when first promulgated by the previous administration just after school reformers had won a majority on the board, the rhetoric was real. True decentralization into ten areas, each with an area director, combined with the devolution of at least some budget authority down to the princi-pals, provided an environment in which the Reading One-One innovation could grow. However, since that time, a new school administration has moved to at least partially undo these reforms.

First, as discussed above, an enormous share of the discretionary Title I money was abruptly removed from the elementary schools. Further, the principals of these schools were strongly steered in the use of the funds they did have. This had the effect of backing away from the ideals of "parental involvement and school-centered education" (site-based man-agement) which had been instituted four years previously. In particular, school-centered decision-making committees composed of parents and teachers, which had been created with much fanfare, had much of their dis-cretionary Title I funding removed. At the same time, principals were "guided" to reassert their authority over these groups.[15]

Second, during summer 1995, the administration eliminated the division of the district into ten areas, replacing this structure with six "clusters."

Five former area directors were demoted. This change appeared to signal a desire to regain some of the control that had been given up by top administrators during the decentralization experiment. At a minimum, it increased centralized control by funneling decisions through only six top administrators. Combined with the general climate of fear among principals, and the ease with which their decision-making has thus far been "guided," we may infer that true decentralized decision-making at the school level has been significantly reduced.

Finally, the district's emphasis upon the accountability system was increased. In spring 1995, the school board voted to have all teachers' annual review be partially dependent upon the accountability system measure of their own students' progress. (That is, their standardized test scores, regression-adjusted for their scores the previous year, as well as for other background variables.) The Dallas public schools are apparently the first school district in the nation to take accountability this far. Incidentally, as publicity associated with accountability has progressed, two other changes have occurred in statistical reporting of the district's test scores. First, districtwide summaries by grade and ethnicity have become more difficult to access. Second, the district now reports all statistics in normal curve equivalents rather than grade-equivalents. It is perhaps not an accident that the former are difficult for laypeople to interpret in absolute, commonsense terms, and even more difficult to compare to previous year results when grade-equivalents were used.[16]

PROGRAM IMPLEMENTATION LESSONS

After reviewing the expansion of Reading One-One during the past five years of "school reform" activities within Dallas, I tentatively reach the following conclusions: First, school district decentralization came in with much fanfare in 1991; it is now on its way out. Strong school administrators have only a limited tolerance for true grass-roots decision-making. As with most educational fads, the half-life of decentralized decision-making may be little more than five years. This observation is reinforced by recent events, where the Chicago mayor has taken over control of the Chicago school system, and the New York mayor has sought to do likewise. (For a discussion of this, see the many articles in the *New York Times* during the summer and early fall of 1995.)

Second, under full decentralization, combined with an emphasis upon test scores such as that provided by a test-based accountability system, a highly cost-effective service innovation—Reading One-One—was able to expand quickly to serve many schools.

Third, unfortunately for the future of this innovation, by the close of the 1994–95 school year the administration had strongly reduced its commitment to decentralized decision-making. At the same time, the administration appeared to tilt against Reading One-One, even though program effects were larger than ever. Many principals who were immensely enthusiastic about the program's positive effect on their students and were strong personal advocates for the program fell immediately into line once their budgets were slashed and the administration's position was made clear.

Fourth, the lesson is that school reforms and service delivery improvements by outside providers will always exist at the sufferance of top administrators, and such sufferance will be short-lived. Truly effective outside providers are always likely to constitute a threat to insiders, and are unlikely to be allowed to continue their efforts over an extended period. Even though the emphasis upon test-based accountability continues stronger than ever, without school-based decision-making outside innovations have little opportunity for adoption.

Fifth, the program continues to operate in Dallas on a reduced scale. It now also operates on a small scale in Brownsville, San Antonio, Salt Lake City, and Richardson (the Dallas suburb containing the University of Texas at Dallas). Experiences thus far have demonstrated that, properly recruited, trained, and managed, paraprofessionals can significantly raise the reading performance of at-risk elementary-school students. However, the future of the program is uncertain. It appears to depend upon bureaucratic politics within a time of large upheavals in the local and national educational picture.

Sixth, efforts at outreach and negotiation across a variety of school districts show that strong opposition to Reading One-One is usually forthcoming from top district administrators concerned with the curriculum, its delivery, and the remediation of low-performing students. This occurs even when program advocates have presented strong evidence of what the program can do and have successfully convinced other educational administrators, including school board members and principals, to give it a try. This opposition seems to result from the preexisting commitments that such administrators have with Reading Recovery, Program Z, and other educational vendors. It also appears to relate to the fact that these administrators fear a loss of control, while seeing little personal incentive to move toward a lower-cost program.

In summary, Reading One-One often serves as a Rorschach test, revealing the focus and interests of school administrators. If parents of low-performing children were directly offered the opportunity for their child to have a university-trained and -managed reading tutor for sixty to one hundred one-on-one sessions, the program might be expected to grow rapidly. At $500 for sixty tutoring sessions for one student, the more than $5 billion annual national Title I budget could serve more than ten million low-performing students. Instead, these funds serve many fewer than this number, and rarely do so effectively. To be more explicit, consider that the U.S. Department of Education estimates that for 1995–96 there were 8.49 million children aged five to seventeen who qualified for Title I services (largely by being raised in low-income households). The national Title I budget during this time period was $5.97 billion, for an average of $703 per child. If Reading One-One-style tutors were used to serve these children, *every child could receive one-on-one tutoring*. No other program can make such a claim. And yet, unless Reading One-One can find a way to successfully cross the political/bureaucratic minefields within the school district bureaucracies of our major cities, its current embattled and marginalized status is unlikely to improve.

Much of the antipoverty literature focuses on designing programs to assist children from low-income households. Reading One-One represents one cost-effective example of such programs. However, I have learned that creating programs such as this one is not enough. Ultimately, we must move toward addressing the systemic functioning of the education system, which makes remedial programs necessary while resisting or mismanaging their implementation.

NOTES

1.   The material in this chapter represents a history reconstructed by the author, who was a participant-observer to the events described. The interpretations are largely based on the evidence of my own eyes and ears.

2.   "Refused to meet" in fact barely begins to describe a long-term pattern of opposition and harassment by central administrators. Incidents include "misplacing" paperwork necessary for Reading One-One to be paid for services rendered under contract with the district, failure to process paperwork in a timely manner so that the university was forced to forward-fund more than one million dollars of Reading One-One expenditures until the end of the school year, and failure to return phone calls I placed to administrators. When business leaders and the University president called to ask for reconsideration of the decision to (in effect) drastically curtail Reading One-One, they were told, "Mind your own business."

3.   Thanks to Linda Perry for this insight.

4.   For example, after we had tutored children in one school for two months, had bonded with them, and were making progress with them, the Title I lead teacher was instructed by the central bureaucracy to make us give her those students to tutor and for us to begin again with other students.

5.   In a previous time period, the same administrators had blocked efforts by Reading Recovery to enter the district.

6.   In fact, the Title I evaluator within the district had performed a statistical analysis that appeared to show that none of the programs had effects statistically different from zero. However, the report included a table in which these not statistically different program effects were rank-ordered, with Reading One-One coming in just below the middle. I wrote a paper critiquing these findings, showing that the study had such methodological weaknesses as to render it useless for the purpose of estimating the effects of these programs. I also reported our own statistical findings on the positive Reading One-One effects (see the previous chapter), and discussed in detail why my methodology *was* reliable. District administrators discussed my paper among themselves, but they never agreed to meet with me to discuss it.

7.   In 1976 the U.S. District Court issued a judgment requiring the Dallas schools to "follow a plan designed to further desegregate the schools." As played out in the ensuing years, this judgment led to the creation of superschool "learning centers," largely in highly segregated African-American neighborhoods. These schools are funded at a much higher per pupil rate than other schools, permitting smaller class sizes and a variety of add-on programs and services. For example, teachers were hired at relatively high hourly wage rates to tutor after school. These programs and funds, along with a districtwide budgeted "desegregation fund," are seen by district employees as being rightfully African-American controlled.

8.   Sources: Conversations with Title I lead teachers at various Dallas schools, as well as tabulations prepared by the Office of Research, Evaluation, and Testing of the Dallas schools.

9.   When I have spoken privately with administrators, they have usually agreed with this observation.

10.   Indeed, teachers-in-training are a potentially excellent source of Reading One-One tutors. They can get practical experience in teaching reading, under the best possible circumstances with only one student at a time, and also support themselves while attending college. And we have had some success in interesting education school professors in the program. Here too, however, we often come up against business as usual and entrenched pedagogical ideologies and affiliation networks, which make program dissemination difficult.

11.   See the special issue of *Educational Psychologist*, Fall 1994, edited by Symons, Woloshyn, and Pressley. For additional very useful discussion, with a particular emphasis upon the process by which normal children become classified as learning disabled or reading disabled, see Spear-Swerling and Sternberg (1996). After seeing reading skills decline substantially, California has recently backed off its prior commitment to whole-language instruction.

12.   That is, they lobby very effectively with district administrators against permitting any sort of demonstration of what might by achieved by the methods of Reading One-One.

13.   This is not completely nonsensical if your goal is to teach the student *Spanish*, since Spanish and English vowels have different pronunciations.

14.   For research showing a similar failure of bilingual education in New York City, see "Bilingual Education Effort is Flawed," *New York Times*, October 20, 1994, p. A20. For a more general treatment, see Porter (1996).

15.   Consider the case of an elementary school where the principal has always been very sensitive to political winds within the district. In 1992 she was quick to recruit Reading One-One to her school, and we ran a very large program there for more than three years. The school also showed dramatic test score gains in reading for the grades we were tutoring. Suddenly, and with no prior discussion, she issued a memo to teachers in spring 1995, that said, among other things, "(a) Reading One-One will not be back next year, and (b) we will use Program Z." After having largely usurped the authority of this committee, and having permitted no discussion with me or the committee, she then went on to announce that the committee "will have much to decide on this spring."

16.   An attraction of the accountability system for central administrators is apparently that it permits them to "declare victory" in the newspapers on an annual basis, while directing attention away from the absolute level of performance of the children. This is so because the calculations of "school improvement" are relative, based on the school's performance the previous year. For example, I have spoken to a former Reading One-One tutor who was employed as an English teacher in what was later reported to be the highest (accountability system) ranked Dallas high school during the 1994–95 school year. She tells me that it was a demoralizing experience. None of her students could read the assigned materials, none was willing to do homework, and the students told her that "the teachers always give us the answers to the tests."

Appendix

Methodology for Constructing Table 10.2

A serious difficulty must be overcome to estimate the full distribution of student reading levels at the close of first, second, and third grades. This is that state regulations exclude a relatively large number of low-performing students from testing in English. Most of these are limited-English-proficient (LEP). To overcome this difficulty, we proceeded as follows. First, we used district records to ascertain the number of students who were and were not tested at the end of each grade, separately by grade and race. (These and all other calculations are for the 1994–95 school year.) The result is shown in Table A1. We see that by far the largest number of untest-

Table A1.   DPS Enrollment vs. Tested Students*^{a}*, End of Year 1994–95

	Grade		
	One	*Two*	*Third*
Black			
Tested	5085	4798	4605
Total students	5558	5339	5225
Percentage tested	91.5	89.9	88.1
Hispanic			
Tested	1590	1579	1943
Total students	6094	5081	5365
Percentage tested	26.1	31.1	36.2
White			
Tested	1447	1382	1264
Total students	1739	1661	1582
Percentage tested	83.2	83.2	79.9
Total			
Tested	8122	7759	7812
Total students	13391	12081	12172
Other ethnicities, total students	239	997	267
District total, total students	13630	13078	12439

^{a} Includes special education students.

195

ed students fall among Hispanics. For this group, the following shares of students were tested: first graders, 26 percent; second graders, 31 percent; third graders, 36 percent.

For tested students there is little problem. District data showing the grade-equivalent distribution of their test scores across (national) decile ranges have already been presented in Table 10.1. For untested students we take advantage of the scores available for all tutored students compiled by Reading One-One, the UTD structured tutoring program. Since most of these students assigned to tutoring were low-performing and approximately 70 percent were Hispanic, they constitute a relatively large sample of students, some of whom were administered the ITBS by the district, and many of whom were not.

To fill in the missing data for Hispanic students, we have assumed that the Reading One-One Hispanic students who were omitted from ITBS testing by the district are representative of all district Hispanic students omitted from testing. Fortunately, *all* tutored students were administered the Woodcock-Johnson Reading Comprehension test both at the beginning and the end of the school year. For first graders, we use the end-of-year distribution of Woodcock-Johnson grade-equivalent scores to estimate the distribution of scores for untested students. The results, applied to the actual number of untested students, are shown for Hispanic first graders in the first panel of Appendix Table A2.

A similar method is used for Hispanic second and third graders. However, for these groups an additional refinement is employed. Rather than just using the Woodcock scores for untested students, these are regression-adjusted to more closely approximate ITBS scores, utilizing a regression of ITBS scores on Woodcock scores plus student personal characteristics from tested students. This is particularly desirable for second and third graders, since it is among these students that we observe a tendency for ITBS and Woodcock scores to drift apart. (Second- and third-grade students tend to "test more poorly" on the group-administered ITBS than on the one-one administered Woodcock.)

Unfortunately, this methodology is not available for black and white students, since there are too few of these who were both tutored by Reading One-One (and thus administered the Woodcock) and also excluded from ITBS testing. For these students we employed the following methodology. We assumed that untested students fell in the below-grade-level categories, with relative shares approximately equal to the relative shares shown for tested students. These shares, expressed as percentages summing to 100, were then applied to the actual number of untested students within each race group. The results are shown in Table A2. This table, combined with Table 10.1, yields the results of Table 10.2.

This methodology for filling in missing scores for untested white and black students is, of course, approximate. However, it should be regarded as conservative, in the sense that it errs in the direction of producing scores that are, on average, *higher* than these students would have achieved if they had been tested. This is because the method treats students in each of the below-grade-level categories as having the same chance of being omitted from testing, whereas actually students in the lowest categories were probably more likely to have been omitted from testing. Beyond this, it should be noted that untested black and white third graders number only 938 students, or 7.7 percent of all third graders. Thus, a 10 percent error in assigning these students to categories would affect less than 1 percent of all third graders.

Table A2. Distribution of Estimated End-of-Year Reading Comprehension Scores for DPS Students Who Did Not Take the ITBS

Grade-equivalent ranges:	K.1–1.19	1.2–1.39	1.4–1.59	1.6–1.69	1.7–1.79	1.8–1.99	2.0–2.19	2.2–2.59	2.6–2.89	2.9–4.7
First grade										
Black: N = 473	67	62	154	66	123					
%	14.2	13.1	32.6	14.0	26.0					
Hispanic: N = 4504	1784	669	669	290	201	245	156	245	89	156
%	39.6	14.9	14.9	6.4	4.5	5.5	3.5	5.5	2.0	3.5
White: N = 292	42	32	90	53	76					
%	14.4	11.0	30.8	18.2	26.0					
Total: N = 5269	1893	763	913	409	400	245	156	245	89	156
%	35.9	14.5	17.3	7.8	7.6	4.7	3.0	4.7	1.7	3.0
Cumulative percentage below grade level	35.9	50.4	67.7	75.5	83.1					

Grade-equivalent ranges:	K.4–1.69	1.7–1.99	2.0–2.19	2.2–2.59	2.6–2.79	2.8–3.09	3.1–3.39	3.4–3.79	3.8–4.59	4.6–7.0
Second grade										
Black: N = 541	112	135	82	129	83					
%	20.7	25.0	15.2	23.8	15.3					
Hispanic: N = 3502	1666	731	544	391	102	51	17			
%	47.6	20.9	15.5	11.2	2.9	1.5	0.5			

Grade-equivalent ranges:	K.4-1.69	1.7-1.99	2.0-2.19	2.2-2.59	2.6-2.79	2.8-3.09	3.1-3.39	3.4-3.79	3.8-4.59	4.6-7.0
White: N = 279	40	57	56	71	56					
%	14.3	20.4	20.1	25.4	20.1					
Total: N = 4322	1818	923	682	591	241	51	17			
%	42.1	21.4	15.8	13.7	5.6	1.2	0.4			
Cumulative percentage below grade level	42.1	63.4	79.2	92.9	98.4					

Grade-equivalent ranges:	1.3-2.09	2.1-2.79	2.8-3.09	3.1-3.39	3.5-3.79	3.8-4.19	4.2-4.69	4.7-5.39	5.4-6.49	6.5-9.7
Third grade										
Black: N = 620	121	161	150	90	99					
%	19.5	26.0	24.2	14.5	16.0					
Hispanic: N = 3422	805	1661	503	327	101	25				
%	23.5	48.5	14.7	9.6	3.0	0.7				
White : N = 318	41	63	75	59	80					
%	12.9	19.8	23.6	18.6	25.2					
Total: N = 4360	967	1885	728	476	280	25				
%	22.2	43.2	16.7	10.9	6.4	0.6				
Cumulative percentage below grade level	22.2	65.4	82.1	93.0	99.4					

References

Aaron, Henry. 1994. "Distinguished Lecture on Economics in Government: Public Policy, Values, and Consciousness." *Journal of Economic Perspectives* 8:3–22.

Adams, Marilyn Jager. 1990. *Beginning to Read: Thinking and Learning About Print.* Cambridge, MA: MIT Press.

Alexander, Karl and Bruce Eckland. 1980. "The 'Explorations in Equality of Opportunity' Sample of 1955 High School Sophomores." Pp. 31–58 in *Research in Sociology of Education and Socialization*, vol. I, edited by Alan C. Kerckhoff. Greenwich, CT: JAI.

Alexander, Karl, Doris Entwisle, and Maxine Thompson. 1987. "School Performance, Status Relations, and the Structure of Sentiment: Bringing the Teacher Back In." *American Sociological Review* 52:655–82.

Allison, Graham. 1971. *Essence of Decision: Explaining the Cuban Missile Crisis.* Boston: Little, Brown.

Alwin, Duane F. and Robert M. Hauser. 1975. "The Decomposition of Effects in Path Analysis." *American Sociological Review* 40:37–47.

Arroyo, Carmen G. and Edward Zigler. 1993. "America's Title I/Chapter 1 Programs: Why the Promise Has Not Been Met." Pp. 73–95 in *From Head Start and Beyond: A National Plan for Extended Childhood Intervention.* edited by Edward Zigler and Sally J. Styfco. New Haven, CT: Yale University Press.

Baker, Michael and Dwayne Benjamin. 1994. "The Performance of Immigrants in the Canadian Labor Market." *Journal of Labor Economics* 12(3, July):369–405.

Becker, Gary. 1964. *Human Capital.* New York: National Bureau of Economic Research.

Benbow, Camilla P. and Stanley, Julian C. 1980. "Sex Differences in Mathematical Ability: Fact or Artifact?" *Science* 210(12, December):1262–64.

Berg, Ivar. 1970. *Education and Jobs: The Great Training Robbery.* Boston: Beacon.

Bernstein, Basil. 1960. "Language and Social Class (Research Notes)." *British Journal of Sociology* 11:271–76.

———. 1962. "Linguistic Codes, Hesitation Phenomena, and Intelligence." *Language and Speech* 5:31–46.

———. 1977. *Class, Codes and Control*, vol. 3. London: Routledge & Kegan Paul.

Blau, Peter. 1977. *Inequality and Heterogeneity.* New York: Free Press.

Blauner, Robert. 1964. *Alienation and Freedom; The Factory Worker and His Industry.* Chicago: University of Chicago Press.

Borjas, George. 1985. "Assimilation, Changes in Cohort Quality, and the Earnings of Immigrants." *Journal of Labor Economics* 3(4, October):463–89.

Bourdieu, Pierre. 1977. "Cultural Reproduction and Social Reproduction." Pp.

487–511 in *Power and Ideology in Education*, edited by Jerome Karabel and A. H. Haley. New York: Oxford.

Bowles, Samuel and Herbert Gintis. 1976. *Schooling in Capitalist America*. New York: Basic Books.

Brooks-Gunn, Jeanne, G. J. Duncan, P. K. Klebanov, and N. Sealand. 1993a. "Do Neighborhoods Influence Child and Adolescent Behavior?" *American Journal of Sociology* 99:353–95.

Brooks-Gunn, Jeanne, P. K. Klebanov, F. Liaw, and D. Spiker. 1993b. "Enhancing the Development of Low Birth-Weight, Premature Infants: Changes in Cognition and Behavior over the First Three Years." *Child Development* 63:736–53.

Brooks-Gunn, Jeanne, P. K. Klebanov, and G. K. Duncan. 1995. "Ethnic Differences in Children's Intelligence Test Scores: Role of Economic Deprivation, Home Environment, and Maternal Characteristics." Paper read at the Meeting on Black-White Differences in Test Performance, Harris School of Public Policy, University of Chicago, May 26.

Brophy, Jere E. and Thomas L. Good. 1974. *Teacher-Student Relationships: Causes and Consequences*. New York: Holt.

Burstein, Paul and Susan Pitchford. 1990. "Social-Scientific and Legal Challenges to Education and Test Requirements in Employment." *Social Problems* 37:243–57.

Cain, Pamela S. and Donald J. Treiman. 1981. "The DOT as a Source of Occupational Data." *American Sociological Review* 46:253–78.

Camic, Charles. 1986. "The Matter of Habit." *American Journal of Sociology* 91:1039–87.

Carliner, Geoffrey. 1981. "Wage Differences by Language Group and the Market for Language Skills in Canada." *Journal of Human Resources* 16:384–99.

Cattell, R. B. 1941. "Some Theoretical Issues in Adult Intelligence Testing." *Psychological Bulletin* 38:592.

Chall, Jeanne. 1967. *Learning to Read: The Great Debate*. New York: McGraw-Hill.

Center for Human Resource Research. Various years. *NLSY Data Documentation*. Columbus, OH.

Chambliss, Daniel. 1989. "The Mundanity of Excellence: An Ethnographic Report on Stratification and Olympic Swimmers." *Sociological Theory* 7:70–86.

Chiswick, Barry R. 1986. "Is the New Immigration Less Skilled Than the Old?" *Journal of Labor Economics* 4(2, April):168–92.

———. 1991. "Speaking, Reading, and Earnings among Low-skilled Immigrants." *Journal of Labor Economics* 9:149–70.

Chubb, John and Terry Moe. 1990. *Politics, Markets, and America's Schools*. Washington, DC: Brookings Institution.

Cicourel, Aaron V. and Hugh Mehan. 1985. "Universal Development, Stratifying Practices, and Status Attainment." *Research in Social Stratification and Mobility* 4:3–27.

Clay, M. 1979. *The Early Detection of Reading Difficulties*. Auckland, NZ: Heinemann.

Coleman, James. 1961. *Adolescent Society*. New York: Basic Books.

Collins, Randall. 1971. "A Conflict Theory of Sexual Stratification." *Social Problems* 19:2–21.

———. 1975. *Conflict Sociology*. New York: Academic Press.

_____. 1979. *The Credential Society: An Historical Sociology of Education and Stratification*. New York: Academic Press.

_____. 1985. *Max Weber: A Skeleton Key*. Beverly Hills, CA: Sage.

_____. 1986. *Weberian Sociological Theory*. Cambridge: Cambridge University Press.

_____. 1988. *Theoretical Sociology*. San Diego: Harcourt, Brace.

Corcoran, Mary and Sharon Parrott. 1992. "Black Women's Economic Progress." Unpublished manuscript. ISR, University of Michigan, Ann Arbor.

Crane, Jonathan. 1995. "Race and Educational Achievement: Evidence That Environment Explains the Entire Gap in Children's Test Scores." Paper read at the Meeting on Black-White Differences in Test Performance, Harris School of Public Policy, University of Chicago, May 26.

DiMaggio, Paul. 1982. "Cultural Capital and School Success: The Impact of Status Culture Participation on the Grades of U.S. High School Students." *American Sociological Review* 47:189–201.

DiMaggio, Paul and John Mohr. 1985. "Cultural Capital, Educational Attainment, and Marital Selection." *American Journal of Sociology* 90:1231–61.

Dornbusch, S., P. Ritter, and L. Steinberg. 1991. "Community Influences on the Relation of Family Statuses to Adolescent School Performance: An Attempt to Understand a Difference between African-Americans and Non-Hispanic Whites." *American Journal of Education* 99:543–67.

Duncan, Greg, J. Brooks-Gunn, and P. K. Klebanov. 1994. "Economic Deprivation in Early Childhood Development." *Child Development* 65:296–318.

Dusek, Jerome B. 1975. "Do Teachers Bias Children's Learning?" *Review of Educational Research* 45:661–84.

Easterbrook, Gregg. 1995. "Blacktop Basketball and *The Bell Curve*." Pp. 30–43 in *The Bell Curve Debate*, edited by R. Jacoby and N. Glauberman. New York: Times Books.

Entwisle, Doris R. and Karl Alexander. 1994. "Winter Setback: The Racial Composition of Schools and Learning to Read." *American Sociological Review* 59:446–60.

Entwisle, Doris R. and Leslie Hayduk. 1982. *Early Schooling: Cognitive and Affective Outcomes*. Baltimore: Johns Hopkins University Press.

_____. 1983. "Young Children's Academic Expectations." *Research in Sociology of Education and Socialization* 4:75–99.

Farkas, George. 1993. "Structured Tutoring for At Risk Children in the Early Years." *Applied Behavioral Science Review* 1(1):69–92.

_____. Forthcoming. "Reading One-One: An Intensive Program Serving A Great Many Students While Still Achieving Large Effects." In *Social Programs That Really Work*, edited by J. Crane. New York: Russell Sage Foundation.

Farkas, George, D. Alton Smith, and Ernst W. Stromsdorfer. 1983. "The Youth Entitlement Demonstration: Subsidized Employment with a Schooling Requirement." *Journal of Human Resources*, 18(fall):557–73.

Farkas, George and Keven Vicknair. 1995. "Reading One-One Program Effects, 1994–95." Paper read at the session on "Raising Children's Test Scores" of the *Conference on Social Programs That Really Work*, sponsored by the Institute of Government and Public Affairs, University of Illinois, October 20, 1995, Chicago.

————. 1996. "Appropriate Tests of Racial Wage Discrimination Require Controls for Cognitive Skill." *American Sociological Review.* (forthcoming)

Farkas, George, Randall Olsen, Ernst Stromdorfer, Linda Sharpe, Felicity Skidmore, D. Alton Smith, and Sally Merrill. 1984. *Post-Program Impacts of the Youth Incentive Entitlement Pilot Projects.* New York: Manpower Demonstration Research Corporation.

Farkas, George, Kurt Beron, Keven Vicknair, and Diane Walters. 1994. "Reforming Compensatory Education with Reading One-One." Paper read at the Annual Meetings of the Association for Public Policy Analysis and Management, Chicago, October 27.

Farkas, George, Robert Grobe, Daniel Sheehan, and Yuan Shuan 1990a. "Cultural Resources and School Success: Gender, Ethnicity, and Poverty Groups within an Urban School District." *American Sociological Review* 55:127–42.

————. 1990b. "Coursework Mastery and School Success: Gender, Ethnicity, and Poverty Groups within an Urban School District." *American Educational Research Journal* 27:807–27.

Featherman, David and Robert Hauser. 1978. *Opportunity and Change.* New York: Harcourt, Brace.

Flesch, Rudolf. 1955. *Why Johnny Can't Read—And What You Can Do About It.* New York: Harper and Row.

————. 1981. *Why Johnny Still Can't Read—A New Look at the Scandal of our Schools.* New York: Harper.

Fordham, Signithia. 1988. "Racelessness as a Factor in Black Students' School Success: Pragmatic Strategy or Pyrrhic Victory?" *Harvard Educational Review* 58(1, February):54–84.

Fordham, Signithia, and John Ogbu. 1986. "Black Students' School Success: Coping with the 'Burden of "Acting White."'" *Urban Review* 18:176–206.

Fraser, Steven. 1995. *The Bell Curve Wars.* New York: Basic Books.

Gans, Herbert J. 1968. "Culture and Class in the Study of Poverty: An Approach to Anti-Poverty Research." Pp. 201–28 in *On Understanding Poverty*, edited by D. P. Moynihan. New York: Basic Books.

Gottfredson, Linda S. 1996. "What Do We Know About Intelligence?" *American Scholar* (Winter):15–30.

Granovetter, Mark S. 1974. *Getting A Job: A Study of Contacts and Careers.* Cambridge, MA: Harvard University Press.

————. 1985. "Economic Action and Social Structure: The Problem of Embeddedness." *American Journal of Sociology* 91(3):481–510.

————. 1994. "The Sociological and Economic Approaches to Labor Market Analysis: A Social Structural View." Pp. 187–216 in *Industries, Firms, and Jobs: Sociological and Economic Approaches*, expanded edition, edited by G. Farkas and P. England. Hawthorne, NY: Aldine de Gruyter.

Greenstone, J. David. 1991. "Culture, Rationality, and the Underclass." Pp. 399–408 in *The Urban Underclass*, edited by C. Jencks and P. Peterson. Washington, DC: Brookings Institution.

Grenier, Giles. 1984. "The Effects of Language Characteristics on the Wages of Hispanic American Males." *Journal of Human Resources* 1:35–52.

Haley, Robert. n.d. "Investigation of an 'Epidemic' of Public School Achievement in Minority Students in Dallas." Mimeo. Southwestern Medical School, Dallas.

Hampton, Robert L. 1987. *Violence in the Black Family. Correlates and Consequences.* Lexington, MA.: D. C. Heath.

Hanushek, Eric. 1986. "The Economics of Schooling: Production and Efficiency in Public Schools." *Journal of Economic Literature* 24:1141–77.

———. 1987. "Educational Production Functions." Pp. 33–41 in *Economics of Education,* edited by G. Psacharopoulos. Oxford: Pergamon.

———. 1994. *Making Schools Work.* Washington, DC: Brookings Institution.

Hardin, Russell. 1995. *One for All. The Logic of Group Conflict.* Princeton, NJ: Princeton University Press.

Herrnstein, Richard and Charles Murray. 1994. *The Bell Curve.* New York: Free Press.

Heyns, Barbara. 1978. *Summer Learning and the Effects of Schooling.* New York: Academic Press.

Hill, M. Anne and June O'Neill. 1994. "Family Endowments and the Achievement of Young Children with Special Reference to the Underclass." *Journal of Human Resources* 29:1064–1100.

Hollinger, David. 1995. *Postethnic America: Beyond Multiculturalism.* New York: Basic Books.

Horn, J. L. 1976. "Human Abilities: A Review of Research and Theory in the Early 1970s." *Annual Review of Psychology* 27:437–85.

———. 1978. "The Nature and Development of Intellectual Abilities." Pp. 107–36 in *Human Variation: The Biopsychology of Age, Race, and Sex,* edited by R. Osborne, C. Noble, and N. Weyl. New York: Academic Press.

———. 1985. "Intellectual Ability Concepts." Pp. 35–77 in *Advances in the Psychology of Human Intelligence,* edited by R. Sternberg. Hillsdale, NJ: Lawrence Erlbaum.

———. 1988. "Thinking about Human Abilities." Pp. 645–865 in *Handbook of Multivariate Psychology,* edited by J. Nesselroade and R. Cattell. New York: Academic Press.

———. 1991. "Measurement of Intellectual Capabilities: A Review of Theory." Chapter 7 in *Woodcock-Johnson Technical Manual,* edited by K. McGrew, J. Werder, and R. Woodcock. Allen, TX: DLM.

Horn, J. L. and R. B. Cattell. 1966. "Refinement and Test of the Theory of Fluid and Crystallized Intelligence." *Journal of Educational Psychology* 57:253–70.

Hult, Karen and Charles Walcott. 1990. *Governing Public Organizations.* Pacific Grove, CA: Brooks/Cole.

Hunter, Alfred. 1988. "Formal Education and Initial Employment: Unraveling the Relationships between Schooling and Skills over Time." *American Sociological Review* 53:753–65.

Jacoby, Russell and Naomi Glauberman (eds.). 1995. *The Bell Curve Debate.* New York: Times Books.

Jencks, Christopher and Paul Peterson. 1991. *The Urban Underclass.* Washington, DC: Brookings Institution.

Jencks, Christopher, James Crouse, and Peter Mueser. 1979. *Who Gets Ahead? The Determinants of Economic Success in America.* New York: Basic Books.

Jencks, Christopher, et al. 1983. "The Wisconsin Model of Status Attainment: A National Replication with Improved Measures of Ability and Aspiration." *Sociology of Education* 56:3–19.

Jones, F. L. and Jonathan Kelley. 1984. "Decomposing Differences between Groups: A Cautionary Note on Measuring Discrimination." *Sociological Methods and Research* 12:323–43.

Juhn, Chinhui, Kevin M. Murphy, and Brooks Pierce. 1993. "Wage Inequality and the Rise in Returns to Skill." *Journal of Political Economy* 101:410–42.

Kilbourne, Barbara, Paula England, George Farkas, Kurt Beron, and Dorothea Weir. 1994. "Returns to Skill, Compensating Differentials, and Gender Bias: Effects of Occupational Characteristics on the Wages of White Women and Men." *American Journal of Sociology* 100:689–719.

Kirschenman, Joleen and Kathryn M. Neckerman. 1991. "'We'd Love to Hire Them, But . . . ': The Meaning of Race for Employers." Pp. 203–32 in *The Urban Underclass*, edited by C. Jencks and P. Peterson. Washington, DC: Brookings Institution.

Kochman, Thomas. 1981. *Black and White Styles in Conflict*. Chicago: University of Chicago Press.

Kohn, Melvin. 1969. *Class and Conformity*, 2nd ed. Homewood, IL: Dorsey.

Kohn, Melvin and Connie Schooler, with J. Miller, K. Miller, and R. Schoenberg. 1983. *Work and Personality: An Inquiry into the Impact of Social Stratification*. Norwood, NJ: Ablex.

Korenman, Sanders, Jane Miller, and John Sjaastad. 1994. "Long-term Poverty and Child Development in the United States: Results from the NLSY." Working paper, second revision (August). Humphrey Institute of Public Affairs, University of Minnesota, Minneapolis.

Kossoudji, Sherrie. 1988. "English Language Ability and the Labor Market Opportunities of Hispanic and East Asian Immigrant Men." *Journal of Labor Economics* 6:205–28.

Lamont, Michele and Annette Lareau. 1988. "Cultural Capital: Allusions, Gaps and Glissandos in Recent Theoretical Developments." *Sociological Theory* 6:153–68.

Lang, Kevin and William T. Dickens. 1988. "Neoclassical and Sociological Perspectives on Segmented Labor Markets." Pp. 65–92 in *Industries, Firms, and Jobs: Sociological and Economic Approaches*, edited by G. Farkas and P. England. New York: Plenum.

Lareau, Annette. 1987. "Social Class Differences in Family-School Relationships: The Importance of Cultural Capital." *Sociology of Education* 60:73–85.

———. 1989. *Home Advantage: Social Class and Parental Intervention in Elementary Education*. London: Falmer.

Leiter, Jeffrey and James S. Brown. 1985. "Determinants of Elementary School Grading." *Sociology of Education* 58:166–80.

Lieberman, Myron. 1993. *Public Education: An Autopsy*. Cambridge, MA: Harvard University Press.

Locke, John. [1692] 1947. *Some Thoughts Concerning Education*. Pp. 205–388 in *John Locke on Politics and Education*, edited by Howard R. Penniman. New York: Walter J. Black.

MacLeod, Jay. 1987. *Ain't No Makin' It. Leveled Aspirations in a Low-Income Neighborhood*. Boulder, CO: Westview.

Madden, Nancy A., Robert E. Slavin, Nancy L. Karweit, Lawrence J. Dolan, and Barbara A. Wasik. 1993. "Success for All: Longitudinal Effects of a Restructuring Program for Inner-City Elementary Schools." *American Educational Research Journal* 30:123–48.

Marsden, Peter. 1988. "Homogeneity in Confiding Relations." *Social Networks* 10:57–76.

McGrew, Kevin, Judy Werder, and Richard Woodcock. 1991. *Woodcock-Johnson Technical Manual*. Allen, TX: DLM.

McManus, Walter, William Gould, and Finis Welch. 1983. "Earnings of Hispanic Men: The Role of English Language Proficiency." *Journal of Labor Economics* 1:101–30.

McPherson, Miller and Lynn Smith-Lovin. 1987. "Homophily in Voluntary Organizations." *American Sociological Review* 52:370–79.

Mehan, Hugh. 1992. "Understanding Inequality in Schools: The Contribution of Interpretive Studies." *Sociology of Education* 65(1):1–20.

Meier, Kenneth and Joseph Stewart. 1991. *The Politics of Hispanic Education*. Albany: State University of New York Press.

Meier, Kenneth, Joseph Stewart, and Robert England. 1989. *Race, Class, and Education: The Politics of Second Generation Discrimination*. Madison: University of Wisconsin Press.

Mincer, Jacob. 1958. "Investment in Human Capital and Personal Income Distribution." *Journal of Political Economy* 66:281–302.

———. 1974. *Schooling, Experience, and Earnings*. New York: National Bureau of Economic Research.

Moore, Kristin and Nancy Snyder. 1991. "Cognitive Attainment among Firstborn Children of Adolescent Mothers." *American Sociological Review* 56:612–24.

Moynihan, Daniel P. 1968. *On Understanding Poverty*. New York: Basic Books.

Murnane, Richard. 1975. *The Impact of School Resources on the Learning of Inner City Children*. Cambridge MA: Ballinger.

Murnane, Richard J., John B. Willett, and Frank Levy. 1995. "The Growing Importance of Cognitive Skills in Wage Determination." *Review of Economics and Statistics* 77(2, May):251–66.

Natriello, Gary and Sanford M. Dornbusch. 1983. "Bringing Behavior Back In: The Effects of Student Characteristics and Behavior on the Classroom Behavior of Teachers." *American Educational Research Journal* 20:29–43.

———. 1984. *Teacher Evaluative Standards and Student Effort*. New York: Longman.

Natriello, Gary, E. McDill, and A. Pallas. 1990. *Schooling Disadvantaged Children: Racing Against Catastrophe*. New York: Teachers College Press.

Neckerman, Kathryn M. and Joleen Kirschenman. 1991. "Hiring Strategies, Racial Bias, and Inner-City Workers." *Social Problems* 38(4):433–47.

Nisbett, Richard. 1995. "*Race, IQ, and Scientism.*" Pp. 36–57 in *The Bell Curve Wars*, edited by S. Fraser. New York: Basic Books.

O'Neill, June. 1990. "The Role of Human Capital in Earnings Differences between Black and White Men." *Journal of Economic Perspectives* 4(4):25–46.

Ogbu, John. 1974. *The Next Generation: An Ethnography of Education in an Urban Neighborhood.* New York: Academic Press.

———. 1978. *Minority Education and Caste: The American System in Cross-Cultural Perspective.* Orlando, FL: Academic Press.

———. 1986. "The Consequences of the American Caste System." Pp. 19–56 in *The School Achievement of Minority Children,* edited by U. Neisser. Hillsdale, NJ: Lawrence Erlbaum.

Orr, Eleanor W. 1987. *Twice as Less: Black English and the Performance of Black Students in Mathematics and Science.* New York: W.W. Norton.

Parcel, Toby and Elizabeth Menaghan. 1994. *Parents' Jobs and Children's Lives.* Hawthorne, NY: Aldine de Gruyter.

Parcel, Toby and Charles Mueller. 1989. "Temporal Change in Occupational Earnings Attainment, 1970–1980." *American Sociological Review* 54:622–34.

Parsons, Talcott. 1959. "The School Class as a Social System: Some of Its Functions in American Society." *Harvard Educational Review* 29:297–318.

Patterson, Orlando. 1995. "For Whom the Bell Curves." Pp. 187–213 in *The Bell Curve Wars,* edited by S. Fraser. New York: Basic Books.

Pinnell, Gay Su, Carol Lyons, Diane DeFord, Anthony Bryk, and Michael Seltzer. 1994. "Comparing Instructional Models for the Literacy Education of High-risk First Graders." *Reading Research Quarterly* 29(1)8–39.

Pinnell, Gay Su, Diane DeFord, Carol Lyons, and Anthony Bryk. 1995. "Response to Rasinski." *Reading Research Quarterly* 30:272–75.

Porter, Rosalie Pedalino. 1996. *Forked Tongue: The Politics of Bilingual Education.* New Brunswick, NJ: Transaction.

Rasinski, Timothy. 1995. "Commentary: On the Effects of Reading Recovery." *Reading Research Quarterly* 30:264–71.

Rehberg, Richard A. and Evelyn R. Rosenthal. 1978. *Class and Merit in the American High School.* White Plains, NY: Longman.

Reynolds, Arthur. 1992. "Mediated Effects of Preschool Intervention." *Early Education and Development* 3:157–70.

Rist, Ray. 1973. *The Urban School: A Factory for Failure.* Cambridge, MA: MIT Press.

Rosenthal, Robert and Lenore Jacobson. 1968. *Pygmalion in the Classroom.* New York: Holt.

Sadker, Myra and David Sadker. 1986. "Sexism in the Classroom: From Grade School to Graduate School." *Phi Delta Kappan* 67(7, March):512–15.

Schultz, T. W. 1960. "Capital Formation by Education." *Journal of Political Economy* 68:571–83.

———. 1981. *Investing in People.* Berkeley: University of California Press.

Sennett, Richard and Jonathan Cobb. 1972. *The Hidden Injuries of Class.* New York: Random House.

Sewell, William H. and Robert M. Hauser. 1975. *Education, Occupation, and Earnings.* New York: Academic Press.

———. 1980. "The Wisconsin Longitudinal Study of Social and Psychological Factors in Aspirations and Achievements." Pp. 59–100 in *Research in Sociology of Education and Socialization,* vol. I, edited by Alan C. Kerckhoff. Greenwich, CT: JAI.

Sexton, Patricia C. 1961. *Education and Income.* New York: Viking.

Shuan, Yuan. 1989. *Teacher Characteristics and Student Success.* Ph.D. dissertation, Graduate Program in Political Economy, University of Texas at Dallas.

Slavin, Robert. 1989. *Effective Programs for Students at Risk.* Needham Heights, MA: Allyn and Bacon.

Slavin, Robert, et al. 1994a. "Success for All: Longitudinal Effects of Systemic School-by-School Reform in Seven Districts." Paper presented at the Annual Meeting of the American Educational Research Association, New Orleans, April.

Slavin, Robert, Nancy Madden, Lawrence Dolan, and Barbara Wasik. 1994b. "'Whenever and Wherever We Choose . . .' The Replication of Success for All." Paper presented at the annual meeting of the American Educational Research Association, Atlanta.

Slavin, Robert, Nancy Madden, Lawrence Dolan, Barbara Wasik, Steven Ross, Lana Smith, and Marcella Dianda. 1995. "Success for All: A Summary of Research." Paper presented at the Annual Conference of the American Educational Research Association, San Francisco, April 22.

Slavin, Robert, Nancy Madden, Nancy Karweit, Lawrence Dolan, and Barbara Wasik. 1990a. "Success for All: First-year Outcomes of a Comprehensive Plan for Reforming Urban Education." *American Educational Research Journal* 27:255–78.

————. 1990b. "Success for All: Effects of Variations in Duration and Resources of a Schoolwide Elementary Restructuring Program." Report No. 2, Center for Research on Effective Schooling for Disadvantaged Students, Johns Hopkins University, Baltimore, MD.

Smith, James P. and Finis R. Welch. 1989. "Black Economic Progress after Myrdal." *Journal of Economic Literature* 27:519–64.

Smith, Michael. 1990. "What Is New in 'New Structuralist' Analysis of Earnings?" *American Sociological Review* 55:827–41.

Spear-Swerling, Louise and Robert J. Sternberg. 1996. *Off-Track: When Poor Readers Become "Learning Disabled."* Boulder, CO: Westview.

Spearman, C. 1904. "'General Intelligence,' Objectively Determined and Measured." *American Journal of Psychology* 15:201–93.

Spence, A. Michael. 1974. *Market Signaling.* Cambridge, MA: Harvard University Press.

Spenner, Kenneth. 1983. "Deciphering Prometheus: Temporal Change in the Skill Level of Work." *American Sociological Review* 48:824–37.

Stinchcombe, Arthur. 1990. *Information and Organizations.* Berkeley: University of California Press.

Stolzenberg, Ross. 1990. "Ethnicity, Geography, and Occupational Achievement of Hispanic Men in the United States." *American Sociological Review* 55:143–54.

Strong, Edward K. 1934. *The Second Generation Japanese Problem.* Stanford, CA: Stanford University Press.

Summers, Anita and Barbara Wolfe. 1977. "Do Schools Make a Difference?" *American Economic Review* 67:639–52.

Swidler, Anne. 1986. "Culture in Action: Symbols and Strategies." *American Sociological Review* 51:273–86.

Tainer, Evelina. 1988. "English Language Proficiency and Earnings among Foreign-born Men." *Journal of Human Resources* 23:108–22.

Terman, L. 1916. *The Measurement of Intelligence.* Boston: Houghton Mifflin.

Wasik, Barbara A. and Robert E. Slavin. 1993. "Preventing Early Reading Failure with One-to-one Tutoring: A Review of Five Programs." *Reading Research Quarterly* 28(2):178–200.

Wechsler, D. 1981. *Wechsler Adult Intelligence Scale—Revised.* New York: Psychological Corporation.

Weir, Dorothea. 1993. *School Resources, Classroom Content, and Student Achievement in the Primary Grades.* Ph.D. dissertation, Graduate Program in Political Economy, University of Texas at Dallas.

Williams, Trevor. 1976. "Teacher Prophecies and the Inheritance of Inequality." *Sociology of Education* 49:223–36.

Willis, Paul. 1977. *Learning to Labor.* London: Gower.

Wilson, James Q. 1995. *On Character,* expanded edition. Washington, DC: American Enterprise Institute.

Wilson, William Julius. 1987. The Truly Disadvantaged: The Inner-City, the Underclass, and Public Policy. Chicago: University of Chicago Press.

Woodcock, Richard. 1990. "Theoretical Foundations of the WJ-R Measures of Cognitive Ability." *Journal of Psychoeducational Assessment* 8:231–58.

Index

211